Isaac Williams

The characters of the Old Testament; in a series of sermons

Isaac Williams

The characters of the Old Testament; in a series of sermons

ISBN/EAN: 9783337086039

Printed in Europe, USA, Canada, Australia, Japan

Cover: Foto ©Lupo / pixelio.de

More available books at **www.hansebooks.com**

THE CHARACTERS OF THE OLD TESTAMENT

In a Series of Sermons

BY THE
REV. ISAAC WILLIAMS, B.D.
LATE FELLOW OF TRINITY COLLEGE, OXFORD

NEW EDITION

RIVINGTONS
London, Oxford, and Cambridge
1870

PREFACE

THE Sermons in this Volume, with the exception of that on Job, are arranged according to the order of the Sunday Lessons; and indeed the selection of the characters has been regulated in some measure with this view. The concluding Sermon on Antichrist was not written with any reference to this series; but, independently of other reasons for its introduction, it is so connected with some of the subjects as to render it a suitable termination for the Volume.

While such works are in some sense offered to the public, yet rather would the Writer in this as in all other things wish to look up more entirely to the Author of all good; and, as the "lad with five barley loaves," present these through His Church to the gracious Eye of his Divine Master; if peradventure He would look on them and accept them, and, if he might say it without presumption, take them into His all-hallowing hands, and multiply and sanctify them to the great ends of giving food to His people.

STINCHCOMBE,
October, 1856.

CONTENTS

SERMON I

ADAM

For as in Adam all die, even so in Christ shall all be made alive.
—1 CORINTHIANS xv. 22 1

SERMON II

ABEL AND CAIN

By faith Abel offered unto God a more excellent sacrifice than Cain, by which he obtained witness that he was righteous, God testifying of his gifts.—HEBREWS xi. 4 12

SERMON III

NOAH

And he called his name Noah, saying, This same shall comfort us concerning our work and toil of our hands, because of the ground which the Lord hath cursed.—GENESIS v. 29 . . 23

SERMON IV

ABRAHAM

And the angel of the Lord called unto him out of heaven, and said, Abraham, Abraham.—GENESIS xxii. 11 34

SERMON V

LOT

Then Lot chose him all the plain of Jordan; and Lot journeyed East: and they separated themselves the one from the other.—GENESIS xiii. 11. 45

SERMON VI

JACOB AND ESAU

Was not Esau Jacob's brother? saith the Lord: yet I loved Jacob, and I hated Esau.—MALACHI i. 2, 3 56

SERMON VII

JOSEPH

The archers have sorely grieved him, and shot at him, and hated him: but his bow abode in strength, and the arms of his hands were made strong by the hands of the mighty God of Jacob.—GENESIS xlix. 23, 24 67

SERMON VIII

MOSES

                                                                       PAGE

Now the man Moses was very meek, above all the men which were upon the face of the earth.—NUMBERS xii. 3 . . . 79

SERMON IX

AARON

And no man taketh this honour unto himself, but he that is called of God, as was Aaron.—HEBREWS v. 4 . . . 90

SERMON X

PHARAOH

And the Lord hardened the heart of Pharaoh.—EXODUS ix. 12 . 103

SERMON XI

KORAH, DATHAN, AND ABIRAM

And the Lord spake unto Moses, saying, Speak unto the congregation, saying, Get you up from about the tabernacle of Korah, Dathan, and Abiram.—NUMBERS xvi. 23, 24 . . . 114

SERMON XII

BALAAM

Let me die the death of the righteous, and let my last end be like his!—NUMBERS xxiii. 10 126

SERMON XIII

JOSHUA

And he gave Joshua the son of Nun a charge, and said, Be strong and of a good courage: for thou shalt bring the children of Israel into the land which I sware unto them: and I will be with thee.—DEUTERONOMY xxxi. 23 138

SERMON XIV

SAMSON

And the woman bare a son, and called his name Samson; and the child grew, and the Lord blessed him.—JUDGES xiii. 24 . 149

SERMON XV

SAMUEL

She bare a son, and called his name Samuel, saying, Because I have asked him of the Lord.—1 SAMUEL i. 20 . . . 160

SERMON XVI

SAUL

But the spirit of the Lord departed from Saul, and an evil spirit from the Lord troubled him.—1 SAMUEL xvi. 14 . . . 171

SERMON XVII

DAVID

To whom also He gave testimony, and said, I have found David the son of Jesse, a man after Mine own heart.—ACTS xiii. 22 . 183

SERMON XVIII

SOLOMON

Did not Solomon king of Israel sin by these things? yet among many nations was there no king like him, who was beloved of his God.—NEHEMIAH xiii. 26 195

SERMON XIX

ELIJAH

Elias was a man subject to like passions as we are.—ST. JAMES v. 17 206

SERMON XX

AHAB

But there was none like unto Ahab, which did sell himself to work wickedness in the sight of the Lord, whom Jezebel his wife stirred up.—1 KINGS xxi. 25 215

SERMON XXI

ELISHA

And Elisha said, I pray thee, let a double portion of thy spirit be upon me. And he said, Thou hast asked a hard thing; nevertheless, if thou see me when I am taken from thee, it shall be so unto thee.—2 KINGS ii. 9, 10 224

SERMON XXII

HEZEKIAH

He trusted in the Lord God of Israel; so that after him was none like him among all the kings of Judah, nor any that were before him.—2 KINGS xviii. 5 234

SERMON XXIII

JOSIAH

Because thine heart was tender, and thou didst humble thyself before God, when thou heardest His words against this place, and against the inhabitants thereof, and humbledst thyself before Me, and didst rend thy clothes, and weep before Me; I have even heard thee also, saith the Lord.—2 CHRONICLES xxxiv. 27 244

SERMON XXIV

JEREMIAH

Oh that my head were waters, and mine eyes a fountain of tears, that I might weep day and night for the slain of the daughter of my people! Oh that I had in the wilderness a lodging place of wayfaring men; that I might leave my people and go from them!—JEREMIAH ix. 1, 2 255

SERMON XXV

EZEKIEL

And, lo, thou art unto them as a very lovely song of one that hath a pleasant voice, and can play well on an instrument: for they hear thy words, but they do them not.—EZEKIEL xxxiii. 32 267

SERMON XXVI

DANIEL

And He said unto me, O Daniel, a man greatly beloved.—
DANIEL x. 11 279

SERMON XXVII

JOEL

The word of the Lord that came to Joel the son of Pethuel.—
JOEL i. 1 292

SERMON XXVIII

JOB

*Ye have heard of the patience of Job, and have seen the end of the Lord.—*ST. JAMES V. 11 302

SERMON XXIX

ISAIAH

*These things said Esaias, when he saw His glory, and spake of Him.—*ST. JOHN xii. 41 313

SERMON XXX

THE ANTICHRIST

PAGE

Let no man deceive you by any means: for that day shall not come, except there come a falling away first, and that man of sin be revealed, the son of perdition.—2 THESSALONIANS ii. 3 . 323

ADAM

For as in Adam all die, even so in Christ shall all be made alive.—1 CORINTHIANS xv. 22.

THE state of our first parents in Paradise must always be a mystery to us; we can form no conception of a condition in which there was no death, and none of the sad company of death, sin and fear and care and pain. But in this our ignorance all has been told us which it is good for us to know; and their trial and fall is so like what we ourselves experience, that we understand it but too well. We find in ourselves the like mystery of evil when we sin against better knowledge, forfeit our great strength, choose death instead of life, and give up our God in exchange for some passing temptation.

First of all, then, we read that God made man in His own image and likeness, capable of knowing and loving Him as the inferior creatures could not; He set him in dominion over them; He endowed him too with every gift which the perfection of his nature required; He imparted to him an intimate knowledge of all the creatures, so that he could give them suitable names such as God approved; He placed him in a garden, which He is described as, in some especial and pre-eminent manner, furnishing very richly for his use; He added also an associate, whom, as a part of himself, he might cherish with a more intimate love; and, more than all, God Himself conversed with him, without his being overcome with shame or fear, and, as it is described, walked with him in the garden. Thus He made him to be like His own image below, crowned above all the creatures with understanding, and adorned with gifts both within and without. But this was not all—for God made with Adam a covenant of everlasting life, dependent on his obedience, annexing to that obedience the gift of immortality; for in addition to all other gifts was the Tree of Life, and hard by it in the midst of the garden, the Tree of Knowledge, to be the trial of obedience. Thus was he called by this covenant of grace from all earthly pleasures and endowments, to the "more excellent way" of charity; that charity which is "proof against" all temptations; charity which "never faileth;" charity which is content to be without the "knowledge that puffeth up;" which obeys because it loves, and loves because it trusts, and is therefore ever wont to look up to and to lean on God; till faith, "rooted and grounded in love," when perfected by obedience, might be translated to a higher and securer state of bliss with God Himself in Heaven. And the place of this covenant of grace was "in the midst of the garden:" as the sun is the centre of the universe, which without him would be dead; so did obedience to this one command give order and beauty to that Paradise, when all was obedient to man, because man was obedient to God.

Thus were they in a state of perfect innocence and happiness: but their life was not in themselves, it was dependent on God, and they were made to feel this their dependence upon Him, in their liability to fall; it was therefore a life of faith, because it was a condition of trial and obedience. Their happiness was in the love of God, in Whose likeness they were made; and while they had that love, faith in Him would be their strength, and obedience their delight. The free gift is made them that they "may eat of every tree of the garden," except one only; and when that one exception is made, it is with the promise of life on their obedience. If they eat not of that forbidden tree they shall live; and therefore with that Tree of Knowledge is the tree of Life. And as God giveth not as man giveth, but liberally and abundantly beyond words, we may conclude that therein was implied that such obedience would lead to a more perfect and blissful immortality. For their present life on earth was then precarious, and dependent on means from without, that Tree of Life to which they had access; it was not of that "Well of Life" which is with God, which is from within, ever "springing up into everlasting life."

Moreover, another peculiar gift is spoken of. It is said that God "breathed into his nostrils the breath of life," and in consequence "man became a living soul," i.e. a soul capable of that better life which is in God. For what was this breath of God but that He infused into him of His Divine Spirit, clothed him with that vesture of immortality, whereby after having been created in the similitude of God, he might look up to Heaven, as "waiting for the revelation of the sons of God," and the crown and fulness of that angelic nature? Thus then was it that God had not only "set him over the works of His hands," but He "visited him," and "crowned him with glory and worship." He had set His love on the man He had formed, and in this the greatness of His love, He sought for the love of man in return, his free love and choice, which could only be shown by this obedience.

And now we come to the mysterious origin of evil,

which has been ever since so intimately with us, which wraps us about as our very clothing, enters into us as the food we eat, as the air we breathe, is with us, in us, and about us, and lets not go its hold on us till we die. But "the serpent said unto the woman, Yea, hath God said, Ye shall not eat of every tree of the garden?" Here, then, we have disclosed in its fulness the existence and craft of an evil spirit bent on our ruin; and his entering into the serpent, as afterwards, by our Lord's permission, the devils entering into the swine, sets before us how they may take possession of those whom God hath made, and hence of the body and of the soul of man. Add to which that his making the creature the instrument of evil, seems to account for the animal creation around us being united and sharing, for some mysterious reasons, in the sufferings of mankind.

"And the woman said unto the serpent, Of the fruit of the tree which is in the midst of the garden, God hath said, Ye shall not eat of it, neither shall ye touch it, lest ye die." Now though Eve was as yet sinless, we may see in this reply the first faint tendency to her falling away from God. The command which God had given to Adam was, "Thou shalt not eat of it," but Eve adds here the words, "Neither shall ye touch it." She overstates, as it were, the prohibition; like the Pharisees afterwards whom our Lord condemned, she thus added to the word of God. Nor is this all; for at the same time she diminishes from it, for God had said to Adam, "Thou shalt surely die," or "Dying thou shalt die," which is a very strong expression; but she softens it down, and says merely, "Lest ye die." She adds to God's word like the Pharisee—she takes away from it like the Sadducee. She adds to the command—takes away from the warning.

Thus all is gradual, the serpent insinuates a poisonous question, then Eve doubts God's word, and then the serpent denies it. "Lest ye die," says Eve. "Ye shall not die," adds the tempter.

While this is at work in the heart, what follows? "I have made a covenant with mine eyes," says Job, taught by the sad experience of mankind; but not so was it now. "The woman saw that the tree was good for food, and that it was pleasant to the eyes, and a tree to be desired to make one wise." All her life and bliss was in God, and in union with God; but now she desired something out of God. For these three things contain all the temptations to which mankind are subject, as St. John states them, "the lust of the flesh," for it was good for food; "the lust of the eyes," for it was pleasant to behold; and "the pride of life," for it was to be desired to make one wise, yea, as gods. "All these," says St. John, "are not of the Father, but are of the world;" and "if any man love the world, the love of the Father is not in him[1]."

Thus are these temptations put in motion by Satan; he stealthily approaches like a serpent wherever he finds access, advancing by little and little with great subtlety, first through the creature, then by the weaker vessel; tempting the woman by the fruits of the garden, in which as a serpent he lay hid, and thus winding his way to the man as it were on the weaker side, by his love for the woman, through that new and great gift, the love of his espousals. And what is the first result of this act of disobedience? Instead of the likeness of God, Eve puts on the likeness of Satan; she at once takes part with the serpent; she also now acts as a tempter, and, in so doing, brings death on one whom she loved; "She gave to her

[1] 1 John ii. 15, 16.

husband, and he did eat." So is it with sin at all times; no one falls alone; those nearest and dearest are often injured by every sin of ours—and, oh! terrible thought, may lose on our account life eternal. Here in the germ is the fulness of all sin; some secret presumption that goes before a fall; then the devil tempting; then doubt of God; and then evil curiosity; and then the influence of example which spreads the sin, that fearful net of the wicked one, entangling all around in the society of evil.

Their innocence was gone—their covenant with God was broken—of their better nature shame alone remained; in this shame alone is their hope[2], inasmuch as it is an acknowledgment of sin, and might therefore lead to repentance. Disobeying God, their own nature was no longer obedient to themselves, and they were ashamed of it, for it had other desires than the will of God, " another law in their members bringing them into captivity to the law of sin[3]." And whereas before they knew nothing but good, they now know both good and evil, the knowledge which it would have been infinitely better never to have had, the knowledge of evil spirits, of the good they have lost, of the evil they have chosen. "They saw that they were naked," for not till then were they divested of God's righteousness; the clothing of His sanctifying Spirit, when without shame or fear they conversed with God: but now they seek for covering from that shame; such has ever been the effort of mankind, with the fading leaves of worldly objects to cover themselves; secretly conscious of their nakedness and deep internal poverty without God. "They cover with a covering," says the Prophet, "but not of my Spirit, that they may add sin to sin[4]."

[2] St. Ambrose, De Paradiso, cap. xiv.
[3] Rom. vii. 23; St. Aug. vol. x. 612. 1303. [4] Isa. xxx. 1.

And they "hid themselves from the presence of the Lord God amongst the trees of the garden. And the Lord God called unto Adam, and said unto him, Where art thou?" Into what abyss of misery art thou fallen? from what grace and hope art thou lost[5]?

And now if Eve had before acted as Satan the tempter, so Adam is now as Satan the accuser, for he says, "The woman whom thou gavest to be with me, she gave me of the tree, and I did eat." Here is no humiliation—no confession. Yes, I did eat; the woman gave me, and Thou gavest me the woman; it is all from Thee! Oh, sad change! what a return to God for all His gifts! They hide among the trees, they cover their shame with leaves; and now with pretext and excuse.

"And the woman said, the serpent beguiled me and I did eat." She too, as Adam, cast the guilt upon another; yet here indeed there is in some sort confession of sin; and therefore gives ground for pardon[6]. But oh, how much has mankind to suffer before they come to that true contrition of heart which says with the Psalmist, "I said, Lord, have mercy on me; heal my soul, for I have sinned against thee[7]." The afflictions of Job; the trials of Joseph; the endurance of Moses; the contrition of David; the confessions of Daniel; the sorrows of the Prophets; the tears of St. Peter; the travails of St. Paul; the sufferings of Saints and the blood of Martyrs; have yet to prove this humiliation of man, in order that he might be accepted in the Second Adam; and these answers of our first parents may be undone or amended. And this healing is in the merciful sentence, "in sorrow shalt thou

---

[5] St. Ambrose.   [6] St. Ambrose.
[7] Ps. xi. 5; St. Aug. vol. iii. 467.

bring forth:" and "in sorrow shalt thou eat," "till thou return unto the ground." Yea, the very voice of the accepted One shall be heard as it were from the ground, and speaking from the dust of death, "I am a worm and no man." Thus not in sorrow only but in death itself shall be found the means and hope of restoration; when "love shall be stronger than death;" and dying in Christ; yea, exercised in dying shall bring forth more abundant life; for in conformity to Christ's death is life.

Thus, in taking the shame, and the sorrow, and the death, Christ restores again to the Paradise of God. For this Paradise is the Church of God, "the garden inclosed," on which, as "the winds blow, the spices flow out;" wherein is the "well of living waters[8]." And there too is the Tree of Life which hath "leaves," it is said, "for the healing of the nations;" there is also in it a river not from the ground as in that Eden of old, but "proceeding out of the throne of God and of the Lamb." Wherein He Himself says, "I will give to him that overcometh to eat of the tree of life, which is in the midst of the Paradise of God." For, in Him they shall, He says, "have right to the tree of life[9]." In the centre of that garden; yea, "in the midst of the Paradise of God," restoring all again to love, and harmony, and peace, is He Himself; in whom is there a better knowledge and a better life which He will impart to them that love Him; for in Him are all the treasures of wisdom and knowledge; and "our life is hid with Christ in God." In that Paradise He Himself walks again with man, for it is said, "I will walk among you, and be your God, and ye shall be My people[1]."

[8] Song of Sol. iv. 15, 16.   [9] Rev. ii. 7; xxii. 14.
[1] Lev. xxvi. 12.

Yea, He hath clothed their shame again with the covering of His righteousness, and hath said, "They shall walk with Me in white²." And "they shall see His face." He hath again renewed them in His image. Nay more, by another transcendental endowment of which that in Paradise was the sign, on His rising from the dead, He hath "breathed into their nostrils the breath of life³," by the gift of His Spirit: that in the likeness of His resurrection, "putting on the new man," they may be again "created after God in righteousness and true holiness⁴;"—that like Adam of old, they may keep His commandments, and by keeping them in this Paradise of trial which is His Church, they may at length be fitter for a better Paradise, and the Presence of God in Heaven.

From the creation of man unto this day his history has been, in those words of the Psalmist, "In my prosperity I said, I shall never be moved: Thou, Lord, of Thy goodness hast made my hill so strong. Thou turnedst away Thy face, and I was troubled⁵." And then, troubled and exercised with many sorrows under the displeasure of God he hath come to learn indeed to know both good and evil; —the evil of departing from God; our only good to be in Him; His goodness and His love in Christ; good and evil, the depth and fulness of which we shall know even yet far better when we depart from the body, when it is known what heaven and hell are; when Satan's words shall become true in a way he little thought, to the elect of God, when knowing both good and evil they shall be as gods, shall be "made partakers," as St. Peter says, "of the divine nature," shall be made one with the Son of God, "shall be

---

² Rev. iii. 4.   ³ St. John xx. 22.   ⁴ Eph. iv. 24.
⁵ Ps. xxx. 6, 7; St. Aug. vol. iii. 445.

like Him," and "awaking up after His likeness shall be satisfied with it."

One word more in conclusion. As man fell by pride, his return must be by humility: his pride was the poison of Satan, "that ye may be as gods;" but in order that we might be restored, He who was indeed Very God emptied Himself of all His glories that He might become man for our sakes. Instead of the forbidden Tree of Knowledge "He learned obedience by the things which He suffered." He has given us an example by which we might overcome in Him; and has set forth in Himself as it were, an epitome of our life-long conflict, in a trial corresponding to that in which Adam fell, when in the wilderness He encountered and overcame that old serpent; not in a garden but in a desert; not in abundance but in hunger; not in manifestation of His Divine power, but meekly shielding Himself against all temptations by the written Word of God; showing us by what means we are to overcome,— that we have each of us in like manner with our first parents, an enemy to contend with, a trial to undergo, a Paradise to lose, a kingdom of Heaven set before us to obtain. And in order that we may be in Him equal to this conflict, He, "the last Adam," has for us "been made a quickening Spirit," and has given us to eat of His Body and Blood, as the antidote of death, and indwelling of immortality, that "as in Adam all die," all in Him may "be made alive." And this with a pledge that in greater fulness He will "give to him that overcometh" to partake of that life which is in Him, admitting even by death itself into a greater nearness with Himself and saying to the dying thief, "To day shalt thou be with Me in Paradise."

These things are not then afar off, my brethren; He

Himself in death shall lead us unharmed by the "flaming sword" of the "Cherubims;" yea, even this day, or tomorrow, or next week, you or I, if found worthy, may, by God's mercy, be admitted into that His mysterious Presence, of which He spake under the name of that garden of old.

ABEL AND CAIN

By faith Abel offered unto God a more excellent sacrifice than Cain, by which he obtained witness that he was righteous, God testifying of his gifts.—HEBREWS xi. 4.

THE fall of our first parents is soon followed by a consummating act of wickedness, such as it will continue to be to the end of time, the very type and sign of the world that slew Christ, even a brother's murder. But though crime has again thus speedily appeared in a form so intense, yet in one respect it has assumed a more consoling character, for there is now a bright and a dark side ; together with Cain there is Abel with the praise of God and the crown of goodness : from the same fountain-head there are now two streams parting asunder, which from henceforth flow on to the end of the world, deepening and enlarging as they go. So soon were they to know both good and evil, the result of that first sin. Between those born of the same womb and nurtured at the same breast, a separation is made.

It is to be observed that Holy Scripture keeps this act in continual remembrance, as containing in itself all that character of evil which still survives and goes on. Our Lord speaks of Abel, saying to the Jews, that his blood should be required of that generation[1] ; when God visits it will be again brought to mind. St. Paul, mentioning Abel

[1] St. Matt. xxiii. 35, 36.

as the first in the catalogue of saints, uses the memorable words that "being dead, he yet speaketh;" which seems to attach an emphatic teaching to his death; and afterwards, when speaking of the Blood of Christ, he adds, "which speaketh better things than that of Abel." Whereby he implies that the death of Abel does still speak, as does that of Christ, although it speaks of judgment. Thus he comes down to us with a voice which is heard from the ground. And with him necessarily Cain also. St. John brings the first murderer into especial remembrance, when speaking of one that loves not his brother, "Not as Cain," he says, "who was of that wicked one." Our Lord seems to allude to him in that warning to the Jews, "Ye are of your father the devil: he was a murderer from the beginning." And St. Jude as crowning the corruption of the last days, "They have gone in the way of Cain." Thus did the dimensions of this crime at once fill as it were the earth and all time; like some fiery rocket, which, culminating in an instant, has risen to the sky, and falls again in a thousand fragments to the earth, holding in itself and scattering abroad all lesser crimes of ill will.

Moreover, great as is this crowning deed of wickedness, yet herein is given "the valley of Achor for a door of hope[2]," while we behold in Abel the very type of all acceptableness, and in contrast with his brother Cain, in the strongest manner, are good and evil set before us; that in the black cloud which then came on the morning of the world, we may see the bow of promise, the power of God's grace, and by cleaving to Him suck out the riches of His goodness. The testimony of Holy Scripture to the character of Abel is very clear and decisive. Our Lord Himself calls Abel "the righteous Abel;" St. John says

[2] Hos. ii. 15.

that Cain slew him because "his works were righteous;" and St. Paul, that "by faith he offered a more excellent," or as it is in the original, "a more abundant sacrifice," and "obtained the testimony of God that he was righteous." Thus goodness and faith are in him combined; and the same appears in the account in Genesis, for God says to Cain, "If thou doest well, shalt thou not be accepted?" from which it is clear that the acceptance of Abel was because he did well. And the very nature of his offering expressed an acceptable faith; it was "the firstlings of his flock, and the fat thereof," of the first and the best he offered to God, the crown and flower of his substance; "the firstfruits" and "the fat," both of which God Himself afterwards prescribed in the Law, taking this act of Abel as the pattern of after piety. Moreover it was the Lamb of the flock by whose skins they were covered from the shame of sin by God Himself. Such an offering by one of a meek and blameless life expressed both thanksgiving to God: and by sacrifice an acknowledgment of death, and of himself worthy to die: it was a call for mercy, a pleading with God for pardon. And He who reads the heart and called him by His grace knew it to be expressive of Christ. The act of itself speaks and must speak; and this he had to perfect by a yet higher sacrifice, that of himself; for, on account of his acting in this manner towards God he suffered even unto death, the first of martyrs.

And all this appears the more from the contrast with Cain; he also brings an offering, though it be not the earliest or the choicest, it is of the fruits of the ground which he tilled; here also is worship, and it might have been acceptable; the Law also has its offering of the fruits of the ground: but so it is, it has not the savour of Christ, the Lamb, and the Blood; it has not that which should go with a sacrifice, penitence; nor that which can alone give value to a gift, the heart of the worshipper. "If thou bring thy gift to the altar, and there remember that thy brother hath ought against thee, leave there thy gift." It pleaded not for mercy; and it gave not mercy, which is the better part of sacrifice. In the words of the Law it has not the salt, nor the oil, nor the incense, was without goodness, without grace, without prayer. He is wroth, and his "countenance is fallen," turning to the ground on which the curse of sin was; whereas, Abel was all love, and his countenance was lifted up on high, as looking for and expecting what God would do. Nor is Cain without warning, for God Himself expostulates with him, and shows him the better part. He is not, he says, his brother's keeper; be it so; such is even now the language of the world; but Christ and they that are in Him are of another mind; His attribute is the good Shepherd that layeth down His life for the sheep; He is the keeper of His brethren, even at the cost of His own life. And Abel is His prototype and martyr, and in some sense His representative, offering up a sacrifice as the High Priest of God in a fallen world. It matters not whether any thing was then explicitly revealed respecting Him Who should bruise the serpent's head; the Covenant of God sometimes influences the heart in a way which passeth understanding. And of the highest saving faith, our Lord says, "Flesh and blood hath not revealed it unto thee, but My Father which is in heaven." The Father draws unto the Son, and the Son brings unto the Father, in mysterious ways, without express knowledge. It is not knowledge that characterizes faith, but trust in God, which receives though it knows not, but in receiving knows with a better knowledge, that God is love. And this may have been Abel's faith. An ancient bishop says of his sacrifice, "Isaiah preached of the Lamb dumb before His shearers: John the Baptist pointed out the Lamb of God: Abel by offering up the Lamb in significancy set forth the same[3]."

Whatever his knowledge might have been, it is enough that his offering was for Christ's sake accepted, and that offering is the Lamb which must needs speak of that Lamb which was slain from the foundation of the world: for all was ordered of God in him who was first predestined, and called by His grace, and by His grace sanctified, and perfected by His grace, and accepted.

And here observe from the very beginning the mark of the elect and of the reprobate: the love of God is the sign of the elect: and cupidity or self-love of the evil. Cain kept to himself the first and the best; Abel offered the first and best to God. Nor was this all, it was in faith, and it was the offering of one who did well, and was in life acceptable with God: it was himself that he had first given to God, and of this that sacrifice was the sign; and he was allowed to prove this by having his own life also made to be a yet more acceptable sacrifice and more lively token of the death of Christ: as the Christian martyrs who gave first their goods, and then themselves also to die.

The crime of Cain was precisely that of the Jews, envy; "the chief priests had delivered Him from envy;" and perhaps more than any other it partakes of the likeness of Satan, who was bent on the destruction of mankind, not from anger, lust, or covetousness, but from envy and hate of goodness. Cain was the first Antichrist, and an image of the last. He already sets forth "the synagogue of Satan" and the Jew, which preserves his likeness unto the end. "And the Lord said unto Cain, Where is thy

[3] St. Greg. in Job xxxviii. 31.

brother? And he said, I know not." Thus like him who was "a liar and a murderer from the beginning," he would deny what he had done, if he could; but so is it with the Jew unto this day, he has slain his brother, even Him who was, like himself, of the seed of Abraham; and he is asked, Where is He? even by the voice of God, speaking through the Scriptures unto this day. And he answers, "I know not." Yet it is he who might and should have been his brother's keeper. Law and Prophets had consigned Him to his keeping; but cast out from the presence of God he wanders forth unto the end of the world, bearing witness to what he hath done,—the second Cain who hath slain the great Shepherd of the sheep. And God hath set His mark upon him that he dies not. Other nations and other religions melt into each other, and are lost and changed, but the Jewish people are preserved, and change not, for they have on them the mark of God. They wander through the earth, and find no rest, for "they understand not the Sabbath of the heart[4]," which is Christ. "I shall be a fugitive and a vagabond," says Cain, and it is the sentence of God that he shall be so: "the wicked are like the troubled sea, when it cannot rest. There is no peace, saith my God, to the wicked[5]." Already, like Judas, he hath found the weight of his sin: "My punishment is greater than I can bear;" and hath the fear of death, for "every one," he says, "that findeth me shall slay me;" as a sign of what shall be hereafter, fearing death, he shall not be able to die.

True it is that there is another character and appearance in the eyes of the world, for with them "these are the ungodly, these prosper in the world[6]." The greatest of

---

[4] St. Aug. vol. viii. 382. 385, and vol. vii. 860.
[5] Isa. lviii. 20, 21.   [6] Ps. lxxiii. 12.

all cities, even that city of Rome which put to death Christ and His martyrs, is said to have been founded by one who slew his brother. So it is with Cain. It is added, and "he builded a city, and called it after his son's name." He continues to live on to old age, he begets children, and sees his children's children; the founders of mighty cities, wherein the harp and the organ are heard, and their cattle range on a thousand hills, inventors in brass and iron are there, of works of art, of music, and poetry; "they planted and builded, they married and gave in marriage;" but Abel is cut off childless in the morning of his days. So is it as the world judges; but oh, how far otherwise in truth! for he is with God, he lives to God and with God. While they, filling up the measure of their sin, are heaping up unto themselves wrath "against the revelation of the righteous judgment of God," till the windows of Heaven shall be opened, and the great deep rise from below, and wash them all away. It is an awful sign to live on adding sin to sin. It was as the voice of God already going forth upon earth, to teach mankind that there was a better life hid with God, that life upon earth was not life without Him, but death. If the sinner continued to live on, it was but as a sign of the long-suffering of God that He was not willing that any should perish, but that all should come to repentance.

Thus early was there given to the world, as it were, an expressive image of Christ's death, whereby He should bruise the serpent's head, while he attacked His heel—a more worthy representation than that of slain beasts. Cain, the firstborn, is of the earth, earthy; Abel, the sign of the heavenly, speaks of the Lord from Heaven. As Isaac, the child of promise, was born after the son of the bondwoman; as Jacob was after Esau; as the Jew was the elder brother, and the believing Gentile the younger; as the first Adam was of the earth, and the second Adam of Heaven, so was it now foreshown in Cain and Abel. And "cut off from the land of the living" he bears witness that the inheritance is not of earth, but with God; that in death and after death is his victory. And while thus in mystery he speaks of Christ's death, Seth is given to mankind on earth, whose children are called "the sons of God." Thus it may be said, "he shall see his seed, he shall prolong his days[7]." And yet further, for while Seth is made to be a pledge of Christ's resurrection, His ascension is set forth in Enoch, who walked with God and was translated, having first borne witness that "the Lord cometh, with ten thousand of His saints, to execute judgment[8]."

Nor is it only in sign and figure that Christ's death is set forth in Abel the first of martyrs, but he is also given to be the example of all acceptable faithfulness. In him have we the firstfruits of the City of God; the fulness of the last and crowning beatitude; "Blessed are they which are persecuted for righteousness' sake, for their's is the kingdom of Heaven." "For not only," says St. Augustine, "from the bodily presence of Christ and His Apostles, but from righteous Abel unto the end of time, amidst the persecutions of the world, and the consolations of God, the Church advances onward in her pilgrimage[9];" "Always enduring earth and hoping for Heaven[1]."

"Thy brother's blood," said God to Cain, "crieth unto Me from the ground;" and so it continues to do until the end; the blood of righteous Abel, says our Lord, shall be required when God visits: the blood of Abel, says St. Paul, is still speaking; with the souls of those that are

[7] Isa. liii. 10.
[8] Jude 14, 15.
[9] St. Aug. vii. 860.
[1] St. Aug. iv. 2264.

under the altar it cries with a voice ever louder and more loud, "How long, O Lord, Holy and True, dost Thou not judge and avenge our blood on them that dwell on the earth[2]?" The blood of Abel thus cries from the ground, "and the Heavens above," says St. Ambrose, "and all things that are in Heaven, Sun, Moon, and Stars, Thrones, Dominions, Principalities, and Powers, Cherubim and Seraphim[3]," take up the cry, and absolve not the guilt. But although the blood of Abel thus cries from the ground, yet it is not Abel himself that thus speaks. It signifies rather that the wrongs of Abel and of all the meek upon earth are thus remembered of God. He puts their tears into His bottle, and these things are noted in His book; their sufferings and woes for His sake are numbered by Him, and not forgotten. "Here is the patience of the saints[4]." All things are with God which have been done to them "whose names are written in the book of life of the Lamb slain from the foundation of the world[5]." "Right dear in His sight is their death:" and He whom Saul persecuted is slain in Abel.

The very silence of Abel is expressive; it seems to speak of Him who as a sheep before his shearers was dumb, and as a lamb brought unto the slaughter, opened not His mouth. His blood calls from the ground, but he himself is silent; he appeals not for vengeance even in death, as if saying, "My cause is in Thy hands; Thou shalt answer for me, O Lord my God." He "committed himself unto Him that judgeth righteously." All that is said of Abel, and all that is left unsaid by him would indicate that he in character laboured to be like that meek and innocent victim which he offered up in sacrifice to God. And such

[2] Rev. vi. 10.   [3] De Cain et Abel, lib. ii. cap. 10.
[4] Rev. xiv. 12.   [5] Rev. xiii. 8.

Abel seems to represent in all times and countries unto the end; them to whom the Father, it may be in some hidden manner unknown of man, reveals His Son, and by some secret bond in the mystery of godliness, knits them unto Him. They are not their own; they are of Him, and in Him, and depart to be more intimately with Him. The world knoweth them not as it knew Him not—it knoweth not from whence they come nor whither they go. These are strangers upon earth; the world hateth them because they are of God. Their treasure and their heart are with Him; their treasure, because they give Him the first and best; and their heart, because their affections must needs follow their actions. They devote to Him the first and the best of all; the first and best of their substance, the first and best of their time, the first and best of their affections.

Thus in every age and nation Abel yet speaketh; each carries on his example, confirms it by others of like character and circumstance, and leaves it yet to speak as it will unto the end; every place has those that "have gone in the way of Cain," and also those that patiently suffer; even among children there is often, alas! a Cain and Abel —in families, in every village and neighbourhood—among nations, and in the wars of nations. It goes on like one continued chain, still adding link to link; when the last is added it reverberates unto the first; evil as well as good are as parts of one body; and each may find in himself whether he has mostly the marks of Cain or of Abel.

When St. John states that, "Whosoever hateth his brother is a murderer," and connects this with Cain[6], he seems to refer to our Lord's own declaration, that though in the Law of Moses it is written, "Thou shalt do no

[6] 1 John iii. 12. 15.

murder," yet in the eyes of the all-seeing Judge, "Whosoever is angry with his brother without a cause[7]," shall come under the like condemnation. It is this which adds such force to that early deed, that there is a lesson connected with it which comes to us, not on tables of stone, but by the finger and Holy Spirit of God, inscribed on the fleshly tables of the heart, containing in itself the new and better law of love—a law written in the blood, not of Abel, but of Christ.

[7] St. Matt. v. 21.

NOAH

And he called his name Noah, saying, This same shall comfort us concerning our work and toil of our hands, because of the ground which the Lord hath cursed.—GENESIS v. 29.

AFTER the death of Abel mankind multiplied, cities were built, the arts increased, iniquity abounded and God was forgotten; and then we see one man amidst the universal corruption building an ark, and in so doing set at nought and mocked. This was Noah, and we may now inquire what was the character of one so pre-eminent. We cannot know the deep things of the Spirit of God, nor the heart of a good man in which as in deep waters His footsteps are; but on meditating on what is written we may gain much.

The first point which strikes us in Noah is his extreme solitude; he stands alone in a fallen world; when the great wickedness is described, it is added, "But Noah found grace in the eyes of the Lord," the one and only one; and again, "The Lord said unto Noah, thee have I seen righteous before Me in this generation." It is for this that he stands out so remarkable beyond all the Saints in Scripture, that it was amidst the utter corruption of that generation. He stands alone, like one solitary pillar in the midst of a ruin. But this is not all, for his character is given yet more particularly, "Noah was a just man and perfect in his generations, and Noah walked with God." This remarkable and beautiful expression that he "walked with God," had been used of Enoch before God took him. Moreover the righteousness of Noah and his consequent power with God is shown by the mention of him in Ezekiel, "Though these three men, Noah, Daniel, and Job, were in it, they should deliver but their own souls by their righteousness, saith the Lord God[1]." Now as Job was remarkable for intercession, interceding first of all "continually" for his sons; and then afterwards by the express command of God for his three friends[2]; and as Daniel is known as the signal intercessor with God for his people; so we may conclude from Noah's being mentioned thus together with them that he was especially known of God for his intercessions in behalf of that wicked world in which he lived. And as such prayers are certain in some way to be answered of God, it is probable, that to these, his prayers, his own family were given him, to be the origin of a new world, and in whom the covenant of God might stand.

In addition to these there is also another circumstance which we know of Noah; he is mentioned by St. Peter as "a preacher of righteousness." This description taken with all the rest has great weight; for it indicates that he was not only, like Samuel and Daniel, engaged in mourning and praying for others, not a silent sufferer only as Abel; but that like the Prophets and Apostles he pleaded with them, preaching righteousness. And this might have been during the hundred and twenty years wherein God gave warning of what He was about to do, as St. Peter says, "When once the longsuffering of God waited in the days of Noah, while the ark was a preparing[3]." Or it might

---

[1] Ezek. xiv. 14. [2] Job. i. 5; xlii. 8. [3] 1 Pet. iii. 20.

have been all his life before that time; until at last when his preaching had been long in vain, that sign was given, when, as St. Paul speaks of it, "being warned of God, moved with fear, he prepared an ark to the saving of his house; by the which he condemned the world[4]." All these things serve to indicate what the life and character of Noah was.

But it is on his Name,—the signification of it, and the emphatic mention of it in Scripture, as given by prophetic inspiration when he was born, that I would most dwell. And his father Lamech, it is said, "called his name Noah," i.e. "rest," or "comfort," "saying, This same shall comfort us concerning our work and toil of our hands, because of the ground which the Lord hath cursed." Scripture then, by this account, draws our attention to the "rest" and "comfort" which Noah imports amidst the troubles of the world. The words seem to imply some great alleviation from the evils of the fall. But yet if we look to the mere surface of the history, it is, as St. Ambrose observes, rather the contrary, for in his time wickedness advanced to such an accumulation and height of misery as to bring down the destruction of the world[5]. To this point I would more especially turn, not only because the mention of it in Genesis seems to draw attention to that circumstance, but also because our Lord Himself has in so memorable and marked a manner mentioned Noah and his days as the sign of the days of the Son of Man; and it has always been observed in the Church that the history of Noah is quite full of type and prophecy respecting the Church of Christ in the latter days. Indeed even among the tombs of the early martyrs unto this day some of the most frequent emblems of the Christian faith are taken from Noah, and the ark, and the dove. And that the

[4] Heb. xi. 7. [5] See St. Amb. De Noe et Arcâ, lib. i. cap. 1.

very name of rest and comfort, in its fuller acceptation, signifies Christ, is obvious unto all. Woe to him who looks to any one else for his comfort and rest.

Thus Noah seems to imply that there will be "a man" in Whom there will be rest and comfort in a perishing world. "And a man shall be," as the Prophet Isaiah says, "an hiding place from the wind, and a covert from the tempest[6]." In the first ages of the world there was a strong expectation that the great Deliverer was already come or coming; and in answer to this expectation men were given to be signs of Him. Four persons especially stand forth in the old world as it were the pillars of it on account of this faith; as Abel is the sign of Christ's Death; Seth of His Resurrection; Enoch of His Ascension; so Noah sets forth the rest and comfort which is to be found in Christ in the latter days when "iniquity shall abound." He is the depository of the promise, as God says to him, "With thee will I establish My covenant[7]." Of him Christ shall be born; and St. Paul designates him as the "heir of the righteousness which is by faith[8]."

Thus Noah stood alone in the world as it were the Second Adam, the New Man, the type of Him in Whom alone the Father is well pleased; of Him Who is alone "perfect" before God and "righteous;" of Him Who hath found grace, walking with God, for "God was with Him[9];" of Him Who hath promised to be with His Church unto the end; Who in His ministers and the stewards of His mysteries is warning, and preaching to, and interceding for a fallen world. With Noah the covenant is again renewed; and by an express warrant from God all the creatures are made subject to him. "And the dread of

[6] Isa. xxxii. 2.
[8] Heb. xi. 7.
[7] Gen. vi. 18.
[9] Acts x. 38.

you," it is said, "shall be upon every beast . . . into your hands they are delivered[1]." Thus was he the type of the Second Adam, of Whom it is said in the 8th Psalm, "Thou hast put all things in subjection under His feet; all sheep and oxen; yea, and the beasts of the field."

As there were the second tables of stone, the first being broken; a second covenant with man after the fall, when the first in Paradise had been forfeited; a second temple after the first was destroyed; a second people taken into covenant with God when the Jews were rejected; so now there is a second world which has the promise, the first being lost, in token of "the new heavens and new earth wherein dwelleth righteousness;" wherein, as St. John says, "there shall be no more curse[2]." "This same shall comfort us because of the ground which the Lord hath cursed."

Of this great redemption Noah is the sign, and as it were the second parent, as it is stated in the Evangelical Prophet, "For this is as the waters of Noah unto Me;" and then in explanation it is added, "for the mountains shall depart, and the hills be removed, but My kindness shall not depart from thee, nor the covenant of My peace be removed, saith the Lord that hath mercy on thee[3]." The same is again exhibited to us in a very beautiful and striking figure in the Prophet Ezekiel, which is afterwards renewed in the revelation of St. John, when Christ is represented as sitting on the throne of His Kingdom. "Upon the likeness of the throne," says the Prophet of Chebar, was "as the appearance of a man," and "round about was as the appearance of the bow that is in the cloud in the day of rain[4]." St. John says, "and there

[1] Gen. ix. 2.
[2] Rev xxii. 3.
[3] Isa. liv. 9, 10.
[4] Ezek. i. 26. 28.

was a rainbow round about the throne in sight like unto an emerald⁵." Thus "the faithful witness in Heaven" given to Noah still continues unto the end, because it speaks of the everlasting Gospel. "The bow shall be in the cloud, and I will look upon it," said God, "that I may remember the everlasting covenant⁶."

And hence more particularly in Noah, "the Spirit that beareth witness," sets forth "the Water and the Blood," or the two Sacraments: one in the flood and the ark, as St. Peter says, "The like figure whereunto baptism doth now save us by the resurrection of Jesus Christ." And the other Sacrament afterwards in the blood at that time so expressly set apart, as so emphatically repeated in the Law: "Be sure that thou eat not the blood, for the blood is the life thereof⁷." "For it is the blood that maketh an atonement for the soul⁸." Thus our Lord Himself said, "For My flesh is meat indeed, and My blood is drink indeed. He that eateth My flesh, and drinketh My blood dwelleth in Me, and I in him."

Thus strongly then is Christ represented to us in Noah; and these are great matters for our contemplation, when we consider His own awful words, in calling our attention to Noah. For when He Himself says, "as it was in the days of Noah, so shall it be in the days of the Son of Man," this resemblance in the times should rivet our attention to the resemblance to Himself also. Now a promise of rest and comfort, indicated by the name of Noah, implies great and signal need of comfort and rest, and therefore times of tribulation and trial, not necessarily to all men, but to the good; and this is shown in our Lord's own words, for the rest and comfort in Himself

⁵ Rev. iv. 3.
⁷ See Deut. xii. 23—28.
⁶ Gen. ix. 16.
⁸ Lev. xvii. 11.

which He promises is to them that are much weighed down and oppressed: "Come unto Me, all ye that travail and are heavy laden, and I will give you rest."

The times to which our Lord likens these the latter days are then the days of Noah, that is, the hundred and twenty years of his preaching: these are the days wherein He Himself warns men of coming judgment, wherein, if we may so apply the words of St. Peter, "the longsuffering of God waits in the days of the Son of Man, while the ark of Christ's Church is a preparing, wherein few are saved;" and the point of resemblance which our Lord takes is not the violence or great crimes then in the world; but a general forgetfulness of approaching judgment while mankind are taken up "with the cares and pleasures of this life." "They bought, they sold, they planted and builded, they were marrying, and giving in marriage until the day." They are precisely the same things which our Lord described as the reasons why men would not receive the Gospel, and which have been fulfilled from the time in which He spake even unto this day. For though He likens the Gospel to a feast, and though Noah signifies "rest" and "comfort," and the ark a place of refuge, yet they all, He says, with one consent began to make excuse; and these excuses, He states to be the very same reasons which He mentions in the days of Noah: "I have bought a piece of land, and must needs go and see it;" or, "I have married a wife, and therefore I cannot come."

Moreover, while all this is going on, this indifference and carelessness respecting the future, we have the same God, the same Jesus Christ, in the Book of Genesis as we have in the Gospels, mourning with infinite tenderness and compassion over mankind. In the former are the wonderful and affecting words, "And it repented the Lord that He had made man on the earth, and it grieved Him at His heart." This exactly corresponds with what we read in the Gospels of our Lord Himself, as in those His expressions: "Woe unto thee, Chorazin! woe unto thee, Bethsaida!" and the like: and in that memorable account that when He saw Jerusalem He wept over it, and said, "O Jerusalem, Jerusalem, how often would I have gathered thy children together as a hen gathereth her brood under her wings," i. e. foreseeing their danger which they knew not of, "but ye would not;" and in the evangelical parable He calls His angels together over one sinner that He has rescued, saying, "Rejoice with Me, for I have found the sheep which I had lost."

It is then in such days of great outward worldliness and sensuality, while God is "grieved," and His "Spirit striving" in vain with man, warning him of that Judgment which in the "evil imaginations of his heart" he sets aside and will not consider, that the example of Noah is given us. Now when our Lord tells us that if we come to Him He will give us rest; yet at the same time He teaches us that this coming to Him implies our taking upon us His yoke; and though He adds that that "yoke is easy," and that "burden light," yet in other places He speaks of it as the very Cross itself, which, though His martyrs and saints have indeed found full of joy and comfort, yet to flesh and blood it must be in itself burdensome and grievous. The dove of Noah returned to him because she could find no rest for the sole of her foot elsewhere, and he put forth his hand and received her into the ark with joy; but she had returned to the confinement of the ark instead of that liberty which was abroad in the world; and there is not a soul on earth but has oftentimes occasion to say, "Oh that I had wings like a dove! for then would I fly away, and be at rest. Lo, then would I get me away far off, and remain in the wilderness!" But of these very few indeed are they whose prayers in the Holy Spirit take the wings of the dove,—which though it hath lien among the pots yet is covered with silver wings,—and depart from the world to be with Christ.

And thus if Noah signifies comfort, and the great Comforter now in the world, yet he was one that had taken upon him the yoke of God, he was "a righteous man," "perfect in his generation," "walking with God." In building the ark he was, says St. Paul, "moved with fear," in faith receiving the awful warning "of God of things not seen as yet." The difference between him and the world around him was that he realized, expected, looked to the judgment which God was about to bring; but the world was as it is to this day, in the glass of God's Word, shutting its eyes and ears against warnings of the future. "They did eat, they drank, they married and gave in marriage, till Noah entered into the ark, and the flood came." The maxim of the world always is, as it then was, "Let us eat and drink, for to-morrow we die." But the Christian's precept is, "Let us fast and watch, for to-morrow we die, and after death the judgment;" or, in his Master's words, "Take heed that your heart be not overcharged with surfeiting and drunkenness, and the cares of this life, and so that day overtake you unawares." "Watch and pray, for ye know not when the time is."

To accept in faith and fear the doctrine of a sudden, speedy, and eternal Judgment will fill any one with disquietude, and make him feel his need of rest and comfort; and to such it is that this promise is given. He will feel his need of far other consolations than these which the world supplies from without; and most men have had this impression, and felt this want for a time ; as, for instance, when the dead body of a friend or near relative has been lying before them. For in that case they know the Judgment hath in some sense already overtaken, and that too speedily; and they see it must shortly be so with themselves, and they are moved ; and while this impression lasts they seek and find rest in Christ, and comfort in the great Comforter; but when the storm has been stilled, and the waters of that affliction abate, they again, like Noah's dove, leave the ark and, may be, return to it no more.

And now to look more closely at the example of Noah, and consider it in conjunction with the warnings of God ; it is evident that a deep and abiding, nay, an overwhelming sense of coming Judgment, under which the Christian is to live, is to affect the heart in the world, and not out of the world ; or rather is to have the effect of taking him out of the world while he is in the world. And this is the difficulty, he is to walk with God, i. e. with Christ risen, whilst in the world. For Noah himself, while he "walked with God," yet was engaged in those earthly occupations which it is said in the case of the rest of mankind withdrew their heart from the great hereafter. He married and gave in marriage. He was "a husbandman, and planted*." Nay, as he was a "righteous man," this implies that he had dealings with mankind, wherein righteousness or integrity is shown : he bought and sold as other men. It is then in these very same occupations, even in the same field, in the same mill, and the same bed, one shall be taken and the other left, when the separation is made. It depends on the keeping or not keeping of the heart in the same employments : as St. Paul states the same : "Brethren, the time is short : it remaineth, that both they that have wives be as though

* Gen. ix. 20.

they had none;... they that rejoice as though they rejoiced not; they that buy as though they possessed not; ... for the fashion of this world passeth away[1]." And thus when the Psalmist speaks of those who "forget God" being "cast into hell," he adds, "but the patient abiding of the meek shall not perish."

It is not then in taking us out of these things, but by taking the heart out of them, that the change is needed: and so far from such avocations being made an excuse for neglecting the Gospel, and its great injunction of watchfulness and prayer, they are the most urgent reasons for them. Instead of its being said, "I have bought a yoke of oxen," or the like, "and therefore I cannot come," when God calls, it should be said, "I have bought or sold, and therefore I needs must watch and pray more earnestly, for death is found in such things to all who do not. I am engaged in domestic concerns, and therefore I must watch and pray the more continually, lest I be too much taken up in them, and be found sleeping when the time comes." We daily need bread for the body, because we have earthly work to do; shall we not equally need daily bread for the soul, because we have also heavenly work to do, and the night cometh when no man can work—that work which if found undone, must be left undone for ever?

[1] 1 Cor. vii. 29–31.

ABRAHAM

And the angel of the Lord called unto him out of heaven, and said, Abraham, Abraham.—GENESIS xxii. 11.

THERE is nothing in Holy Scripture, unless it be in the Gospels themselves, of such awful and moving interest, as the life of Abraham; and when he has come to that crowning trial of all, and God calls to him out of Heaven, repeating his name, nay, as if not content with that, like one among men, who, on some great crisis of joy and thankfulness, hastens to repeat again his deep sense of what has been done, when, I say, God calls to him a "second time out of Heaven," saying, "By Myself have I sworn, saith the Lord, for because thou hast done this thing, and hast not withheld thy son, thine only son : that in blessing I will bless thee." So thrilling and overwhelming is this awful moment of interest, that there is nothing equal to it in the history of man. He has obtained the victory of all victories, and the highest praise of God ; he has, in the course of a few hours, done an act of which the consequences are felt unto the end of time. It is as if the Heavens themselves had been in deep and awful suspense, watching what he would do, whether he would be equal to that great trial of all trials that God had put upon him : and when he "stretched forth his hand to slay his son," then all the creations of God and the Angels of Heaven rejoiced with a great and mighty rejoicing. The Angel of the Covenant, nay, God Himself, called aloud from Heaven, repeating his name, and again a second time declared and confirmed the blessing. No occasion has been like this; and probably none will be till that awful moment itself which resembles it, when it shall be said by Christ Himself to him that has overcome, the true son in the faith of the faithful Abraham, "Well done, thou good and faithful servant, . . . enter thou into the joy of thy Lord."

This transcendent consummation of all trials had this in it above all, that it was made to have a resemblance to the act of the Almighty Father Himself, in giving up His Only Beloved Son to die for mankind, to be an imitation of the perfection of Divine love itself. Here is a father for God's love willing to be fatherless; and in that willingness made the father of nations, and of all that are in Christ. O wonderful old man! O wonder of all wonders! O joy of all joys! Well indeed may that child be to thee the name of joy and wonder; God hath indeed "made thee to *laugh*," and his mother, and "all that hear shall laugh[1]" with thee, "at the strangeness of that salvation." O faith without parallel, grounded in love! O love, strong as death, high as Heaven, image of the love of God for man! The death-pang of trial is over, and the crown is won. And, oh! who but God can know what those three days of travail were to Abraham? and what it was when "on the third day he lifted up his eyes, and saw the place afar off," what the struggle between faith and affection, between nature and grace, the yearnings of all that was human, and the constraining power of all that was Divine? the tender child on the one hand, and on

[1] Gen. xxi. 6.

the other the knife, the cords, and the wood; the child of his love, the son of his old age, the heir of the promise, the child on whom were centred the hopes of all that God had given, and was about to give; "thy son, thine only son, whom thou lovest," as God Himself said; the child by his side, with the affecting, simple inquiry, "Father, where is the lamb?" But blessed be God Who called him by His grace, and gave him to hear His call, and to persevere unto the end! His "light affliction" was but "for a moment," and hath wrought for him "an eternal weight of glory."

And now as He Who put upon him this great burden knew that he would attend to His voice, and gave him power to do it, let us consider how from step to step through his life God had called him on by little and little, and he had answered every call, till it was given him to hear and to answer this great summons, the perfection and crown of all. As he "rose up early in the morning," and had three days of painful trial before him, till he came to the Mount of God, in like manner had his whole life from the first been a preparation for this great act. Even from childhood we may suppose that God had been dealing with him, and as the looks of a loving child answer the light of a father's countenance, so grace answered to grace; and among the Chaldees, his family and kindred, he habituated his heart to listen to, and hear and understand that still small voice that pleadeth with every man, till the call came and the trial. Then he arose at God's bidding, leaving Ur of the Chaldees, the seat of his childhood and youth, and dwelt at Haran. Then came from God a second call to leave his country, and his kindred, and his father's house, and leaving Haran, he "went forth to go into the land of Canaan; and into the land of Canaan he came². " Most, if not all persons, have had these first and early calls by God's Spirit, but in most cases these calls have not been answered by the heart, and therefore what the advance onward would have been has not been known. We have been all called from the first to leave the country wherein we were born, to seek "a better country, that is an heavenly," though we be in it for a time but strangers, with the enemy in the land. Nay, we know not beforehand not only not the sufferings we have to undergo, but above all, we know not the treasures and delights of that kingdom of grace, as they become afterwards known to the true believer. For obedience comes first, and knowledge afterwards; God calls, and faith obeys the call, knowing that when God commands He gives grace to fulfil.

Now from this beginning in Abraham what was not to be expected? He had already cast the world behind him from an unconquerable trust in God; poor in all things as yet, but rich in faith, "he went out, knowing not whither he went;" and when he came to the place where he was promised a possession, he had "not so much as to set his foot on." And again, it was to be "an inheritance to his seed," but "he had no child³." To all but the eye of faith there was nothing but disappointment, and he was deceived of his high expectations; but he strengthened himself by beholding Him that is invisible; it was this disappointment and frustration of his hopes, this very weakness, that made him strong; and when he found it thus, "he looked for a city which hath foundations, whose Builder and Maker is God⁴." The enlargement of his heart, the raising of his spirit, the strengthening of his soul, was from this, which would have otherwise been straitening, depressing,

² Gen. xiii. 1. 5.   ³ Acts vii. 5.   ⁴ Heb. xi. 10.

weakening; and he confessed himself "a stranger and a pilgrim upon earth[5]." He put his soul as it were into his hand, and left the issue with God. As he could not look to the objects of sight to rest on, he looked upwards to the things of faith, nay, rather he looked upward to God alone. God became to him his all, his treasure, his home, his country, his inheritance for ever; this was the secret of his endurance, and God Himself, answering his heart's desire, said to him, "I am thy exceeding great reward[6]." He loved God, and therefore he loved what God loved; he hated father, and mother, and child, yea, and his own life also; not that he loved them the less by dwelling in the very Fountain of Love Itself, but that his love for himself and his own was but as hate compared with his love of God. Or rather shall we say with Scripture, his fear of God, his fear of losing Him, of losing His love, of displeasing Him, as the voice from Heaven said to him, "Abraham, Abraham, now I know that thou fearest God[7]."

Now not to dwell on all the particulars of the life of Abraham, we know that he is pre-eminent above all men for faith, and faith is to the Christian all in all; faith marked and crowned the life of Abraham as its great characteristic; this faith is always referred to when Abraham is spoken of, whereby he is made "the father of the faithful," the chosen father of Christ in the flesh, the type of the accepted ones, the first in the kingdom of Heaven. This faith is described in the Epistle to the Hebrews as seen in all the great acts of his life, all leading on to the great consummation in the offering up of his son. But now we may observe how this faith in God, like that charity which St. Paul describes, was "fruitful in every

[5] Gen. xxiii. 4; Heb. xi. 13.   [6] Gen. xv. 1.   [7] Gen. xxii. 12.

good word and work," was seen in every virtue and grace that can adorn the Christian character.

First of all, with regard to his devotion, we must have noticed how it occurs, incidentally as it were, in his history, that his removal from one place to another is scarcely ever mentioned without this circumstance, so frequent as to be quite peculiar to him, so emphatic and brief the mention as to indicate some acceptable and distinguishing act of faith. Thus, "And Abram passed unto the place of Sichem, . . . and there builded he an altar unto the Lord, Who appeared unto him." And the next verse, "And he removed thence unto a mountain on the east of Bethel, . . . and there he builded an altar, and called upon the name of the Lord[8]." And again the next chapter, "And he went on his journeys from the south even to Bethel, . . . unto the place of the altar which he had made there at the first, and there Abram called on the name of the Lord." And a little afterwards, "Then Abram removed his tent, and came and dwelt in the plain of Mamre, . . . and built there an altar unto the Lord[9]." This is in the earlier mention of him.

In the next place he was tried by prosperity and not found wanting. His heart was with God. He was "very rich[1]," and amidst his riches, says St. Augustine, was poor in spirit. In possessing he was as though he "possessed not." So much so that in our Lord's parable it was into Abraham's bosom that poor Lazarus was received; it was Abraham who pleaded for him with the rich Jew, saying, "Thou in thy lifetime received thy good things, and Lazarus evil." Of this his freedom from covetousness several instances may be mentioned. Thus, when on account of their increasing substance it was necessary for

[8] Gen. xii. 6—8.   [9] Gen. xiii. 3, 4. 18.   [1] Gen. xiii. 2.

himself and his brother's son to separate, "Abram said unto Lot, Let there be no strife, I pray thee, between me and thee, for we are brethren:" and then when he might fairly have claimed to himself the choice of the better land, he offers all this to his nephew, and Lot chose for himself the rich plain of Jordan, flourishing "as the garden of the Lord." The same liberality and greatness of soul is seen again when the king of Sodom, on his rescuing his people from captivity, says to him, "Give me the persons, take the goods to thyself," but Abraham's answer is, "I will not take from thee a thread even to a shoelatchet." On the same occasion the like integrity towards God appears when to Melchizedeck, the Priest of the Most High God who met him at the same time and blessed him, he gave tithes of all. A similar disinterestedness is afterwards shown in his dealings with the Hittites for the cave of Machpelah. To which we may add, that his example for hospitality is referred to by the Apostle: "Be not forgetful to entertain strangers, whereby some have entertained angels unawares."

And no less remarkable was his courage as seen in that signal instance when he arose and rescued Lot from Chedorlaomer and the kings; when he fought not for himself, but for another; not for possession or glory, but from brotherly affection. There is also throughout his whole life a singular meekness, as may be observed in all his conduct, to Lot, to Sarah his wife, to all others; to Melchizedeck, to Abimelech, to Ephron the Hittite; he bowed down himself before them and said, "I am a stranger and sojourner with you². " There is a remarkable patience and humility in all his words and deportment. And again, what compassionate love is seen as filling all his character

² Gen. xxiii. 4. 7.

in all that long intercession for the sparing of Sodom! To these things must be added one point which God Himself is pleased to single out in Abraham as the great cause of His favour, and that is the religious care of his household: "I know him, that he will command his children and his household after him, and they shall keep the way of the Lord[3]." And we may observe a remarkable instance of this in "the eldest servant of his house," whom he sends for his son's wife: a great piety and devotion marks his whole conduct so as to be very like Abraham himself[4].

But it is indeed when he turns to God more especially that all the wonderful depth and sweetness of Abraham's character is seen; it comes forth as it were upon his countenance, and lights it up as when friend meets a friend; as on that occasion of interceding for Sodom, what love, what reverential awe and humility! "And Abraham drew near, and said, Wilt Thou also destroy the righteous with the wicked?" And then, "Abraham answered and said, Behold now, I have taken upon myself to speak unto the Lord, which am but dust and ashes." And again, "And he said unto Him, Oh, let not the Lord be angry, and I will speak." And then even once more with the same affecting words. How is all this which so marks the character of Abraham contained in the proverbial expression that "he was called the Friend of God[5]!" How does

---

[3] Gen. xviii. 19.

[4] Ancient writers on Abraham's going down to Egypt with his wife, and their saying indeed the truth, though not all the truth, speak of that occasion as a beautiful instance of his faith in God, and that God by His protection of him and the pleading of his cause showed that his trust in Him was not disappointed.—St. Aug. iii. 613; vii. 689; viii. 596. St. Amb. De Abr. lib. i. c. 11. s. 9. "Pulcherrimus est hic locus ad incitandum studium devotionis," &c.

[5] James ii. 23; Isa. xli. 8; 2 Chron. xx. 7.

this beautiful confiding trust break forth in that gentle inquiry when all earthly promises seemed against him: "Lord God, what wilt Thou give me?" There is the same lowliness of mind and love, when on a later occasion he fell on his face and laughed in surprise and wonder. Hence there appears through his words and actions such a remarkable indifference, as if his heart were elsewhere. But he had we know a hidden joy, of which our Lord has Himself testified, "Your father Abraham *rejoiced* to see My day, and he saw it afar off and was *glad.*" Hence I say this great unconcern in matters of self, and his great earnestness in things of God. Zeal and alacrity mark where the heart is. On three occasions this may be noted in Abraham, in his haste to receive his three guests with welcome; in his hastening to rescue Lot; and when he "arose up early in the morning" to sacrifice his son in obedience to God.

Thus did Abraham advance onward, and gained strength as he advanced: as he waited on God, and waited for God, so did God watch over him: as at every stage he built an altar and called on God, so also again and again did God appear unto him, bringing sunshine on his path on every occasion of difficulty or trial; first at Ur of the Chaldees[6]; then with great promise of blessing at Haran; then when he came into the land of Canaan and found the Canaanite there, did God appear unto Abraham with the promise of that land to his seed. And when Lot parted from him and he was left alone, then still more emphatically with the assurance, "Lift up thine eyes and look Northward, and Southward, and Eastward, and Westward," "all thou seest" on every side is thine for ever. And then after his victory, living as he must have done amidst angry

[6] Acts vii. 2.

kings and foes, God again appears to him, saying, "Fear not, Abram, I am thy shield[7]." Yet his faith is marked with an absence of definite knowledge throughout, but a full reliance on God; when he left his country, he knew not whither he was to go; when the promises were made, he knew not how they could be fulfilled. As his faith increased, so did the promises, but they were of things still further off, and on God he reposed: first, his seed was to fill the land of Canaan; then came the promise that the nations of the earth are in him to be blessed; his seed after the flesh are to be as the sand on the shore; and to fill the earth; and then again they are to be as the stars and to people Heaven also. But when he wished for a sign and for clearer knowledge, "a horror of great darkness fell upon him," as setting forth the great tribulation, and a light that divided; it was, says St. Augustine, the sign and the sight of Antichrist; it was a sad vision; enough to raise his mind to Heaven, that he might not seek rest on earth, and might see that in mercy God veils the future from our eyes[8].

Thus then is given us the wonderful pattern of a soul that would live to God, in God, and for God—the life of faith. God calling and commanding, and giving him power to perform what He commanded, and blessing and crowning His own work in him. God proceeding with promise, and Abraham with faith: till Abraham was no more himself, no more his own; but faith in God filled all his soul, all that he did, all that is recorded of him.

It was this faith that lighted up his character with every virtue and grace; it was like one light brightening

---

[7] Gen. xii. 6, 7; xiii. 14; xv. 1.
[8] Gen. xv. See St. Aug. Civ. Dei, vol. vii. p. 696.

up jewels of many colours; faith was in his generosity; faith in his courage; faith in his humility; faith in his devotion; faith in the care of his household; it was all one and the same faith burning more and more intensely, till it had purged the dross and alloy of human affection; and God had become to him his only rest. God looked upon him, and a ray from the light of His countenance warmed and lit up his heart; and that illumination was faith. His "eye was single," and therefore his "whole body was full of light," his whole character full of God.

LOT

Then Lot chose him all the plain of Jordan; and Lot journeyed East: and they separated themselves the one from the other.—
GENESIS xiii. 11.

OUR Lord has said, "Remember Lot's wife;" if He had not, men might have thought there is nothing we know of Lot's wife which has any thing to do with Christianity, nor indeed with religion at all; what we are told of her is a mere matter of fact like any other incident in history, that on looking back in escaping from Sodom, "she became a pillar of salt." But now our Lord has marked it as an especial warning to us in these last days, as speaking of the dangers of a half-repentance, of one that has been once saved by God's mercy, and assisted by His grace, casting back the eyes to that state from which he has been once delivered. It is an incident which says of itself, in other words, that "no man having put his hand to the plough, and looking back, is fit for the kingdom of God[1]." If then it be the case with that one circumstance, we may be sure that the whole of that awful history is full of instruction for us, and contains admonitions from God. Nay, further, our Lord has Himself given us to understand that the destruction of Sodom is a figure of the last Judgment, which will come at a time

[1] Luke ix. 62.

when lawlessness shall abound, and faith be scarce found. Lot therefore is, as St. Augustine says, a sign of the Body of Christ at that time[2], of the Christians who shall be grieved at the wickedness of the world around, and by God's mercy escape the great condemnation. Full of interest then to us is the character of Lot, who is saved; and it is one that affords much matter for reflection from its imperfectness, and God's mercy notwithstanding.

St. Peter speaks of Lot as a righteous man. "And delivered just Lot," he says, "vexed with the filthy conversation of the wicked: for that righteous man dwelling among them . . . vexed his righteous soul[3]." Here he is spoken of as a righteous man in comparison with that wicked people among whom he dwelt[4], and as knowing the true God. St. Paul also perhaps alludes to his hospitality[5], as well as that of Abraham; and it is something to have been the friend of Abraham, who was "the friend of God." But on the other hand, St. Paul makes no mention of Lot in the catalogue of those whom he records as by faith inheriting the promises. And in this history nothing is said of Lot being in himself accepted except for Abraham's sake; "God remembered Abraham," it is said, "and sent Lot out of the midst of the overthrow, when He overthrew the cities in the which Lot dwelt[6]." "Scripture reminds us," says St. Augustine, "that it was for the merits of Abraham that Lot was delivered[7]." The history of his deliverance shows God's extreme care for Lot; the Angel waits long and presses him, and great as is the guilt, loud the cry of Sodom, he says, he can do nothing till Lot is in

[2] St. Aug. viii. 598.   [3] 2 Pet. ii. 7, 8.
[4] St. Aug. iii. 619.   [5] Heb. xiii. 2.
[6] Gen. xix. 29.   [7] Quæs. in Gen. xlv. vol. iii. 619.

a place of safety: but it is mentioned as of God's especial mercy to him. No approbation is expressed of him. It is for Abraham's sake who was probably at the time interceding for him with God.

It would appear as if Scripture had purposely interwoven the histories of Abraham and Lot, in order to show us by placing them together the difference between a perfect and imperfect faith. The beginning of Lot's history is one with that of Abraham; they both leave their country and home, both go to a strange land. We read, "Abraham went and Lot with him;" this is repeated; under the shadow of Abraham we behold him, one with Abraham, learning of him self-sacrifice, hospitality, trust in God. But as the companion and nephew of Abraham, as living under his guidance and protection, there is as yet in Lot no proof of an independent faith. Many are brought up under the shelter of a parent's roof in godly habits, while all the while their own faith is not as yet put to the proof. It may be as good as his under whose shade they dwell, time and temptation will show; they may be merely as shoots from a parent stem, having no root in themselves but from connexion with the deeper and stronger stock, and when severed from it, then will come the trial of inherent life.

The first indication of this difference between the two is seen when, on account of their increasing herds, they are obliged to part asunder; then there appears in Lot a worldly eye, a sense of his own advantage. "And Lot lifted up his eyes, and beheld all the plain of Jordan, that it was well watered every where, before the Lord destroyed Sodom and Gomorrha." "Then Lot chose him all the plain of Jordan," "and pitched his camp toward Sodom. But the men of Sodom," it is added, "were wicked and sinners before the Lord exceedingly." Thus they are now parted asunder in the earthly Canaan, but still more in their road toward the heavenly. Lot is governed by sight, Abraham by faith. There is nothing perhaps more frequently decides the eternal condition of the soul than the use of worldly goods. All the dealings of God with Abraham had been to separate him from the wicked nations; but Lot chooses to live among the worst of them, and contracts marriages with them, because their land was "as the garden of the Lord." He thinks more of the rich land than of the wicked people. He lifted up his eyes, and he saw the rich beauty of the land, and pitched his tent toward Sodom; now the men of Sodom were exceedingly wicked. The passage is remarkable, as implying so much, and saying so little.

From this point came the change and the trial. While Abraham continued with his eyes turned more and more to God; more free from worldly cares and temptations; more at rest and peace with God; with light burning more and more bright to the perfect day; God's presence a "shield" against every temptation; His love a "reward exceeding great," beyond all things on earth; while he is seen with all his family and household walking with God, with step more and more firm as he advances onward, and is lost from our view in the light of God's countenance and the heavenly Jerusalem; in the meanwhile the best thing which an Apostle can say of Lot is of his being vexed from day to day on account of those scenes into the midst of which he had placed himself by a too keen estimate of worldly good. And what was his family? and what his care of them? His sons-in-law were of Sodom; his wife a memorial to all ages of a doubting faith; from his daughters were sprung the great enemies of God's people. Abraham waited in faith and looked to God, and God gave in His own good time; Lot waited not, but chose for himself, and lost what he thus obtained. Lot was next seen with the king of Sodom, joined with him in the evils that came upon him; Abraham with the king of Salem, which is Peace, and receiving the blessing of Melchizedeck, the Priest of the Most High God.

On every change of life, on every proof of duty and self-sacrifice, God appears to Abraham with some manifestation of favour, and he goes on his way rejoicing. But far otherwise with Lot; God has been pleased to mark his course with disappointment in those very things which he for himself had chosen. This indeed is always a sign of God's mercy; it is in tribulation that God speaks, and in tribulation man listens to His voice. But were it not for Abraham he would have lost all, and ended his days as a captive, for it so pleased the Almighty that all his deliverances should be through the means of Abraham, who trusted in God. We just now read that "Lot lifted up his eyes, and saw as it were the garden of the Lord, and chose him all the plain," "and dwelled in the cities of the plain towards Sodom;" but the next thing we hear of him is that Chedorlaomer, the king of Elam, had overcome and slain the kings of Sodom and Gomorrha; "and they took Lot," it is added, "Abram's brother's son, who dwelt in Sodom, and his goods, and departed." Thus was he admonished and warned of God. But God has for him, and in him for us all, a yet more awful warning, to stand as a record to all ages, for a sign of what is yet to be.

It had been said at first that Lot "pitched his tent toward Sodom;" but it would appear as if he afterwards ceased to dwell in tents, as Abraham and his children did, indicating thereby, says St. Paul, that they were strangers and pilgrims upon earth, looking for a more abiding city.

But many must have this lesson written on them as it were by fire. Lot lifted up his eyes and saw the well-watered plain—as it were the garden of the Lord—and beautiful must it have been indeed to look on. What fulness of beauty and abundance, with its pure waters and skies, and morning and evening suns! But wait awhile and look again; Lot cannot look to it, he may not look to it, he cannot escape sufficiently far from it; we may look to it in the gracious light of Christ's goodness, and behold in it the Judgment day, and the soul salted with fire. What a change on that scene! the smoke rising up as from a furnace, the brimstone, the ashes, and the salt, which is no salt, but bitterness; the dead sea, and the dead land are there; nay, the land of the dead unto this day.

But while these marks of God have taken place on the objects of Lot's choice, let us consider what is more important, what changes are going on within the soul; what indications there are of the inner life. I observed that Lot's character was of interest to us from its very imperfection; and for this reason, that when we read of the highly-approved Saints of God, much of the interest is lost from our considering them so much beyond us; and when we come to those whom Scripture strongly condemns, as Pharaoh, and Saul, and Ahab, we think we are not such as they, so that their example does not so much rivet our attention; but that of Lot is very near us, as resembling that of so many among Christians; such as we should many of us be content to be, for we think that he has with him signs of salvation and of God's mercy.

Now in considering Lot our thoughts are mostly turned to those events to which our Lord has so signally invited our attention, the overthrow of Sodom. Yet surely the account of Lot himself is rendered on that occasion full of fear by his very imperfection and the consequent difficulty of his deliverance. Seasons of prosperity and temptation, with intervals perhaps more or less of ease, together with worldly carefulness and pleasures, may be passing over us through life and producing changes on our minds which we do not notice at the time; but they await the occasion of some great trial, which will probably overtake us before we die or at the time of death itself, perhaps in sickness or some great bereavement or tribulation, and then these changes which have been long silently going on will appear. Then it is that their effects on the soul will tell; and the way in which all the sins and infirmities of a whole life may then be shown will be in the want of faith; that is all in short which unites the soul to God being impaired and weakened; the very heart as it were of the heart itself, our religious being, the only strength of our spiritual life, being eaten out and corrupted. This trial came on Lot unexpected and irretrievable; sudden, short, speedy; it was come and gone ere he had time to reflect; and in this respect it has been left by our Lord as the sign and resemblance of that great season of change which we have all to undergo. Such indeed have been usually the great trials of faith, as in Esau's lost inheritance, in the trial of Moses, in Saul's disobedience, in David's sin, in Lot's wife, in St. Peter walking on the waters and his denials in the hall of Caiaphas, and again in the Rich Young Man, and in Judas Iscariot, they overtook when unexpected, weighed the soul in the balance, and were gone. And indeed the imperfections of Lot on that terrible night have been considered by St. Augustine to have been owing to great perturbation of mind arising from the suddenness of the trials that then crowded together upon him, from the wickedness of man and the judgments of God. The state of his mind appears to have been twofold, as formed by opposite influences; there was in him Abraham's faith which had become like part of his better self, as seen in his knowledge of God, his kindness and reverence for his Angel-guests, his strong and hospitable welcome to them; but with this there appears also the effect on his soul of long residence amongst the ungodly; so that compared with them of Sodom he was a righteous man, the "just Lot;" but compared with Abraham he was not what he might have been. He was grieved at the wickedness of the city, for they were past warning and beyond hope, given over of God to a reprobate mind; but he went out to his own sons-in-law at the Angels' bidding with the offer of preservation and life; as if in them there was yet hope, and the voice of God speaking to them and within them: but even here too his influence with them was none at all. "He seemed," it is said, "as one that mocked to his sons-in-law." He grieved over some; and warned others; and so far he was a witness of God. But it next appears that there was a lingering reluctance in his own heart; for it is added, "Then the Angels hastened Lot, saying, Arise, . . . lest thou be consumed in the iniquity of the city." But notwithstanding he "yet lingered," and God of His great mercy met him, as it were, and aided him in that his weakness.

"And while he lingered, the men laid hold upon his hand, . . . the Lord being merciful unto him; and they brought him forth, and set him without the city." But though without the city, he is not yet safe, nor will be, unless God is yet further gracious to him, for there is still the like weakness, a feebleness of heart that makes his knees totter and his strength fail. "And it came to pass, when they had brought them forth abroad, that he said, Escape for thy life; look not behind thee, neither stay thou in all the plain; escape to the mountain, lest thou be consumed. And Lot said unto them, Oh, not so, my Lord: behold now, thy servant hath found grace in thy sight, and thou hast magnified thy mercy, which thou hast showed thy servant in saving my life; and I cannot escape to the mountain."

Now true faith is marked by a strong sense, not of the goodness only, but still more of the power of God. What is the meaning of a weak faith, a weak Christian? It is one that is weak in God. It was a belief in His power that our Lord most of all required, and most approved of in the Gospels. "I can do all things," says St. Paul, "through Christ strengthening me." Lot looks to the mercy, not to the power. And how different is his conduct from that of Abraham! Abraham when bidden, arose early and went to the mountain to slay his son, strengthening himself in beholding Him that is Invisible. Lot is bidden to flee to the mountain, that he may save his life; but he lingers and has not power to do so, not faith that He who commands would give power to perform. It is said to him, "Escape to the mountain, lest thou be consumed," but he says in answer, that he cannot escape to the mountain, lest he die. Nor is this all, for he then soon after "feared to dwell even in the little city which God had spared for him, and promised him security therein[8];" showing thereby, as St. Augustine observes, what little strength his faith had, so that even from thence he went up to the mountain and the cave.

Thus then did Lot "escape for his life," with his life

[8] St. Aug. Quæs. in Gen. xlvii.

only—his "life given him for a prey," all else lost—saved as by fire—as a brand plucked from the burning—scarce saved, as the Apostle says, apparently with an allusion to him, "if the righteous scarcely be saved."

Many indeed would be well content to be as Lot, and if but saved at last, think that all will be well. But consider, to be but scarcely saved, is to be well-nigh lost, and what if not saved, but lost! Lot had Abraham to look to, and fell short; but he that looks to Lot, and falls short even of that, as he surely will do, can have not even a Zoar allowed him to escape to. Lot lingers and hesitates, and with difficulty advances. The next thing to this is to look back, and then, "Remember Lot's wife." No doubt the example of Lot is given us by the side of Abraham for our warning and avoidance; the uncertainty, the temptation, the dangers, the suspense, the terrors of that night may well indicate the state of a soul such as that of Lot in the great crisis we may all have to undergo.

These are both instances of faith—Abraham and Lot. But look at this and look at that; see the peace of the one—the disquietude of the other; godliness hath the promise of the life which now is, and of that which is to come; to him that seeketh first the kingdom of God all things needful for this life shall be added; nay, more, to self-sacrifice is promised manifold more in this present time, as well as everlasting life hereafter; it hath "peace and joy in the Holy Ghost;" but this is all to one thoroughly religious, to the life of faith; to the half-religious it is not so, but doubt often, and care, and inquietude. Joys of sense are not compatible with joys of the spirit; gladness is spoken of with singleness of heart; but these are not found with "fulness of bread," which gave rise to the sin of Sodom.

Now where shall all who are met here on this day find

themselves described in the awful picture of this history? You are not as they of Sodom; nor are you probably as Lot's sons-in-law, who mocked at his entreaties; neither are you such as Abraham; then you must be either as Lot or as Lot's wife; in a state of uncertainty for good or evil, and one in which faith may be strengthened or weakened; and if in either of these states now and at the last, then your end will be one of these two; in one case, that you are very nearly lost, but not quite—in the other, that you are very nearly saved, *but not quite!*

JACOB AND ESAU

Was not Esau Jacob's brother? saith the Lord: yet I loved Jacob, and I hated Esau.—MALACHI i. 2, 3.

IT is said that, "the Heavens are not clean in God's sight;" and that "His Angels He chargeth with folly," much more "them that dwell in houses of clay[1]." Among the Saints in the mirror of God's Word there is not one that appears as it were "without spot or wrinkle." In some cases Scripture itself bears witness to this, as in the sin of Moses, of David, of Hezekiah, the denial of St. Peter, and the error of St. John in wishing to bring down fire from Heaven, and with his mother in asking for the chief place. But where the Word of God has expressed no censure it is better not to judge; as in the apparent act of intemperance in Noah, the conduct of Abraham towards Pharaoh, and that of Jacob in obtaining his father's blessing. A good Bishop of our own has strongly condemned this last, and noticed the retribution that followed on Jacob and his mother: that he became an exile in consequence, and she never saw him again; that he was himself soon after deceived in a very remarkable manner by Laban; that he was imposed upon by his own sons in his old age, and that as he had deceived his aged father

[1] Job xv. 15; iv. 18, 19.

with a kid, so his son Joseph's coat was brought to him dyed with the blood of a kid[2].

Such are the reflections of one much revered among us; but the ancient Fathers are very unwilling to attribute sin to Jacob in this matter, knowing how high he stands in the favour of God. We know not how much may be left unexplained to us in that transaction; for it is evidently the setting forth of a great mystery, the sacrament of our redemption; we know not what interposition of God may have taken place with respect to Rebekah, or how far she and her son may have been acting under the influence and hand of God. She had been told of God beforehand that "the elder should serve the younger[3]:" she knew that Jacob valued in faith the covenant that God had made with Abraham respecting Christ, and that Esau despised it, and had sold his birthright: she takes it all upon herself, saying, "Upon me be thy curse, my son:" as knowing that it was no curse but a blessing. Neither does Isaac express any blame on Rebekah or on Jacob; but on the contrary immediately confirms and repeats the blessing. It is said that on finding what he had done he "trembled very exceedingly," this is explained by the Church of old as signifying that by a sudden inspiration from above he perceived the Divine interposition and the hand of God; and then he does willingly what he had before done in ignorance. And not only does he then at the time acquiesce in and establish the blessing he had given, but afterwards he carries out the same, when he sends him to the East; when the account is, "And Isaac called Jacob, and blessed him," "and said, God Almighty bless thee, ... and give thee the blessing of Abraham."

It is indeed in these two brothers God now shows that

[2] Bp. Wilson.   [3] Gen. xxv. 23.

the covenant of grace and salvation which He had made with Abraham is only to stand by faith; and this transaction is the representation of that great mystery. Hence in Jacob we have the Gentile, the younger son, coming and obtaining the blessing of the elder; the Old Testament, the Law and the Prophets represented by Isaac, appeared as if they would confer the blessing on the Jew, for they seemed to address the Jews, to give them the promises. But their father's "eyes were dim" by reason of age, "so that he could not see," i. e. the Law and the Prophets were not understood, they were veiled by a cloud. But Rebekah, she that had been called and come from afar, i. e. the Church of God from the beginning, substitutes the younger son, in the raiment of the elder; he stands in the place of the elder, having received the birthright; but covered with the skins of the slain kid, i. e. having put on Christ, the savour of life, "as the smell of the field which the Lord hath blessed," fruitful in all good works. But the voice is still the voice of Jacob, it is that of the Gentile who by subtlety as it were presses into the kingdom; it is still our nature, which inherits not by right, but through the merits of our elder brother, the First-born, which is Christ. Then he draws near and receives from his father the sacramental kiss of peace, which Esau did not[4]. But as the Jew persecuted the Gentile unto the death, so Esau, it is said, would have slain Jacob; but Jacob fled, having "suffered the loss of all things," but having his father's blessing; like the early Christians, "as deceivers and yet true," "having nothing and yet possessing all things," "persecuted but not forsaken."

It is true that all this does not of itself justify Jacob

[4] St. Chrysostom.

in that transaction because it was thus overruled of God; but this, and some other things of the same kind in the character of this patriarch, we may be content to leave with God, not venturing to judge where God has not judged for us. And in the meanwhile may be mentioned some reflections which should dispose us to think favourably of Jacob, as far as we are allowed to do so. Isaac says by inspiration, "Blessed be he that blesseth thee," we would share in this blessing. We would wish to love what God loves and to hate what God hates; and surely this is a strong expression in the text, which is repeated by St. Paul, "Jacob have I loved." And to come to particulars, he seems to have the praise of God in this very point in which we are inclined to condemn him, for what men attribute to Jacob is deceitfulness; but before mentioning that mysterious transaction Scripture states, as it were intentionally, says St. Augustine[5], that "Jacob was a plain man," i.e. one void of guile and deceit, in contrast to the craft of the "cunning hunter." Which character of Jacob is, as the same writer observes, confirmed by our Lord Himself, for when He says of Nathanael, "Behold an Israelite indeed, in whom there is no guile!" He evidently implies that Israel of old was thus free from guile; even as those who had great faith He spake of as being true children of Abraham. And indeed in this very account itself there seems a shrinking from guile and simplicity of heart in Jacob's words, when he draws back, saying to his mother, "I shall seem to him as a deceiver, and bring on myself a curse, and not a blessing."

But to take a yet larger view of the subject, Jacob is not only one in that "cloud of witnesses," by which, as

[5] Sermon iv. 15, 16.

St. Paul says, we are "compassed about," as examples in that race which is set before us, but he is one of those three chosen ones selected of God for an especial mention of the highest kind as associated with Himself. For we must remember that God is known for ever as the God of Abraham, and the God of Isaac, and the God of Jacob. He is not ashamed to be called their God. And our Lord Himself explains this to mean that they still live with Him, for He is the God of the living, not the God of the dead. They are with Him. And they who by faith enter into Christ's kingdom are said by Him to sit down in the kingdom of Heaven with Abraham, Isaac, and Jacob. Nay, more than this, He is pleased to be spoken of as "the God of Jacob." Such a one then must not be lightly judged or with disparagement. Add to which the very singular care which God seems to have of him, His communing with him so often, so often appearing unto him, to support, direct, and increase him. He hardly moves from place to place without a Divine interference; when he went to the East, when he was to return from thence, when he removed into Egypt, it was under the especial guidance of God. All these things render his life one of peculiar interest; and are seen in strong contrast with the history of Esau; for Jacob evidently throughout valued and loved the promises of God, which Esau despised.

It is true that Jacob's faith is not to be considered such as that of Abraham; for Jacob says, "If God will be with me, and will keep me, . . . then shall the Lord be my God[6]." It was indeed conditional; whereas in Abraham there was nothing of this, for he served God with a full and free heart, never saying, "If God will keep me." Yet

[6] Gen. xxviii. 20, 21.

even this in Jacob was faith acceptable with God; he thus spake when he left his country with a staff in his hand and with a stone for his pillow, and thus he put his faith to the proof. He was not disappointed, and he never forgot that promise. Indeed gratitude and thankfulness seem to mark the whole of his after-life; he continually alludes to it, even to the last; as when in blessing the sons of Joseph, he says, "The God which fed me all my life long unto this day, the Angel which redeemed me from all evil." And he attributes all to the same source; "I had not thought," he says to Joseph, "to see thy face: and, lo, God hath showed me also thy seed[7]." And he alludes especially to that God's first protection of him, as when before meeting with Esau, he says, "O God of my father, . . . the Lord which said unto me, Return unto thy country, and to thy kindred, . . . I am not worthy of the least of all the mercies, and of all the truth, which Thou hast showed unto Thy servant; for with my staff I passed over this Jordan; and now I am become two bands[8]."

It has been said that they who note providences shall never want a providence to note. So it was with Jacob; his life was compassed about with special providences, because he had eyes to observe them.

In furtherance of this we may notice, that what Jacob is more especially known for is his beholding visions of God—the very name given him, that of Israel, has been supposed by some to indicate this[9]. And all his history is a beautiful account of it; the visions of Jacob fill the whole, visions of what was spiritual and Divine in the highest degree, as to a pilgrim and sojourner unto that heavenly Jerusalem, the name of which is supposed to

---

[7] Gen. xlviii. 15, 16. 11.   [8] Gen. xxxii. 9, 10.
[9] St. Aug. in Ps. lxxv. 3, et passim.

signify "the vision of peace." He had faith, and to faith was it given to behold the things of the kingdom of God. It was no light privilege to be visited of God, and to behold His angels, and to be met by them in going out and coming in on the great stages of life. On his leaving the holy land he has a vision of angels; and with a corresponding glad welcome did the angels greet him on returning, at the very threshold of the same. "And the angels of God met him. And when Jacob saw them, he said, This is God's host[1]." It is indeed as if God had "given his angels charge over him, to keep him in all his ways," and had bidden them as it were to "encamp round about" him. What could be more expressive of Christ's kingdom than the ladder of Jacob? our Lord Himself has mentioned it as signifying the highest gifts of His Presence in His Church on earth, for after speaking of Nathanael as an Israelite indeed, He says to him in allusion to this, "Hereafter ye shall see Heaven open, and the angels ascending and descending on the Son of Man." And this his first vision was accepted by Jacob in all its fulness, and understood by him; for he said on awakening, "Surely the Lord is in this place, and I knew it not. And he was afraid and said, How dreadful is this place! this is none other but the house of God, and this is the gate of Heaven." How full of significancy beyond all thought is this expression as spoken of the Holy Land! How true of Israel after the flesh afterwards at Christ's coming, that God was there, though he knew it not, and the very gate of Heaven! It is indeed like a representation of what St. Paul says of the Christian, the true Israel, "That he has come to the Mount Sión, and to an innumerable company of angels."

And again, how full of spiritual wisdom is that account

[1] Gen. xxxii. 1, 2.

of Jacob on his return wrestling with the angel, or with
One greater than an angel, whose Name was Secret, until
the breaking of the day; when in mystery, he saw the face
of God, and prevailed; and in token of that his prevailing
with God had his name changed to Israel. How does it
set forth the wrestling and struggling of a soul with God
in prayer, which beholds His face, and will not let Him
go without a blessing; while "the kingdom of Heaven
suffereth violence," and "the violent take it by force."
When in the power of that blessing he prevails, not with
God only, but also with man, for on the morrow he converts and changes the heart of Esau by humility and
kindness, overcoming evil with good [2].

But Jacob's character is not to be considered only by
itself, but as it comes before us in Scripture in strong contrast with that of his brother Esau, who is declared to be
"a fornicator and profane person [3]," and at enmity with
God. Now there was nothing of this kind which we have
been speaking of in Esau; no wrestling with God, no
visions of angels, no promises, no warnings, no communi-
cations from Heaven; for he evidently had no ears to hear,
nor eyes to see the things of God, because he had no heart
to value them. The first mention of him is as causing
grief to both his parents by his marrying with the daughters
of Canaan; it was a very grievous sin, for it was quite contrary to all faith in God, Who had done so much in calling
forth Abraham, and separating him from the nations. And
when he sells his birthright there is the same contempt of
God; it is said, "He did eat and drink, and rose up, and
went his way;" the account is expressive of the carnal man
which sets at nought God and His promises; "thus Esau,"
it is added, "despised his birthright." And then when

[2] St. Aug. vol. v. p. 50, chap. i. Ser. v.   [3] Heb. xii. 16.

he loses the blessing also, and lifts up "the great and exceeding bitter cry," it is because the blessings of earth, such as he valued, went with a father's blessing; there is no repentance towards God. "They were but transitory things," says St. Gregory, "which he desired in that blessing[4]." And then, like Cain, he envies the blessing which he loses, and purposes in his heart to kill his brother. It is a strange meeting which he has prepared for an only brother, returning from a far country after more than twenty years' absence, when he hastens to encounter him with four hundred men. It is true that he afterwards relents, when Jacob had "bowed himself to the ground seven times" before him, he "ran to meet him, and embraced him, and fell on his neck, and kissed him: and they wept[5]." This is very affecting; it showed that he had strong natural feelings, even to compunction; like as Saul had when David had overcome him in the same manner. But these are mentioned in such characters to caution us not to trust in the like; for the New Testament has held out Esau for our warning as one under the displeasure of God, and a profane person. And while God restrained him from injuring Jacob, yet we may observe it is not even as with Laban the Syrian, by appearing to him on this or any other occasion, being the very opposite to Jacob, who had visions of God.

It is not indeed to be maintained that Jacob was a perfect and blameless character, but that as a certain reverence is due to fathers in the flesh, so to those who may be considered as our fathers in the Spirit, whom Scripture represents as chosen and beloved of God, there is some degree of consideration due when we speak of them. If Jacob describes his life to Pharaoh as a sad pilgrimage,

[4] In Job lib. xi. 13. [5] Gen. xxxiii. 3, 4.

whose days where few and evil, this is but the lot of Christians. His life was that of faith upon the whole, not of sight. Amidst much increase of substance and outward prosperity, it does not appear that he was ambitious or worldly-minded. His prayer to God is that He would give him "bread to eat, and raiment to put on;" and "having food and raiment," says a Christian Apostle, "let us be therewith content[6]." Amidst the abundance and riches of Egypt he forgot not the land of the covenant and promise, but by Divine inspiration portioned it out to his children; as looking forward to the time "when Shiloh should come[7]." "Fruitful in his offspring," says a holy Latin Bishop, "but more fruitful in riches of the Spirit, he bound that offspring with the chains of prophecy[8]." And it is this which the Apostle to the Hebrews has mentioned as the great proof of his faith. "By faith Jacob, when he was a dying, blessed both the sons of Joseph, and worshipped[9]."

To conclude, Esau is in Scripture the type of those who live after the flesh, and shall die: Jacob of "the pure in heart," who "see God," and shall see Him hereafter. When our Lord said to Nathanael that he should witness the realization and fulfilment of that vision of the patriarch in the angels ascending and descending on the Son of Man, it was in immediate connexion with the character which He had given him of one free from guile, and as such a true child of Israel. In Esau and Jacob, as both sons of Abraham, are set before us the carnal and spiritual, the bad and good Christian, where we see that in spite of good feelings and visitings of remorse, there is a broad line between them, that in the spiritual-minded there may be natural

[6] 1 Tim. vi. 8.
[8] St. Greg. in Job, b. iv. 63.
[7] Gen. xlix. 10.
[9] Heb. xi. 21.

infirmities, yet the bent of the whole life is towards God, and consists of faith in God. For the world imagines that it sees faults in good people, and much that is amiable in the worldly; and therefore it would confound good and bad; and thinks that there is no great difference with God, nor will be in the end. But God and Scripture teach us very differently; that notwithstanding appearances there will be seen a difference as deep and broad as the great gulf fixed between Heaven and hell. It is very awful to contemplate two brothers, of the same father and mother, born at the same birth, brought up together under the same roof, yet divided at length by a vast and eternal separation.

One word more with regard to the text; they are the opening words of the last Prophet, Malachi, the last warning before that silence which preceded Christ's coming; he thus begins, "I have loved you, saith the Lord. Yet ye say, Wherein hast Thou loved us? Was not Esau Jacob's brother? saith the Lord: yet I loved Jacob, and I hated Esau." He thus reminds the Jews that they, as Jacob had been, were then the peculiar objects of God's love and choice. But when St. Paul afterwards quotes this passage, saying in his Epistle to the Romans, "It is written, Jacob have I loved, but Esau have I hated[1]," the reverse had become the case; Esau represented Israel after the flesh, who was rejected, and Jacob the Christian, who by faith had become possessed of the birthright and the blessing. How awful is this change continually going on, whereby the last becomes first, and the first last. "Be not high-minded," adds the Apostle, "but fear;" and one greater than the Apostle, "Hold that fast which thou hast, that no man take thy crown[2]."

[1] Rom. ix. 13.   [2] Rev. iii. 11.

JOSEPH

The archers have sorely grieved him, and shot at him, and hated him: but his bow abode in strength, and the arms of his hands were made strong by the hands of the mighty God of Jacob.—GENESIS xlix. 23, 24.

THESE words contain Jacob's own account of his beloved son Joseph, and shortly comprise all his history. No doubt the reason why Holy Scripture has told us so much of Joseph, and rendered the account of him so singularly attractive is, that the example may sink deep into our hearts and lives, suited as it is for every age and condition of life. And the example comes down to us Christians, hallowed and enforced by the remarkable figure which Joseph is given to bear of our Lord Himself; so that it is Christ speaking to us through Joseph of old, and we are constrained to think of our Lord Himself throughout. The dreams of Joseph, of the sheaves bowing down to his, and the sun, moon, and eleven stars doing obeisance to him, at once raise our mind to One greater than Joseph, at whose Name "every knee shall bow, of things in Heaven, and things in earth, and things under the earth[1]." Joseph had to bear his cross; he was "a man of sorrows, and acquainted with grief;" he was stripped of his raiment like our Lord Himself, and cast

[1] Phil. ii. 10.

into the pit as if dead; he is known, like our Lord Himself, as described in Isaiah, by his garments dyed in blood[2]; his brethren, "moved with envy[3]," delivered him up to the Egyptians, as the Pharisees, moved with envy, gave up Christ to the Gentiles; he was sold by one of them whose name was Judah or Judas; and as if to confirm the figure, he is again cast into the dungeon, "as a dead man out of mind," as "free among the dead," and "out of remembrance." He also might say with Christ, "Let not the pit shut her mouth upon me;" "I am so fast in prison that I cannot get forth;" "I am become as an alien unto my brethren;" "Thou hast made me to be abhorred of them;" "false witnesses did rise up against me, they laid to my charge things that I knew not." He was "numbered with the transgressors;" to one of those fellow-sufferers he promises life, to the other not. Then he is raised on high among the Heathen, saving life and giving bread, the bread that saveth from death; setting forth Him Who giveth the true Bread from Heaven; married to a daughter of Egypt, as Christ's Bride, the Church, is taken from among the Gentiles; then receiving his brethren as one "alive from the dead," and with words like those of our Lord Himself after the resurrection, when they were "troubled at His presence," and "supposed that they had seen a spirit[4]," but Joseph says, "Come near to me, I pray you. And they came near. And he said, I am Joseph your brother." And then who is this Benjamin the younger brother, but St. Paul himself, "of the tribe of Benjamin[5]"? And oh, with what tenderness, what love is he welcomed and singled out beyond the rest! "Behold, your eyes see, and the eyes of my

[2] Isa. lxiii. 1—3.
[3] Acts vii. 9.
[4] Gen. xlv. 3. 12; St. Luke xxiv. 37.
[5] Rom. xi. 1.

brother Benjamin, that it is my mouth that speaketh unto you." And in all these things it was with Joseph as with Christ, that his exaltation is brought about by those very means which they took to destroy him, and render the prophecies of none effect.

Now it is to be observed that Christ speaks to us not only in the Gospels and in the New Testament, in what is there written of Himself, of what He says and does, but also throughout the Old Testament in manifold ways; the Prophets mention many things concerning Him as accurate in description as history itself; and the Psalms speak of Him, and express the thoughts of His heart as the Son of Man, as much as they do of David and his own history. We have had occasion to notice how God has made the characters of the Old Testament to represent Him; as Abel speaks of His death; Enoch of His ascension; Noah speaks of Him as our place of refuge; Melchizedeck of His everlasting Priesthood; in Moses He is our Lawgiver; in Joshua the Captain of our Salvation; in Samuel He is the Intercessor; in David our King; Samson speaks of His victory in death; Solomon of His wisdom in His Church, in hymns, and parables, and precepts; Daniel of His honour among the Heathen; Elijah of His miracles and ascension; Elisha of His quickening the dead; and both of these of His mission to the Gentiles*; and Joseph, as we have just observed, of His humiliation, and subsequent exaltation to the right hand of God. These are figures and prophetic types of the events of our Lord's Incarnation; but this is not all; the Saints of old exhibit severally some point in our Lord's character, as the Son of Man, for "of His fulness have all we received, and grace for grace;" some grace corresponding to His as moulded by

* St. Luke iv. 25. 27.

the same Spirit, representing as it were, however faulty, some feature of His countenance, some gesture however imperfectly of His body, some ray from the indwelling of the same Spirit. For they received in measure, He without measure. Thus then again, Abel speaks of His innocence; Enoch of His walk with God; Noah of His "endurance in hope[7];" Job of His patience; Abraham of His obedience; Moses of His meekness; David of His communion with God; Daniel of His humiliation for our sins; Hezekiah of His "strong crying and tears to Him that was able to save Him from death;" Jeremiah of His weeping over His people; Isaiah of His beholding the glory that should be revealed; Elijah of His constant calls to repentance. Thus they in part and measure bring forth to us the fulness and perfection of Christ, one in this way and another in that. For "every one that is perfect shall be as his master[8]," in some respect resembling Him. And therefore we may ask in what particular point of view Christ speaks to us, not only in the history, but also in the character of Joseph? For the narrative of Joseph's life is indeed of itself most engaging and full of interest; it would be so whether we were Christians or not; but it comes before us greatly heightened, when through the same Christ speaks to us of Himself; it is then sacred and Divine; the interest is much increased; it is doubled in every part, deepened in every line. It is as when persons trace in the countenance of a child or a distant kinsman something that reminds them of a great or good man to whom he is related. They love to be reminded of him: it is from their reverence or affection for him that they notice it. How much more when it is one and the same Spirit speaking to us through them; manifold intima-

[7] St. Greg. in Job.   [8] Luke vi. 40.

tions of the Living Word, the same yesterday and to-day!

To speak a little more particularly, our Blessed Saviour's character as the Son of Man, as the Pattern and Perfection of man in the image of God, is a subject for continual contemplation; some point in it for our meditation is found, now in a Prophet, now in a Psalm, now in a history or narrative; some point is thus brought out to our attention more fully than the brief notice of it in the Gospels. As for instance in the 53rd chapter of Isaiah the picture of His bodily sufferings is filled up with some incidents not mentioned by the Evangelists; some circumstance of His secret grief we find in Jeremiah, which the Gospel confirms, but had not brought so distinctly to view; some expression of His sorrows in a Psalm, as throughout the 22nd, which we should not otherwise have considered, for we have in these "the mind of Christ" suffering in the flesh. And the question now is what good thing there was in Joseph which may speak to us of Christ? for as his sufferings were hallowed by their resemblance to those of Christ, as Christ was with him in those sufferings, much more in his soul also may be traced the footsteps of his Lord. This will come out more clearly as we consider Joseph's history.

The first thing which strikes one in the account of him, is the remarkable manner in which God was with him throughout. He was forgotten of man, but not of God. This indeed is incidentally mentioned, but is impressed on his history throughout as its pervading lesson. Thus we read, "And Joseph was brought down to Egypt." "And the Lord was with Joseph." "And his master saw that the Lord was with him." "And the Lord blessed the Egyptian's house for Joseph's sake." And then in the same chapter, when the scene is changed from the court to the dungeon, it is again and again repeated that "the Lord was with Joseph[a]." So much was this the case, that St. Stephen, in speaking of Joseph, selects this for especial mention, "The patriarchs, moved with envy, sold Joseph into Egypt: but God was with him[1]." But now what is there in the heart of man that corresponds to or answers this singular and peculiar Presence of God so emphatically mentioned? It is a feeling and recognition of that Presence; and this we shall find one of the most peculiar marks of Joseph's character. For God is every where alike; but the effect of this Presence is not alike to all. The sun may be on many objects alike, but some things cast aside and reject his beams, or are hardened or cracked by them, while other objects drink in his influence, and are made by it full of life. What we most observe in Joseph is an unceasing sense of God's Presence; thus when tempted by Potiphar's wife, the temptation fell off in an instant. "How can I do this great wickedness, and sin against God?" God's eye was upon him; he felt and knew it. Come what will he was shielded by that. Then next in the prison, to his sad fellow-prisoners he instantly refers all wisdom to God. "And Joseph said unto them, Do not interpretations belong unto God[2]?" And what he was in the prison he was in the palace; his answer to Pharaoh is the same, "It is not in me: God shall give Pharaoh an answer of peace[3]." Yet none are so apt to forget that wisdom is from God as the wise, who attribute it to themselves. It was otherwise with Joseph. Again, the same instant recognition of God occurs when each of his sons is born[4]. As he afterwards also says, "These are

[a] Gen. xxxix. 2, 3. 5. 21. 23.   [1] Acts vii. 9.
[2] Gen. xl. 8.   [3] Gen. xli. 16.   [4] See Gen. xli. 51, 52.

the sons whom God hath given me[5]." But it comes out more strongly still in his intercourse with his brethren. He refers every thing to God. It takes the sting from every wound, the power from every temptation. "God did send me before you to preserve life." And again, "So now it was not you that sent me hither, but God." And again, "Go up to my father and say, God hath made me lord of all Egypt[6]." And at last, "Ye thought evil against me, but God meant it unto good[7]." Thus we may say, as "God was with him," so he was with God in all things.

Now our Blessed Saviour was different from all men in this respect, that in His days on earth He was compassed about and penetrated with such an intense consciousness, so to speak, of God's Presence. It was as it were the very Heaven of Heavens to approach Him, for it was to approach God. But of this we cannot speak. In that mysterious union of the two natures of God and man the light is so transcendent and Divine, that we cannot contemplate it as we should do, any more than we could gaze upon the sun; but this light comes to us softened, the lesson comes down to ourselves, when He Himself speaks to us in the example of Joseph: so far as Joseph was of this mind, we are to contemplate in him, not himself, but Christ. For even of Christ Himself the Apostle thinks it meet to say, "He went about doing good, for God was with Him[8]." This intense realizing of God's Presence was no doubt in Joseph connected with his chastity, for to the pure in heart it is given to see God.

Another point akin to the former and inseparable from it to be considered in Joseph, is his singular sweetness and

[5] Gen. xlviii. 9.
[7] Gen. l. 20.
[6] Gen. xlv. 5. 8, 9.
[8] Acts x. 38.

affection; forgiving injuries before the law of that forgiveness was given by Christ Himself; with a fellow-feeling for the sorrows of others, attracting to himself the love of all his masters by his dutiful love for them. When in prison, with what sympathy does he ask of his fellow-prisoners the occasion of their sadness! And in his interviews with his brothers, where shall we find such filial and brotherly affection? He cannot even endure to witness their mutual reproaches for the wrong they had done him, and the intolerable sufferings their malice had occasioned, but in exceeding tenderness and affection turns aside to weep—more than once in secret to weep, on seeing their sorrows. And afterwards he will not allow them to ask for pardon, but says, "Now therefore be not grieved, nor angry with yourselves, that ye sold me hither[9]." And long after, when their father was dead, and under the fears of their evil conscience, they besought his forgiveness, it melted again his compassionate heart. "And Joseph wept when they spake unto him[1]." "Am I in the place of God?" Ask forgiveness of God, not of me. "And he comforted them," it is added, "and spake kindly unto them." And what had filled his heart with such pity instead of resentment? What had borne him up and sustained him under such trials? It was this constant sense of God's Presence—it was beholding His hand in all. In that "fiery trial" he was "made partaker of Christ's sufferings," though he knew it not, and the glory of Christ was in him revealed[2].

Such was love in Joseph, with such power to sweeten domestic troubles, to hallow incidents of life, to render him meek and gentle, when "the iron entered into his soul." Content to love, yet not to be loved; to save, yet

[9] Gen. xlv. 5. [1] Gen. l. 17. [2] 1 Pet. iv. 12, 13.

to be forgotten; full of love when humbled to the pit, and to the dungeon, and full of love when thence in due season exalted of God. And combined with this love was wisdom. St. Stephen speaks of his wisdom[3]; and Pharaoh says to him, "There is none so discreet and wise as thou[4]." There is in St. John the like union of love and wisdom, but not that human tenderness, that affectionate yearning and sympathy. And a like difference may be seen between Joseph and Daniel; there is in the latter love and wisdom, but it is more lofty, as of one more separate from mankind. There is also love and wisdom in David, which is in some respects still nearer to that of Joseph, but the sweetness and gentleness of Joseph is peculiarly his own. Every star has a hue, every flower a fragrancy, every countenance an expression different from that of another; so is it with Divine charity, the one light of the Heavenly Jerusalem, kindling jewels of many colours.

It would then be a matter of much interest to dwell on the many incidents recorded of our Lord which indicate how Divine Love showed itself in things of this kind—not on occasions great and kingly as David; not in intercession for a whole nation as Daniel; but in the more homely scenes of domestic life; in His intercourse with those around Him; His sympathy with the sorrows of others; His entering into all their wants, as in the marriage feast at Cana; at the grave of Lazarus; in His tender expostulation with Martha who was troubled about many things; in His eating and drinking with publicans and sinners; in His being much grieved at those fears and troubles in His disciples which indicated a want of faith in Himself; in His weeping over those that were about to slay him; in His discourse with the Twelve at the Last

[3] Acts vii. 10.   [4] Gen. xli. 39.

Supper; in His being often as one that needed sympathy but found it not. In wonderful lowliness and much sorrow; rejected of His own but received of strangers; while His brethren said, "He is beside Himself," and they of Nazareth would have put Him to death; as of Joseph they said, "Behold, this dreamer cometh:" yet these things did not stop the current of His loving-kindness towards them: while it was seen in every word and work how "God was with Him," and it was His meat to do His Father's will.

But there is one point in the history of Joseph which requires some explanation; why it was that he delayed so long making himself known to his brethren; kept them as it were at a distance in suspense and fear, prolonging a trial so painful both to himself and them. St. Chrysostom has supposed that it was owing to his fears for his brother Benjamin; apprehending that they may have put him also to death. He had certainly cause for such misgiving, to say nothing of his father's own safety. But this is hardly sufficient to account for his conduct, especially as he continues in the same after he is aware of Benjamin's safety. St. Augustine observes that much as it adds to the sweetness and interest of the narrative, yet this will not explain it, but there must be grave and wise reasons for its being thus recorded, and it may be, he thinks, that it contains something of great mystical import[5]. But may we not suppose as Joseph was so distinguished for his wisdom, both the wisdom of Egypt and the wisdom of God, and therefore in his knowledge of the human heart and modes of dealing with mankind, that he had some great object and design worthy of his love and wisdom; that it was in order to bring them to repentance,

[5] St. Aug. Quæs. in Gen. xlvii. vol. iii. 655.

as knowing that without repentance there could be nothing good? We shall, I think, find all things directed to this end, in a manner worthy of that great wisdom attributed to him; he maintained the long struggle so painful to his own feelings, to bring them to some proof of repentance towards God, in order that "judging themselves they might not be judged of the Lord." And thus when he found them expostulating with one another, self-accused and self-condemned, and at length confessing their guilt so long past and forgotten; this was the part of repentance, and he was much moved, even unto tears. And then after a further trial, when he found them loving Benjamin, tender of his life and safety, and of his father's life bound up in that of the lad; then was there satisfaction indeed: and when at last Judah who had sold him wished himself to be put in bonds, at length was the trial completed. Upon this it is added, "Then Joseph could not refrain himself before all them that stood by him, . . . and he wept aloud, and the Egyptians and the house of Pharaoh heard. And Joseph said unto his brethren, I am Joseph, . . . come near to me, I pray you."

Now a wise and good man deals with others in some measure as God does; not making a show of his feelings, nor acting upon them, but counselling discreetly for their real good. And this behaviour of Joseph in the treatment of his brethren may receive illustration in that of our Lord Himself, especially in His keeping persons so long waiting while He called forth into definite act their repentance and faith; it is His mode of dealing with us all unto this present hour. He knows us, but we know Him not; He makes Himself strange to us, He speaks roughly to us; nay, may we not venture to say it from the expressions used in His prophets, that on our showing signs of repentance, He turns away that He may weep? How many questionings arise with regard to the ways of God's mercy which are like those that occur to us respecting this conduct of Joseph? Why does God so long hide His face from us? Why is He as a stranger, knowing us not? Why does He leave the storms to arise, and for us to toil so long in the dark, and to be troubled, before He says, "It is I; be not afraid"? Why does He leave Lazarus to continue sick and to die, and his sisters to mourn? Why does He leave Mary Magdalene to seek Him so long and be perplexed, before He says to her, "Mary, weep not"? Or to come to this very history, why was Joseph so long a slave and in prison? Why was Jacob left so long to mourn in a hopeless sorrow while his son Joseph was all the while alive? We can only say with St. Augustine, when he speaks of Joseph and his brethren, that the light affliction was but for a moment, and not to be compared with the joy to be revealed. And oh, the glad and wonderful recognition and restoration to his father! What a mysterious resemblance does it seem to bear to our Lord Himself coming alive from the grave, and in Him to every penitent sinner whom He brings with Him from death, when "there is joy in Heaven;" and a voice is heard, "Rejoice with Me:" "for this my Son was dead and is alive again: He was lost and is found."

"When the Lord turned again the captivity of Sion, then were we like unto them that dream. . . . . Then said they among the Heathen, the Lord hath done great things for them." "He that now goeth on his way weeping, and beareth good seed, shall doubtless come again with joy, bring his sheaves with him."

MOSES

Now the man Moses was very meek, above all the men which were upon the face of the earth.—NUMBERS xii. 3.

SUCH is the judgment of God respecting Moses, yet men might have thought otherwise, for Moses was by nature ardent and impetuous. Thus God said to St. Paul, "My strength is made perfect in weakness;" and St. Paul testifies of himself, "when I am weak then am I strong[1]." So was it with many of the Saints of God[2]. St. Peter, for instance, was called the Rock, from his firm faith in the Godhead of Christ; but this had to be perfected in weakness: it was from want of firmness that St. Peter sank in the deep waters, till supported by Christ's hand; from want of firmness he thrice denied, till supported by Christ's look; from want of firmness he erred when rebuked by St. Paul. Thus was it that where most weak there was he by God's help made most strong. As in a besieged town all pains are taken to fortify the weak places until those weak places become its chief strength; so the Spirit of God in the soul of man builds up and establishes where nature was failing, where Satan in consequence was directing his chief assaults. For when good men prayed against their besetting infirmities, the power of God therein was

[1] 2 Cor. xii. 10.
[2] See "On the Study of the Gospels," part vii. sects vii.

given them. Hence, where that which was human failed, it is supplied by that which is Divine; and the power is seen to be of God. Thus at length wherein the soul has been most humbled it shall be most exalted; that man may be nothing, and Christ may be All and in All.

Thus Moses appears to have been naturally of a temper hasty and vehement; as we first read of him in slaying the Egyptian, in defending the daughters of Jethro from the shepherds. There sounds something of impatience in his complaint at the first, "Lord, wherefore hast Thou so evil intreated this people? Why is it that Thou hast sent me[3]?" And "he went out from Pharaoh," we are told, "in a great anger[4]." Again, when on coming down from the Mount he beheld the idolatry of the Israelites, it is said, "Moses' anger waxed hot, and he cast the two tables out of his hands, and brake them beneath the Mount[5]." And on the rebellion of Dathan and Abiram, "Moses was very wroth, and said unto the Lord, Respect not Thou their offering[6]." And the sin recorded of him was when, "being provoked in spirit, he spake unadvisedly with his lips."

It is then out of such a temper when controlled by the fear of God, and moulded by His grace, that the meekest of men is formed; and all the trials he had to undergo through a long life were to form in him this meekness. Thus when reared in the palace of Pharaoh, what a trial to his spirit and temper must it have been to witness the sufferings his brethren had to undergo; then for forty years had he to learn patience in exile and the desert; and yet more when commissioned of God he stood before Pharaoh, while he relented so often and again hardened his heart;

[3] Exod. v. 22.
[5] Exod. xxxii. 19.
[4] Exod. xi. 9.
[6] Num. xvi. 15.

but beyond all what greater trial of temper did any one ever undergo than that of bearing with the children of Israel so long in the wilderness? How often does God Himself speak as unable to bear any longer with them. Such then was the man whom God chose; and such his probation like that of gold in the fire, till at length he came forth as a vessel perfected and made meet for his Master's use.

With regard to his slaying the Egyptian, Holy Scripture does not express approbation of that deed, but St. Stephen says that it was intended as a sign to the Israelites "that God by his hand would deliver them [7]." "As some weeds," says St. Augustine, "indicate a soil rich and good for cultivation, so his zeal on that occasion seemed to point out one meet to be a great Deliverer[8]." Thus God chooses evils of nature to be by His grace converted into good. On the stock of the wild olive is grafted the fruitful Branch. Thus from the Jewish persecutor of His Church He brought forth the great Apostle of the Gentiles; from St. Peter, who drew his sword and deprecated the Cross, the patient Martyr and Confessor; from St. John, who would bring down avenging fire from Heaven, the great Teacher of Divine love.

But mark in Moses the working of this temper, and how it became subdued by Divine grace; for instance, when he came down from the Mount Moses was very wroth, so that Aaron said to him, "Let not the anger of my lord wax hot;" but on this very occasion what a wonderful instance have we of Divine gentleness: we read that on the morrow "Moses said unto the people, Ye have sinned a great sin: and now I will go up unto the Lord; peradventure I shall make an atonement for your sin. And Moses returned

[7] Acts vii. 25.   [8] Vol. viii. 621; vol. iii. 668.

unto the Lord, and said, Oh, this people have sinned a great sin. . . . Yet now, if Thou wilt forgive their sin—; and if not, blot me, I pray Thee, out of Thy book[o]." His anger had been a righteous indignation, a holy jealousy for God's honour; but what meekness did it work in him! Oh that men who are naturally of a temper soon moved to anger would do like this! how would the mercies of God flow in upon the soul, and their peace abound like a river!

In like manner in the other instance we referred to where his anger is spoken of, he appears in meekness to be immediately after deprecating the just wrath of God. "Take a censer," said Moses to Aaron, "and go quickly unto the congregation, and make an atonement for them; for there is wrath gone out from the Lord[1]." Indeed it might be said that it was owing to the exceeding meekness of Moses' interceding for them, that God so long spared them throughout their many provocations and rebellions.

On these occasions, and doubtless others of the same kind, this natural zeal in the disposition of Moses was not disapproved of God, but sanctified and perfected, bringing forth the heavenly temper of Divine charity; but the one sin of Moses for which he was visited of God, and not allowed to enter the land of promise, was that on which this hastiness, as it were, impaired his firm faith in God, when he smote the Rock twice.

True meekness is shown not in acquiescing at the sight of sins that are against God, but in taking meekly offences against oneself; and the case in which the statement of the text is made, that Moses was the meekest of all men, is when Aaron and Miriam murmur against Moses himself, it is then that God interferes to take up the cause of

[o] Exod. xxxii. 31, 32.   [1] Num. xvi. 46.

Moses; and Moses intercedes for Miriam, and she at his intercession is restored[2]. It is on account of this meekness that, as there stated, he is admitted into such familiar intercourse with God. "My servant Moses is faithful in all Mine house. With him will I speak mouth to mouth, even apparently, and not in dark speeches." And indeed on that occasion when he sinned at the Rock there was a jealousy for God's honour, and impatience at the murmuring of the people, when the faith of Moses gave way and was overclouded. It was on their account; when that sin is spoken of, it is said more than once "the Lord was angry with me *for your sakes*." "They angered Him at the waters of strife, so that it went ill with Moses for their sakes[3]."

And here we must observe that this judgment of God on that sin did not imply that He had blotted Moses out of His book of life, or the number of the Saints, or otherwise than forgive his sin. For He continued still to talk with him, and advise with him of the governing of His people, and spake to Joshua that he should be faithful to Him as His servant Moses. That was not the true Canaan from which he was shut out, but only the figure and shadow; and that he was allowed to see; a vision well worthy of all his labours, for the more excellent things signified by it. And that sin and its punishment was itself hallowed in a Divine mystery and signification of Christ's future kingdom. That Rock was Christ; and the rod spoke of His Cross; and the failing of Moses of the Apostles failing in that trial; even those with whom God had conversed face to face, and spoken with as to friends, "even apparently" and openly, and not in proverbs. As Moses wavered at the smiting of the Rock, so Apostles

[2] See also Num. xi. 29.   [3] Ps. cvi. 32. Deut. i. 37; iii. 26.

doubted at the Cross, when the Rock was smitten, and found in it "a stone of stumbling and Rock of offence," as St. Peter thrice denied, and had before deprecated that Cross; and the disciples going to Emmaus said, as having lost hope, "We trusted that it should have been He Who should have redeemed Israel." But at the Resurrection they saw the land of promise, and doubt died. And at the Ascension when they went up the Mount of Olives, they saw as it were still more the promised land, though they entered not in, till death had closed their eyes. And from the Mount of the Transfiguration also they had a view of that promised land of the Resurrection, and of the glory that shall be revealed. And Moses was there as one who shall with them enter into that better land hereafter, though he entered not into that Canaan, which was but the figure of the true. He saw and he bare witness, and he led Israel thither, but he entered not in; and this too in figure, as setting forth that it is not for the Law to enter in, but the grace which follows, and is prefigured in Joshua[4]. "For the Law was given by Moses, but grace and truth came by Jesus Christ." And again, "The Law made nothing perfect, but the bringing in of a better hope did[5]." And indeed the imperfection of the Law was shown in the Lawgiver himself. For that Israel might not glory in man, but look forward to Him that was to come, God has been pleased that one so exalted, and brought so near to Himself as Moses was, should be thus reproved in death, as falling short of the glory of God.

Such then was Moses[6], of whom it is said that he was

[4] St. Aug. viii. 470.   [5] Heb. vii. 19.

[6] The character of Moses is thus beautifully given by St. Augustine: "Hunc Moysen, humilem in recusando tam magnum ministerium, subditum in suscipiendo, fidelem in servando, strenuum in exsequendo; in regendo populo vigilantem, in corrigendo vehementem, in

"a merciful man, which found favour in the sight of all flesh, beloved of God and men, whose memorial is blessed[7]." Great in wisdom, for "mysteries are revealed unto the meek;" and wise in greatness, for the meek are upholden of God. We think of Moses in connexion with the Holy Mount as one above the world; the Mount Sinai where he was alone with God; the Mount Horeb with the smitten Rock; the mountain-top where he interceded against Amalek; the Mount Pisgah where he saw the promised Canaan, and was buried of God; the Mount Sion which he beheld in the distance as the place of the Law; and the Mount Tabor where he was again seen with Christ. Now this may serve by way of similitude to express Moses as compared with other men; he is on the top of the mountain with God; he walks on high with God; he is not as other men, but raised far above, conversing with God, illumined by God's Presence; his ways are on the high mountain, and his feet clad with the Gospel; his stature is seen on the sky glowing in the golden light of the evening sun, and appearing to us below as one greater than man; yet though so eminent and exalted of God, he was not high-minded, but meek, meekest of men.

And thus with regard to the character given of Moses, it is peculiar in this from that of all men; that it is the one character which our Blessed Saviour has expressly taken to Himself, as peculiarly His own; for He says, "Learn of Me, for I am meek and lowly of heart."

amando ardentem, in sustinendo patientem; qui pro eis quibus præfuit, Deo se interposuit consulenti, opposuit irascenti; hunc talem ac tantum virum . . . et amamus, et admiramur, et quantum possumus imitamur."—(Con. Faus. xxii. vol. viii. 621.)

[7] Ecclus. xlv. 1.

Abraham was faithful; Joseph was chaste; Job was patient; Solomon was wise; Daniel a man of love; but none of these characters has our Lord singled out for especial mention as His own, but that of Moses which is meekness, and with the promise that they who of Him learn this meekness shall find rest. Now Moses took them not into that rest, which was signified by the Sabbath, and by the Canaan, which was held out to them of God. He entered not in himself; but in not entering in he was made partaker of that rest of which Canaan itself was but the figure; for on account of his meekness he found rest in God. Thus by being shut out he was in the secret mercies of God more truly admitted into that rest;—like St. Peter, thrice allowed to express his love, because of his threefold denial, and gifted thereby with his shepherd's staff, and his Master's Cross[8];—in judgment he found mercy, and in death, life;- lost the earthly that he might enter into the heavenly Canaan; for he was worthy of a better rest.

But in considering the history of Moses our attention is most drawn to our Lord's own words, "Had ye believed Moses, ye would have believed Me: for he wrote of Me[9]." Moses wrote of Christ, spoke of Christ, represented Christ, and that in ways many and manifold. His history is indeed all of Christ; it is all the Gospel under a veil; by One and the same Spirit; of One and the same Christ; by One and the same Father that revealeth from above to the secret heart. And thus when God first appeared unto Moses, and called him, it was with the Name of the Everlasting God, "I AM." As not to the Jews only, but to us of all time does He speak through Moses. And on the same occasion not only does He proclaim Himself by the

[8] St. John xxi. 18.   [9] St. John v. 46

name of the Everlasting God, but also by a name by which He is to be known for ever, as the God of Abraham, Isaac, and Jacob, as putting on our nature and coming to dwell among us. And then in that Burning Bush from which He spake, the fire was of Heaven, of the Everlasting Light, but the Bush, which it consumed not, was of earth; the Godhead and the Manhood, compassed about with thorns of suffering flesh. And then through Moses in the fires of Mount Sinai He gives forth the Law, which by another and better Pentecost is to be written on the heart in grace and love. The veil is taken away from the face of Moses, and we see in him the meekness of Christ, like that glory from Him which made his face to shine. Moses had said unto them, "A Prophet shall your Lord God raise up unto you, like unto me." Like unto Moses, not only in that Moses bears in many ways the image and figure of the Word made Flesh, but also in this character of meekness.

Thus the Law itself comes to us clothed as it were in "the meekness and gentleness of Christ" our Lawgiver; and the Spirit Himself, who writes that Law on the heart, "intercedeth for us with groanings that cannot be uttered;" and He that gives us the command, gives us also the Spirit of prayer, by which that life-giving command may be obeyed.

Let us consider this a little more particularly. Take the four first of the ten commandments given by Moses on Mount Sinai. These four speak to us of the love of God, and contain within them all the parts and duties of this love. These commandments, we are told by Moses, are to be written on all that we say, and do, and think; they are to be inscribed on all that we possess, or seek, or know; they are to possess ourselves. But now our Blessed Saviour, in His unspeakable meekness, as the Son of Man giving us to partake of His grace, has converted as it were those commandments into a daily prayer. For when in the Lord's Prayer we pray to God as "Our Father," what is this but owning the one and only God, and "none other" but Him, as our God and Father, and seeking from Him in meekness all that this the first commandment would require? And when we add to this, "Which art in Heaven," we set aside all idols, and turn to God Who is a Spirit, and must be "worshipped in spirit and in truth," through Him Who is the only Mediator between God and man. We do what we can to engraft on our hearts through the meekness of prayer the second commandment. And when we next pray, "Hallowed be Thy name," we seek His all-powerful aid to fulfil in all its duties the third commandment of "Not taking God's name in vain." We reverence thereby that Holy Name by which we are called, the Anointed One, Whose Name is upon us, in Whose anointing we partake; we "sanctify the Lord God in the heart." And when we add, "Thy kingdom come," we *remember* in prayer that sabbath of rest which God has promised, we hold in solemn remembrance that kingdom which is a perpetual sabbath, and the coming in of the day of God. Thus it is that the commandments written on tables of stone are impressed on our hearts by the Holy Spirit in prayer, through the meekness of Christ. Thus hath He turned the fires of Mount Sinai into the tender light of Mount Sion. Thus the commandments, which could not give rest, in the New Man become the yoke of Christ, and through meekness bring to Him Who is our Rest. Thus then it is that the character of the Lawgiver himself represents in figure the Mediator of the new covenant, Him on Whose countenance we may look and be transformed into the same image of meekness, through the Spirit of Him Who speaketh to the heart in prayer. Thus God Who gave out the Law amidst the terrors of Mount Sinai, proclaimed at the same time His Name as "the Lord God, merciful and gracious, long-suffering, and abundant in goodness[1];" and as a pledge of His goodness promised another Lawgiver, Who should speak as God, yet should be compassed about with brotherly sympathies; "a prophet from among your brethren," one Who is meek beyond the sons of men, and Whose yoke through that meekness is made easy and His burden light. For He Who is the Lawgiver is Himself the Comforter; He is Himself our Law, and He Himself is Love, and through meekness we partake of Him. He that is most meek prays most; for the life of the meek is of itself a continual prayer; and he that prays most enters most into that "rest which remaineth for the people of God."

Let no one then say, "I am by nature passionate," for so was Moses, the meekest of men; but let him learn to say rather, "It is God that girdeth me with strength of war, and maketh my way perfect." "Thou hast given me the defence of Thy salvation; Thy right hand also shall hold me up, and Thy loving correction shall make me great[2]."

[1] Exod. xxxiv. 6.   [2] Ps. xviii. 32. 35.

AARON

And no man taketh this honour unto himself, but he that is called of God, as was Aaron.—HEBREWS v. 4.

IN considering the history of Aaron we must have been struck with the absence of strength and point in his own character; we might almost say with the want of character altogether. So that gifted as he was in speech beyond Moses, yet no saying of wisdom is recorded of him; and though he bore so eminent a part in the most important history of the world, and the miraculous events which accompanied the establishment of the Law, yet no memorable action is mentioned of himself alone; all is in conjunction with Moses, nothing apart by himself. And even his sins seem to have been owing rather to a want of strength in his character, than from a disposition to evil; his making the golden calf was in obedience to the people; his contention against Moses appears to have been rather at the instigation of Miriam than his own; and when Moses himself failed in faith at the Rock, Aaron was combined with him in that fall; it is spoken of as the sin of both in common[1].

But now what is the reason of this, that God should have chosen one to act a part so eminent, who has in himself so little to arrest our interest or claim our

[1] Num. xx. 12.

admiration? It is no doubt in order that our attention may be turned away from the man to the office. We behold him great indeed, as the "Prophet" of Moses, as speaking from him of the things of God; we see him in "the robe of honour, and clothed with the perfection of glory;" with the golden crown of "Holiness unto the Lord" on his head, and the Urim and Thummim, with the twelve tribes shining in radiant jewels on his breast; "in his coming out of the sanctuary, as the morning star in the midst of a cloud, and as the moon at the full[2]." But in himself and of himself we see him not, either in greatness of mind, or in wisdom, or in goodness. With the censer in his hand he is all-prevailing; with the rod of God the wonder-worker; in his ministrations he is as a continual mediator; but without the insignia of his calling we know him not. And all this, that more clearly may be seen the dignity itself of the Priesthood first instituted in him. As St. Paul says, "we have this treasure in earthen vessels, that the excellency of the power may be of God[3]."

But as Aaron is the prototype and representative of the Priesthood, does this signify the Jewish Priesthood and that of the Law engaged in the services and sacrifices of the Temple? It cannot be confined to this altogether, though it be so in some measure and after a manner. For it is said of the Priesthood instituted in Aaron that it is to continue for ever. The words are, "Thou shalt anoint them," i.e. Aaron and his sons, "that they may minister unto Me in the Priest's office, for their anointing shall surely be an everlasting priesthood[4]." As it is elsewhere expressed, "Moses consecrated and anointed him;" and "this was appointed by an everlasting covenant, so long

[2] Ecclus. l. 5, 6. 11. [3] 2 Cor. iv. 7. [4] Exod. xl. 15.

as the heavens should remain, that they should minister unto Him⁵." This then could not have been the legal Priesthood, for that was then to be abolished, and has now already ceased. It could not, as St. Augustine says, have been spoken of the figure or shadow which was to pass away, but of that substance in which it was to be fulfilled, that this continuance was to be⁶. But now in what is this true fulfilment of the Legal Priesthood? for of itself it "served but as an example of heavenly things, ... according to the pattern shewed in the Mount⁷;" it was but, as St. Paul says of the Sabbath, "a shadow of things to come, but the body is of Christ⁸." Is it then our Lord's own Personal Priesthood, that by which He offered up the one great sacrifice of Himself upon the Cross, and hath entered within the vail; that which he now exercises, unseen by us, in Heaven, as our Intercessor and Mediator on the right hand of God? No, this could not have been the fulfilment of that which was thus ordained in Aaron; for we are told expressly that Christ is the High Priest for ever, "after the order of Melchisedec, and not after the order of Aaron⁹." Of that High Priesthood it must be said, as of Melchizedeck, and as of the Holy Spirit, that we "know not whence it cometh, nor whither it goeth." In what then is to be found the everlasting Priesthood of Aaron? It is no doubt in that which Christ still exercises below in the sight of men by the ordinance of the Christian ministry. This is the anointing "by an everlasting covenant as long as the Heavens shall remain." "For the Law maketh men High Priests which have infirmity¹." Removed by death, they are ever renewed by the anointing of the Blessed Spirit which abideth for ever.

⁵ Ecclus. xlv. 15. ⁶ Vol. vii. p. 741. ⁷ Heb. viii. 5.
⁸ Col. ii. 17. ⁹ Heb. vii. 11. ¹ Heb. vii. 28.

The Levitical Priesthood itself, while the Law declared it to be an everlasting Priesthood, yet was compassed about in all its bearings with death and sin. All things in the institution of Aaron and in the fulfilment of his office indicated this infirmity; the consecrating of Aaron, with all its requirements, the washing, and cleansing, and sanctifying, and the offering for himself before he offered for others². On all is stamped the acknowledgment of sin and weakness, such as could have no place in Him who was the High Priest after the order of Melchizedeck. Such therefore by reason of death could not continue, nor set forth Him Who "abideth a Priest continually," after the power of an endless life. Aaron signifying the Priesthood as well as Moses signifying the Law died first, and neither of them led the people into the land of promise³, leaving that for the true Joshua to do.

Thus the last Prophet, Malachi, when he speaks of our Lord's speedy coming to His temple, says, "He shall sit as a refiner, and purify the sons of Levi;" but as our Lord's coming did away with the temple and its sacrifices, it is evident that it is in His Church He is thus to sit, purifying the everlasting Priesthood He had appointed. And of this we have a lively representation in the Revelation, where our Lord, as the Refiner, in addressing the Angels of the Churches which He holds as seven stars in His right hand, with "His eyes as a flame of fire," and "His countenance as the sun," yet preserves still the figures of the Legal Priesthood, appearing in the midst of the seven candlesticks, clothed "with a garment down to the foot, and girt about with a golden girdle." Thus as He then says of Himself, "I am He that liveth and was dead; and behold, I am alive for evermore," so the same may be

---

² See Lev. xiii. ix. &c.   ³ St. Aug. viii. 356.

said of the visible Priesthood. And this its revival and continuance was beautifully set forth in Aaron's rod preserved in the sanctuary together with the Manna which prefigured the Bread from Heaven. For that Rod speaks at once of the Cross of Christ, budding forth after His death into that Christian Priesthood which He had left to take His place upon earth. That which was dead is alive in a more Divine and glorious form.

And thus when God in the Prophet Malachi says that He has "no pleasure" in those His priests after the Law, "nor will accept an offering at their hands," it is added that "from the rising of the sun even unto the going down of the same," "in every place incense shall be offered unto His Name, and a pure offering." For thus since our Lord's death in the Liturgies of the Church is the incense; and in the memorial of His death the continual sacrifice; while as Priests after the order of Aaron, the Christian minister uses the same form of Benediction which was given to the sons of Levi; as in our Service for the Visitation of the Sick[4].

It is then in connexion with the Christian Priesthood that we consider the history and character of Aaron. And here the first thing that occurs to us is that all the power of Aaron consists in his conjunction with Moses; through Moses and Aaron are carried on all the mighty works, the ordinances, and guidings of the people throughout. Their history comes to us like their names together, "Moses and Aaron." Without Moses Aaron is as nothing in himself, excepting for the Priesthood which he bears. Considering Aaron then as representing the Christian Priesthood, we must look upon Moses in union with him as a figure of our Lawgiver Himself. Thus Aaron is made

[4] Num. vi. 23. 27.

entirely subordinate to Moses and subject to him. This appears in the first mention of Aaron when God says to Moses, "Thou shalt speak unto him, and put words in his mouth." "And he shall be thy spokesman unto the people; and he shall be to thee instead of a mouth, and thou shalt be to him instead of God[5]." Of which St. Augustine says, "Perhaps herein is to be traced a great sacrament of which this bears the figure, that Moses is as mediator between God and Aaron; Aaron the mediator between Moses and the people." "It clearly indicates," he says, "the principal place to be in Moses, the ministration in Aaron[6]." Similar words are again repeated in the Book of Exodus which seem to contain this mysterious allusion to a Divine Mediator. "And the Lord," we read, "said unto Moses, See, I have made thee a god to Pharaoh; and Aaron thy brother shall be thy prophet[7]."

And this indeed marks the whole history; every thing is in conjunction with Moses, every thing in subordination to him. Moses directs, counsels, reproves Aaron. He speaks to God for him, and intercedes in his behalf; and when it is said that "the Lord was very angry with Aaron[8]," Aaron is spared at the intercession of Moses. He speaks to God for him; and he speaks to Aaron from God continually and throughout; in Egypt before Pharaoh; in the guidance of the people through the wilderness; in the institution of the sacred ordinances and laws. Aaron addresses him with deference, though Moses was his younger brother, and calls him "My lord." When the face of Moses shone on his coming down from the Mount, it is said that Aaron as well as the rulers feared to approach him[9]. Moses with the rod of God prevailed against

[5] Exod. iv. 15, 16.   [6] Quæs. in Exod. vol. iii. 670.
[7] Exod. vii. 1.   [8] Deut. ix. 20.   [9] Exod. xxxiv. 30.

Amalek in prayer, but Aaron and Hur had the humbler ministration of sustaining his hands[1]. Through all these things we distinctly read that the Christian Priesthood as represented by Aaron are as nothing of themselves, but in union with and submission to their great Lawgiver; that they are always to be approaching God through the One Mediator which is Christ, they are to do nothing but at His bidding, at His appointment, and in conjunction with Him; they are to receive all at His mouth, and as from His mouth to speak for Him to the people.

It is He that intercedes like Moses on the Mount till the going down of the sun, but He requires that the Christian Priesthood should in lowly co-operation unite with Him, and as it were aid in the lifting up of His hands. He is thus graciously pleased to combine them with Himself.

Thus we learn that in the Christian Priesthood we are not to look for any great wisdom, or power of intellect, or strength of mind beyond other men, of themselves, but as they are in conjunction with Christ, speak to us from Him, and as far as He is Himself with them and confirming their words. "The Priest's lips" are to "keep knowledge;" "for he is the messenger of the Lord of hosts[2]." It is because they speak not their own words but the words of God. "I will be with his mouth," said God, "and he shall be thy spokesman unto the people." "I will give you a mouth and wisdom," says our Lord to His disciples; "it is not ye that speak, but the Spirit of your Father which speaketh in you." Thus all their strength is as being with Christ; speaking from Him, and with Him, as His ambassadors and stewards, His "prophets," i. e. as speaking for Him. He is the Rock on which they are

[1] Exod. xvii. 12.   [2] Mal. ii. 7.

built; His Cross has become their guiding staff by which they go before and guide the sheep; the rod in their hands that works wonders; but the less they are in themselves the more will His strength be seen in them. Nay, more; they of themselves are compassed with infirmities, and this will appear whenever they are apart from Him.

Hence not only is the character and institution of Aaron full of warning and instruction, but so also are the most marked events in his history. When Aaron with Miriam "spake against Moses," the exceeding meekness of Moses himself is mentioned in aggravation of their conduct; there was in him such an absence of self-seeking. "Enviest thou for my sake?" he said on another occasion to Joshua, "would God that all the Lord's people were prophets." We see in Apostles the like tendency to err against the meekness and mercies of Christ; and both occasions continue to carry on the like caution to the Christian ministry. The offence Moses had given was that he "had married the Ethiopian woman," so the stumbling-block to the first Apostolic Priesthood was in the mystery of Christ, that His mercy had espoused the Church of the Gentile.

Again, it is not without surprise and disappointment that we read of Aaron himself, when Moses was absent in the Mount with God, making the golden calf for the people, and joining them in that terrible falling away ; and this too after God had wrought such great miracles by his hand. It is indeed as if he had cast to the ground the rod which God had put into his hands, and it had there become a serpent. His faith failed, and the High Priest of God had become the maker of an idol. There is an occasion which much corresponds with this recorded in the Gospels which we cannot think of without something of the like astonishment. It is when our Lord came down

H

from the Mount of Transfiguration, and found His own Apostles whom He had left below failing in faith, so that they were unable to cast out the unclean spirit from the child; and then too it was in like manner under the pressure of the multitude, and of the scribes questioning and confounding them. And this falling away too was so remarkable, that it drew from our Lord Himself an expression as it were of wonder and disappointment, as it had done from Moses on the former occasion: "O faithless and perverse generation," He exclaimed, "how long shall I be with you? how long shall I suffer you?"

And these two events recorded in Scripture which seem so remarkably to correspond with, and confirm each other, naturally lead on our thoughts to consider whether they may not be intended as a warning, representing to us something to occur in the Christian Church hereafter;—even in these latter days, when our Lord being with God, and absent as it were on the Mount, He shall find on His return His own ministers falling away. For in like manner of surprise or mournful prophecy, when speaking of the great power which His elect have in prayer with God, He adds, "Nevertheless when the Son of Man cometh, shall He find faith upon the earth[3]?"

The circumstance is quite amazing, that Aaron should have made a golden calf for the people to worship, yet in these latter days of which we speak, something occurs which may have a resemblance to it in character, when "the abomination of desolation shall stand in the holy place." Of both alike we may say in the words of St. John in the Revelation, "When I saw I wondered with great admiration[4]." And it may be that as at our Lord's first coming the Jewish Priesthood with Scribes and

[3] St. Luke xviii. 8.   [4] Rev. xvii. 6.

Pharisees, so at His second coming the Christian Priesthood shall be found wanting. For when our Lord spake in those awful terms respecting His last coming, it was St. Peter himself that asked the question whether He alluded particularly to themselves whom He left as His stewards and servants; to which our Lord spake in answer of "that faithful and wise steward" made by his Lord "ruler over His household;" but as if intimating this want of fidelity, He added, " But and if that evil servant shall say in his heart, My Lord delayeth His coming, and shall begin to beat the menservants and maidens, and to eat and drink, and be drunken ; the Lord of that servant will come in a day when he looketh not for him[5]." Now here it is implied that such evil servant will think within himself that his Lord is delaying, and yet He had just said that His return should be very speedy and sudden. In like manner we are astonished to find that when the absence of Moses in the Mount had been for so very short a time, yet it should have given rise to such unbelief and idolatry; for there likewise it is said, "When the people saw that Moses delayed to come down from the Mount, they gathered themselves together unto Aaron, saying, As for this Moses, the man that brought us up out of Egypt, we wot not what is become of him[6]." Yet he had only been out of their sight for forty days. And our Lord's expression of His faithless servant, that he " shall eat and drink, and be drunken," seems to imply that intoxication of the heart which Moses found on his return ; that " music and dancing," when " the people," it is said, " sat down to eat and to drink, and rose up to play." It seems as if the accounts of both these occurrences are thus given to correspond with each other to draw our thoughts to the resemblance.

[5] St. Luke xii. 45, 46.   [6] Exod. xxxii. 1.

But in our Lord's description of the failure of His Priesthood there is another point which we cannot pass over without notice; for the power of His Priesthood, the unction of the Holy One, or as it is expressed in the Law of Moses, "the anointing of the everlasting covenant," depends on the mutual love and union with which they are bound together. For the Priesthood of Aaron when it was ratified in the Christian Church was founded not in one as Aaron, but in twelve. The Urim and Thummim, the light and truth of God, was to be one formed of twelve, and therefore depended on their mutual union and adherence. And this power our Lord represents as broken in the last days, when love waxing cold, the servant whom He hath left as ruler of His household "shall begin to beat his fellow servants." And thus the blessing that came upon the head of Aaron, the anointing oil by which he was consecrated, is spoken of as representing Divine love, or union among brethren. It is indeed this union of Christian fellowship which exhibits that secret anointing of the Spirit to the people, this union especially of the Priesthood; by "this shall all men know that ye are My disciples,"—that ye My Apostles partake of the true anointing,—"if ye have love one to another." It is to this that the increase is promised, and the enduring life. "The precious ointment upon the head, that ran down unto the beard, even unto Aaron's beard; and went down to the skirts of his clothing; like as the dew of Hermon;" "for there the Lord promised His blessing, and life for evermore." Thus therefore it was that while Aaron only represents one Priest separately in his relation to God, and also to the people, or the one Priesthood, yet his very anointing is spoken of by the psalmist as indicating this brotherly concord, in which the unction and power, the goodliness and joy, the sweetness and strength of that Priesthood would consist. For in this the Christian benediction is "the fellowship of the Holy Ghost," in union with which is found "the grace of our Lord Jesus Christ, and the love of God."

In conclusion, it may be observed that there is one circumstance which strikes one in connexion with the history of Aaron with respect to the Christian Priesthood, which may give rise to some awful reflections. Aaron fell into great sins, and these much aggravated by his being a Priest of God, yet for none of these is he punished. Aaron, together with his sister Miriam, rebelled and spake against Moses, "and the anger of the Lord," it is said, "was kindled against them." Miriam was immediately stricken with leprosy. "And Aaron looked upon Miriam, and, behold, she was leprous!" but we do not read of Aaron himself being punished for that sin[7]. And so likewise when Aaron had made the idolatrous calf, the people were heavily visited for that sin, but not Aaron himself. "The Lord plagued the people, because they made the calf, which Aaron made[8]." Now what are we to understand from this but that the sin of the Priest is especially reserved for the judgment of God? it is beyond what human law can reach: indeed human laws are only able to take into account sins that are against society; they cannot punish sins against God. In a peculiar manner "to his own master he standeth or falleth."

Now all these considerations which the circumstances and the character of Aaron give rise to are, I think, especially calculated for the Laity, as leading them to sobriety of thought and expectation respecting the Clergy; that while they " esteem them very highly in love for their

[7] Num. xii. [8] Exod. xxxii. 35.

work's sake," they do not look for too much in their personal powers and endowments, and even in their spiritual attainments; but endeavour in all things to look beyond them to Him whose servants and representatives they are, "the One Mediator between God and man, the Man Christ Jesus;" and especially should these reflections lead them to a more than ordinary compassion for their infirmities and failings, as remembering that they have to give an account of their stewardship to their own Master, and not to His people; and therefore as having, beyond all others, a claim upon their prayers. "If one man sin against another, the judge shall judge him; but if a man sin against the Lord, who shall intreat for him[9]?"

[9] 1 Sam. ii. 25.

PHARAOH

And the Lord hardened the heart of Pharaoh.—EXODUS ix. 12.

THERE is no doubt some great reason why the history of Pharaoh should be so much held up to our remembrance: and the most marked point connected with him is that Scripture, in reference to him, with such remarkable frequency and repetition, uses the expression that God hardened his heart. This then requires our particular attention. It is indeed said in this account that Pharaoh hardened his own heart, or that his heart was hardened; but the point which strikes us, and is no doubt intended to do so, is that of the text.

It may be that the conduct of Pharaoh is so lifted up to our eyes, as casting its shadow over the future, as containing in it the resemblance of other events, as a prophecy; for in Scripture history is often prophecy, and prophecy is often history. There are two occasions which Pharaoh seems to foreshadow; and on both of which the like expression, so startling and impressive, is used, attributing the effect to God. The one is when Israel itself after the flesh takes the place of Pharaoh, and persecutes the Israel after the Spirit, the true children of Abraham, when God brings them out from the falling Jerusalem, "with signs and with wonders," "and with an outstretched arm;" then also this expression is drawn out from the Prophets, and marked by the Evangelists. "But though He had done so many miracles before them," says St. John, "yet they believed not on Him. . . . They could not believe, because that Esaias said, He hath blinded their eyes, and hardened their heart. . . . These things said Esaias, when he saw His glory, and spake of Him[1]." And our Lord Himself frequently refers to the same.

Another point to be observed in this and other like passages of Scripture is, that not only is such stated to be the case, but it is also shown that God had Himself declared beforehand that it should be so. "They could not believe, because that Esaias said." And in Isaiah the commission is expressly given to "Go and harden their hearts, make their ears heavy, and shut their eyes[2]." The same is the case in this history in Exodus. Thus it is said beforehand to Moses, when he is first appointed to go to Pharaoh, that he is to "do all those wonders before" him, "but," it is added, "I will harden his heart[3]." And this, viz. that God had so foretold it from the beginning, is alluded to in the passage of the text, and in other places where the like is stated, that "the Lord hardened his heart, and he hearkened not; as the Lord," it is added, "had spoken by Moses." And again, "And He hardened Pharaoh's heart, as the Lord had said." And before his going unto him it is again repeated, "Thou shalt speak all that I command thee. . . . And I will harden Pharaoh's heart," and "Pharaoh shall not hearken unto you[4]." Thus pains are taken in Scripture not only to express this, that God hardens the heart, but also to point it out as especially God's own doing by the prophecies going before.

[1] St. John xii. 37—40.
[2] Isa. vi. 9, 10.
[3] Exod. iv. 21.
[4] Exod. vii. 13. 2—4.

All this is again shown by St. Paul in the 9th chapter of his Epistle to the Romans, where he dwells on the same at great length, referring in the first place to this hardening of the heart by God Himself in the case of Pharaoh, and then applying it to the Jews, and pointing out especially that God had beforehand foretold this His doing. We may express it in the words of the Psalmist; "God spake once, and twice I have also heard the same: that power belongeth unto God." "And all men that see it shall say, This hath God done; for they shall perceive that it is His work[5]."

The other period on which the account of Pharaoh seems to bear is that of Antichrist; so much so, that in the Revelation, like plagues to those of Egypt are described as then occurring; and like as the magicians worked their false miracles before Pharaoh, it is said, "The spirits of devils, working miracles, shall go forth to kings[6]." Antichrist shall come with "great signs and wonders" to deceive; it shall be with "seducing spirits." But now of those days the like striking expression is used, referring it to God, "God shall send on them a strong delusion, that they shall believe a lie." The same may apply to different ages and countries, after a manner. It has often been observed that before destruction comes on a guilty nation, there goes before a strong infatuation and a hardness of heart against warnings and judgments, so much so that it has passed into a proverb, that God sends madness before destruction.

Before entering more particularly into this subject, we may just notice this awful and impressive circumstance, that under this judicial blindness from God a change takes place before men are aware of it, so that the people of God

[5] Ps. lxii. 11; lxiv. 9.   [6] Rev. xvi. 14.

become the people of Satan. Israel in Egypt bore the strongest stamp of being God's people : their being called out of Egypt to hold a feast or sacrifice unto God in the wilderness ; their being unharmed amidst the evils of Egypt; their light amidst the darkness; the rod of Moses; the passage of the Red Sea ; the Passover, and going forth at midnight in haste, the loins girded, and shoes on their feet, and staff in their hand ; all these, and manifold more, are lively figures of those who are looking for and hastening unto the kingdom of God—they are the very type and parable of the Christian Church. Strange, that while they were in the Psalms speaking of Israel and their deliverance, and especially at the very time of keeping the Passover to commemorate that event, they were themselves taking the place of Egypt, and fulfilling all that is written of Egypt and of Pharaoh. It was at the Passover, when our Lord, as on this day[7], beheld Jerusalem, and wept over it, because the time of their visitation was passed, and the things that belonged unto their peace were hidden from their eyes. They had taken the place of the enemy of God, and that under great aggravations, but they knew it not. From this instance we see what may be the case with a Christian Church or nation, that before they are aware of it they may be falling under that delusion and hardness of heart which we see has taken place in others. It will not therefore be safe to put away the case from us, but we must consider how far it may describe God's dealings with ourselves.

But our object in the history of Pharaoh is as it applies and is intended to apply to individuals ; it is indeed the counterpart and strong description of those that are tried, are borne long with, fall back after many relentings and

[7] Preached on Palm Sunday.

imperfect repentances, and at last perish. It holds up to view in a striking historic picture what commonly takes place with the human soul, as it is expressed in that saying of Solomon: "He, that being often reproved hardeneth his neck, shall suddenly be destroyed, and that without remedy[a]."

Now there is signal mercy shown to Pharaoh; the sin of Egypt had come to the full; the account begins, like that of the Jews when Christ was born, in the slaying of infants under a former king; and under this present Pharaoh the same system is carried on by oppression and heavy bondage, spoken of as the very "furnace" of affliction, "the iron furnace;" but God was long-suffering and gracious to him; He sent him first demands and expostulations, and then warnings; and these signal and repeated, and more and more manifest and awakening; and these judgments too withdrawn, and then repeated after vain repentings and fresh aggravations of sin and cruelty. Now some would suppose that Pharaoh represents the evil spirit; but it is not at all so; it is rather a wicked man, or the world at enmity with God; this is shown by his many repentings, of which there are none with evil spirits. The case may be compared with that of Judas; of him it was distinctly foretold that he should do as he did, and come to that evil end; yet nothing can exceed our Lord's continued expostulations with him, miracles wrought before him, warnings and prophecies. And it is to be noticed that in the same place where our Lord speaks of Jerusalem as having the things belonging to their peace hidden from them, He alludes to his own very earnest dealings with them in calling them to repentance. "How often would I have gathered thy children together as a hen

[a] Prov. xxix. 1.

gathereth her brood under her wings, but ye would not." He had for three years interceded for the tree, dug about it, and laboured in vain, before His word withered up the barren fig-tree. Yet notwithstanding it had been written of them long before: "Let their eyes be blinded, that they see not," "and let them not come into Thy righteousness[9]."

But now, what are we to learn from this doctrine, that God hardens the heart? It is very true that man hardens his own heart, because Scripture says so; it is also true that God hardens the heart, because Scripture says so; yet further it is true that this latter is worthy of much attention, because Scripture repeats it often. With regard to others, this consideration may teach us patience: with regard to ourselves, dependence upon God. Patience to others when we cannot amend them; and dependence on God in the keeping of our own heart. It is indeed of all lessons in the world the most moving and constraining, the most influential on the heart. If an accident or any ill happens to the body, to the goods or outward circumstances, the greatest of comforts is to consider that it is God's doing, to look on it as His; in like manner, when we feel or fear hardness, deadness, coldness coming over our heart, a disinclination to religion, to know that God's hand is in it will move us to turn to Him with all fear and reverence, that He may remove this plague from us, this "plague of the heart." To feel that we are in His hands for life or death, is the most salutary state of mind that a helpless creature can have; to see His hand dealing with us in judgment for past sins; to look to Him to lighten our eyes, that we sleep not in death. In a bodily disease we take all means, we watch, procure medical aid, look to

[9] Ps. lxix. 24. 27.

food, and the like; all this is most necessary; we do so when the sickness is probably even unto death; but at such season of bodily sickness yet more needful is the constant remembrance that all is in God's hand, with Whom are the issues of life and death. It is most needful that this should be inculcated, impressed, brought home to us on such outward trials, for, as the Prophet says, "shall there be evil in a city, and the Lord hath not done it[1]?" But in the case of the soul, this sense of God is of itself restoration and life. "Lord, I am in Thine hands." "I am undone by Thy just judgment. My eyes are blind, so that I cannot see, and that by Thy just judgment; for when I saw, I was as one that saw not. My ears are dull of hearing, and that by Thy just judgment: my knees are weak, I have no heart to kneel, and this by Thy just judgment. But oh, Thou Who hatest nothing that Thou hast made, do Thou create and make in me a new and contrite heart." "O Lord, why hast Thou made us to err from Thy ways, and hardened our heart from Thy fear[2]?" Oh, what a powerful and pity-constraining prayer is this, of all prayers the most appealing to God's compassion; it is like that of David, the most affecting of all in that penitential Psalm, "Cast me not away from Thy Presence, and take not Thy Holy Spirit from me. O give me the comfort of Thy help again, and stablish me with Thy free Spirit." And a still deeper sound is there in that prayer, as of one over whom the pit were about to close her mouth, "Out of the deep have I called unto Thee, O Lord; Lord, hear my prayer."

Now such are the wholesome apprehensions which may be raised in the heart by a sense of this doctrine, as it respects ourselves; if this of all punishments is the greatest,

---

[1] Amos iii. 6.   [2] Isa. lxiii. 17.

to lose the sense and power of good, and if this is God's doing, to whom shall we turn, what else shall we do but to turn to Him? "Of whom may we seek for succour but of Thee, O Lord, Who for our sins art justly displeased?" Look then on your past or present life in this light; you have done this or that sin without remorse, though perhaps it once was otherwise, and such things would have troubled you: well then, this is hardness of heart; but consider it is from God, that it is His punishment on you. Or it may be you do not do this or that which you might and ought to do, yet you are not concerned; now this unconcern is from God, it is a sign of His displeasure. How awful, yet how quickening is this reflection, it is always life and a sign of life to see and acknowledge God's hand and power. You cannot feel, you cannot amend, you cannot change. You are bound by a chain—not imposed by another, but by your own iron will. And that will is with the enemy of your soul, you will what he wills. For from evil will arose evil habit, and habit not resisted became necessity, and necessity a second nature. You have undone yourself. But reflect, the hand of God is also in this; it is He that hath given you over unto death; and He, yea—even He alone can order, even yet, that the stone may be removed, and the grave clothes unloosed; and that your dead and corrupting soul may come forth from the grave. The very thought is already like the quickening of His Spirit, and the hearing of His voice.

Now the reason why Pharaoh did not obey the commands of God, and was not bettered by His miracles, came upon him as a punishment from God[a]. Why do you not love prayer and the Holy Communion? It is a punishment upon you from God, to Him there-

[a] St. Aug. iii. 2621.

fore turn that He may make you love what is your life.

The ten plagues of Egypt seem to represent all the variety of evils that come on us as warnings from God; from the flies, the little annoyances and petty troubles of daily life, to the diseases of cattle and loss of the first-born, its great calamities and bereavements; from the thunder and lightning abroad and the hail-storm to that which climbs up into our secret chambers; from public judgments to private and domestic griefs; all of every kind are to recall us from sin; for "trouble springs not out of the ground," it is of God. Whether great or small, sudden or continuous, abroad or at home, it is of God: thus by little and little does He put us in remembrance; and for the most part it may be observed as in these plagues of Pharaoh, "Wherewithal a man sinneth, by the same also shall he be punished[4]." With what a multitude of troubles like as with the flies of Egypt has your life been beset! this should teach you to remember with the good Mary that one thing only is needful. Your alienation from God has often been a "darkness that may be felt;" what a motive should there be from this judgment to consider the light and health which is in the dwellings of the righteous—in the heart which is at peace with God.

And if in the ten plagues are represented all the chastisements of God, so in Pharaoh are set forth the various shades and changes which there are in impenitence and unbelief. First of all there is rejection of God, "Who is the Lord?" and "I know not the Lord;" but he is not left, the witness of God is sent to tell him who the Lord is. And Moses coming to him so often, what is this but

[4] Wisd. xi. 16.

the many times in which the voice of God meets us? ten times, that is, times out of number. But hardened by judgments, hardened by miracles, hardened by mercies, hardened by forgivenesses and forbearances of God, he brings down upon himself wrath to the uttermost. First of all he rejects the knowledge of God, and he is taught by miracles who the Lord is: and then when given to know Him by His judgments and warnings, he tries every subterfuge; first esteeming religion as idleness and folly: "Ye are idle; therefore say ye, Let us serve the Lord;" "Why do ye let the people from their works?" then he calls in the magicians, he seeks for some false semblance of religion; and then he will do any thing short of what God requires; "Ye may go, but not your women and children;" or again, "Ye need not go, ye may sacrifice in the land;" or, "I will let you go, only ye shall not go very far away. Intreat for me." Or yet further, "Ye may indeed depart;" but then recalling that permission. Such is a description of the world at work in the heart; till he who began by saying, "Who is the Lord? I know Him not," shall know His power in His chastisements; shall preach Him to others by judgments brought on himself which he knows not in a reprobate mind, that prison of darkness in which walk the terrors of night, and in which no star is seen.

Now if the case were one where there was no knowledge of God at all, no warnings, no reproofs, no conscience, and appeals to it, then it would not come home to us in a manner so marked as this of Pharaoh's does; for here is every thing done that can be done; long-suffering, admonitions beforehand, waiting long, and again and again bearing and forbearing. This it is which most strongly characterizes the cases of God's hardening the heart: this it is which renders it so awful and impressive. So was it in every case where this hardening of God is spoken of; there are especial means taken of expostulating, warning, and the like. So was it with the old world, when God said, "My Spirit shall not alway strive with man." So was it with the Heathens whom St. Paul describes, he speaks of conscience and the witness of God long pleading with them, till he says, "As they did not like to retain God in their knowledge, God gave them over to a reprobate mind[5];" so was it with the sons of Eli, of whom it is said, that "they hearkened not unto the voice of their father because the Lord would slay them;" so with Judas Iscariot; so was it with the Jews, "Israel would not obey Me, so I gave them up unto their own hearts' lusts. . . . Oh that My people would have hearkened unto Me; I should soon have put down their enemies[6]." So will it be with the falling away of the Church in the last days. So, alas! is it with every Christian soul that is lost. It is when God has done all, then it is that His taking away His Holy Spirit is thus described; like a binding as it were of hand and foot. As in the Parable it is said of him that had not on the wedding garment—being invited, called, admitted, honoured, made partaker of the kingdom of grace—"bind him hand and foot," for his members belonged to Christ, but have not served Him; "and cast him into outer darkness," for being a child of light he hath not walked in the light.

[5] Rom. i. 28. [6] Ps. lxxxi. 11—14.

KORAH, DATHAN, AND ABIRAM

And the Lord spake unto Moses, saying, Speak unto the congregation, saying, Get you up from about the tabernacle of Korah, Dathan, and Abiram.—NUMBERS xvi. 23, 24.

THE particular characters of these three men, Korah, Dathan, and Abiram, are not given in Scripture; but they seem to represent generally all those who rise up against the powers ordained of God; Korah the Levite against Aaron; Dathan and Abiram of the tribe of Reuben against Moses; but both conspiracies being combined together, indicates that it is the same temper of mind which rejects the ordinances of God whether it be in Church or State. Their signal destruction marks the displeasure of God[1]; it is sudden, extraordinary, and overwhelming. By the "going down alive into the pit," and the "fire coming out from the Lord," it bears some resemblance to the end of Antichrist in the Revelation, where the Beast and the false Prophet are both "cast alive into a lake of fire[2]." And indeed as Moses and Aaron set forth Christ as our Lawgiver and High Priest, their rebellion, though they knew it not, was against the Anointed of God; and so far partakes of Antichrist. Their sin was like that of the fallen angels who from envy, it is supposed, arose against the Son of God. They were

[1] See Prov. xxiv. 22. [2] Rev. xix. 20.

indeed strongly supported, they were no mean adventurers, but themselves chief men, and with them were "two hundred and fifty princes of the assembly, famous in the congregation, men of renown:" but the power which they would establish was from below; that of Moses and Aaron was from above. It was the setting forth of great worldly strength against the ordinance of God. The description also is such as may represent the Christian people of God, for their words are, " Seeing all the congregation are holy, every one of them, and the Lord is among them: wherefore lift ye up yourselves against the congregation of the Lord?" And Moses says to Korah, " Seemeth it a small thing to you, that God hath brought you near to Himself?" "and seek ye the Priesthood also?" We may add, " Seemeth it a small thing to have been made members of Christ, ' kings and priests unto God,' ' a royal priesthood?'" And this reference to the Christian Church is confirmed by the Apostle St. Jude, who, speaking of some in the latter days, says, " Woe unto them, for they have perished in the gainsaying of Core;" that is, they take part with those who were thus condemned of God.

But let us consider how far the case is applicable to ourselves now; as it is in some degree peculiar; for Moses and Aaron had their authority all along confirmed of God by outward signs and miracles. Add to which that their characters were such as less than any other to justify opposition or envy. For Moses was the meekest of men; and Aaron was inoffensive in all his conduct toward them. Their pre-eminence too was in hardship and suffering rather than in wealth or worldly power: in journeyings in the wilderness, not in the riches of Canaan. But these circumstances do not in fact prevent the application to ourselves; for the Pharisees afterwards had no miracles to prove their authority from God; and moreover they were great oppressors and blind guides, covetous and cruel: yet our Lord says of them, "The Scribes and the Pharisees sit in Moses' seat: all therefore whatsoever they bid you observe, that observe and do[3];" and this He says at the very time when He is cautioning His disciples against their wickedness. They had to obey the ordinance of God, though it had neither outward sign nor holiness to support it. And of the Priesthood St. Paul afterwards says, "No man taketh this honour unto himself, but he that is called of God, as was Aaron[4]." And if this was the case with the rulers of Israel, much more with our Lord's own appointed Stewards and Ministers, of whom an early Christian writer[5] says, that they sit in the seat, not of Moses but of Christ. And indeed as if to mark this more strongly, they were called, not Prophets, nor Preachers, but Apostles, "the Sent" of God, the Apostolic Church; sent with the words, "He that despiseth you despiseth Me, and he that despiseth Me despiseth Him that sent Me."

Nor indeed is the Presence of God denied by the company of Korah as being vouchsafed to them under the guidance of Moses and Aaron, they say that "the Lord is among them," as He was seen in the Pillar of Fire and the Cloud, in the Holy Tabernacle, in the Manna from Heaven; but what they complained of was the want of visible fruits and enjoyments, "Thou hast not brought us into a land that floweth with milk and honey;" "Wilt thou put out the eyes of these men?" as men may say now, "We see not our tokens;" where are our spiritual privileges? where is the fulfilment of all the glorious things which the prophets have spoken of the Christian Church?

[3] St. Matt. xxiii. 2, 3.   [4] Heb. v. 4.   [5] Origen.

But if this case is of universal application and for general warning, then the question will arise, are there no allowances, no limitations, to be made; and is there no relief in the case of oppressive Governors and bad Pastors? must all resistance be like that of Korah, Dathan, and Abiram, displeasing to God? and is it never without sin? Let us consider this a little more particularly. If such powers are of God, then He gives such as are suitable to the people over whom they are placed; not necessarily such as they like, or such as are desirable in themselves, but such as are good for them to have, and such as they deserve. For instance, the Roman Emperors during the early days of Christianity, were many of them monsters of cruelty and wickedness; but when we come to inquire into the character of the people over whom they were placed, we find the corruption of morals so deep and extensive, that they were as bad as the tyrants that governed them. Such wickedness could not exist without much suffering, either among themselves or from another set over them; it required an iron rod, and that the sword should not be borne in vain: it was necessary to protect them from one another. And it was to these Romans and living under some of the worst of these Governors that St. Paul says, "Let every one be subject unto the higher powers. For there is no power but of God: the powers that be are ordained of God. Whosoever therefore resisteth the power, resisteth the ordinance of God[6]." And St. Peter unto Christians under the same rule, "Submit yourselves to every ordinance of man for the Lord's sake: whether it be to the king as supreme; or unto governors, as unto them that are sent by him[7]."

Moreover, in consequence of this, we find in Scripture

[6] Rom. xiii. 1, 2.   [7] 1 Pet. ii. 13, 14.

that kings and people are often together condemned and visited alike. Pharaoh and Egypt both together oppressed Israel; both hardened their hearts; both were cut off together. Thus too throughout, both Israel and Judah were visited through their kings. The sins of Solomon and weakness of Rehoboam rent the kingdom in twain; but the visitation was from God, for Israel valued not the ordinances of David; Hezekiah endeavoured in vain to bring them to repentance, and then Manasses was sent, who filled Jerusalem with blood; the reformation wrought by Josiah was found unavailing, as the Prophets testify, and then their succeeding kings were the means of bringing Babylon upon Jerusalem. When the plague came upon David and his people, it might appear from one account that God was displeased with David, and therefore he was tempted to number the people; but it is also evident that God was displeased with Israel, and therefore Satan was allowed to tempt David to that numbering. "The anger of the Lord," it is said, "was kindled against Israel, and He moved David against them to say, Go, number Israel and Judah[a]." It was not merely that David sinned, and his people suffered; but that they sinned, and when God would punish them, it was through the sin of David that this punishment came upon them. Thus then it is with evil rulers, they are not guiltless before God, but in destroying themselves they serve also as a sword[b] or scourge in God's hand. Even as do evil spirits. If thou sufferest, look for the cause in thyself, not in another. Amend thyself, and God will remove what thou fearest. Thus governors and those whom they govern are bound up together, like parents and children; both suffer together, both for themselves and for each other; both have to

[a] 2 Sam. xxiv. 1.   [b] Ps. xvii. 13.

intercede for each other; and to amend themselves, looking unto God in patience.

The same order of Divine Providence applies also to spiritual Governors: it is so with the Church of God in all times and places; the angels of the Churches, and the Churches themselves are tended on, and in each case addressed together as one by their Lord, Who has the seven stars in His hand, while He walks in the midst of the seven golden candlesticks. We only need to look a little more home to ourselves, to see the application of this Law. It is now universally seen and acknowledged, that the Pastors of the Church in this country, of all degrees from the highest to the lowest, have been very negligent of the sacred charge committed to them; something like an extraordinary sleep seems to have been over them for about 150 years; so much so, that the country has sent forth her children to people new worlds, with no thought of supplying them with the means of grace; has possessed herself of vast heathen countries, with no attempt on the part of the Church and nation at large to make them Christians; no Bishop, no blessings of the Church; and at home a vast population increasing, and whole towns grown up, with apparently no thought of any spiritual care for them; but all this while the laity have not perceived it, because they have been no better themselves. The same dark cloud of forgetfulness covered both Priest and people alike.

We may therefore, I say, consider it as a general law of God's Providence, that their rulers both spiritual and temporal will be such as the people are worthy of; that if they need better rulers, the only way in which this can be produced, efficiently and effectively, is by becoming better themselves. As it is contained in that saying of the Wise Man, "What manner of man the ruler of the city is, such are all they that dwell therein." "The power of the earth is in the hand of the Lord, and in due time He will set over it one that is profitable[10]." Now man cannot overturn this rule of God's law; he may change his rulers as he will; he may, as if he were in the place of God, "put down one, and set up another," and thus, by want of submission, the matter may be made worse; as doubtless it always will be by sin; but it cannot be amended, except by obedience, by man's own obedience to God; which obedience must be in the keeping of His ordinances and laws. "In due time," says the son of Sirach, "He will set over it one that is profitable;" but it is "in due time;" like all other Providences of God, it requires waiting on the part of man. "Commit thy way unto the Lord, and He shall bring it to pass." And as the Apostle adds in his injunctions of obedience, "Wilt thou then not be afraid of the power? do that which is good." "For he is the minister of God to thee for good[1]."

How did David suffer from Saul, yet all the while patiently wait upon God for his deliverance, and would not lift up his hand against the Lord's anointed; the life of Saul was precious in his eyes, in order that his own life might be precious in the eyes of God[2].

But a case of doubt and difficulty which may arise is this, if a signal repentance and renovation should take place among the people, the spirit of grace and supplication should be poured out upon them, and there should be a general awakening; then the deficiency of their pastors and rulers will come before them in a striking light; and then will be their great temptation to take the

[10] Ecclus. x. 2. 4.   [1] Rom. xiii. 3, 4.   [2] 1 Sam. xxvi. 24.

amendment of such things into their own hands. But yet not well nor wisely. Surely no reformation can be equal to that which took place suddenly and simultaneously, when the disciples of Christ were yet under the Scribes and Pharisees, yet He said, as they sat in Moses' seat they must be obeyed. Or again, when the Apostles wrote to Christians, that they must submit themselves to the powers that be, while those powers were the most corrupt of heathen governments. It is true that the change had not then become extensive, or leavened the general state of society, but the Law of God's Providence was the same, for it was the gradual progress of that change which would bring over them in God's own good time their own true Governors, such as were meet for them. And in the meanwhile those evil rulers formed a part of that discipline of faith by which they were perfected and established, being purified thereby as gold in the fire.

Moreover, it is observed that the Church of God has flourished more under Heathen than under its own Christian rulers. This consideration may allay our impatience; we are at best so weak and frail, that we need the iron rod more than the golden sceptre; in our present state the Cross is more suited for us than the crown. In prosperity we lean on an arm of flesh, and are weakened; in adversity we lean on God, and are strengthened.

But then it may be said that there is a case far more grievous than this, that of evil ministers in the Church itself, whether it be of Chief Pastors, or of those in their own nearer and subordinate sphere. These are trials peculiarly heavy to a good man; and there are some cases which can only be considered as severe visitations of God, and the scourge of sin. But if God does not afford the power of remedying this great evil, then the same law of patience must be applied. In one ruler or pastor you may read God's wrath, in another His love. You cannot reject either; take His wrath in meekness, and He may show you His love. And in the meanwhile, with regard to any particular case of great trial, we must practise forbearance, and God will remember us in His own good time. The case may be one peculiarly severe, and the heart will often say, "How long?" O Lord! how long? Am I always to forbear? But remember how long our Lord bore patiently, yea, and even lovingly too, even to the last with the false Apostle, Judas Iscariot—and who art thou that dost complain?

It will be often asked, but are there no excepted cases to this rule of submission? Some indeed will always make an exception in their own case, for "rebellion is as the sin of witchcraft." But Holy Scripture is all on the other side; it says, "submit yourselves;" "be patient, brethren;" forbear—wait upon God; "let patience have her perfect work;" "a meek and quiet spirit is in the sight of God of great price." What if in reward for your patience God Himself should come near to you, should Himself, in the failure of outward ordinances, "raise up His power, and come among us, and with great might succour us," being Himself the rest of the meek spirit?

This duty of meekness and patience applies to a case so far as it is one we cannot remedy, like any evil or scourge that comes to us from God's hand, we must take it as our punishment from Him. But then it may be said, when the case is one that implies grievous sin, an example which dishonours God, corrupts Christ's little ones, and poisons the fount of life, are we to acquiesce in this? Does not the love of God constrain us not to resign ourselves to such evil—to lift up our voice and cry—to move Heaven and earth?

This is most true: for surely there is a remedy with God. When He has forbidden one way of redress, He has pointed out another and a better. For redress is required; it is urgent, it is demanded of us; the burden is intolerable, it is one that ought not to be endured, for it presses on our spiritual life, on the means of our union with God. And this brings us to the one practical point of the very greatest urgency and need, most pressing on ourselves at this time, more so than any thing else in the world can be. First of all, that our Pastors may be multiplied, and next that they may be sanctified, whether Bishops or other Parochial Pastors. Our Lord has pointed out the one and only way, and that is the way of Prayer. He did not even Himself send forth Apostles without it. "When He saw the multitudes, He was moved with compassion on them, because they fainted, and were scattered abroad, as sheep having no shepherd. Then saith He unto His disciples, Pray ye the Lord of the harvest, that He will send forth labourers into His harvest[3]." He prayed Himself on this occasion, before He chose His Twelve Apostles, and continued, it is said, the whole night in prayer[4]. So urgent was the need. But He also on this point required their prayers in conjunction with His own, "Pray ye, and He will send." It depended then on themselves: and therefore our not having Bishops so many as we need, or not having them to our mind, or we may say to the mind of Christ, is a sin. For it is certain from our Lord's words, "Ask, and ye shall have," that if we have not, it is because we have not asked. Try this remedy first, and you will need no other until God wills.

[3] St. Matt. ix. 36. 38.   [4] St. Luke vi. 12.

It is a remedy which will make our own hearts most meet to receive such a blessing from God. It may be that we are not yet meet, but that if we pray we shall be; it may be that God is waiting to be thus gracious with us, when we show that we have faith to profit by His gift. It may be as with Cornelius and the first sending of Apostles to the Gentiles; the spirit of prayer and almsdeeds prepared Cornelius for the gift; and St. Peter at the same time was by prayer prepared for conveying it. Nothing is so marked in all the Gospels, as that lesson of God waiting until man asks. Christ more than willing to give—but not giving unless importuned by faith—but passing by. Thus it is doubtless the case that the remedy is in our own hands—not without God, not against God, as in the gainsaying of Core, but with God; it is in our power to move God. If we are importunate, He will rise and give us all that we need. It is indeed most needful—the salvation of many depends upon it.

Many are cast down because the Church is in bonds. It can neither appoint for itself suitable Pastors, nor set aside evil Ministers, nor manage its own affairs, and the government of it is falling into the hands of its enemies. But these are not the great evils to be feared; the one great cause for apprehension is this, whether in the body of the Church at large the spirit of prayer is sufficiently strong to cast off all these impediments; for where prayer is, all such evils from without are thrown off, even as in the spring of the year nature throws off all the chains of winter. The imprisoned eagle may even yet soar aloft, and unfold her wing in the free expanse of Heaven.

When the plague had broke forth on the company of Korah, Dathan, and Abiram, it was not stayed by human means, nor by God Himself without human means, but by

Aaron hastening to stand with the incense between the dead and the living; what is meant by this, but our great High Priest offering up His own prayers and the prayers of His saints?

I have to add one more reflection—the Parable of the importunate Widow, "That men ought always to pray, and not to faint," seems to have an especial reference to the widowed Church in the last days, "when the Son of Man cometh;" where speaking of "His elect which cry day and night unto Him," with the assurance that "He will speedily avenge" their cause, our Lord alludes to the faith of His Church failing in that importunity of prayer. But His promise to her still remains the same, that she cannot pray to Him in vain. If she has not, it is because she prays not.

BALAAM

Let me die the death of the righteous, and let my last end be like his!—NUMBERS xxiii. 10.

THESE words are familiar to us; they express a desire so holy, that it must often come home to the heart, and may well be lodged deeply in the minds of us all. They were spoken by the Prophet Balaam. Nor does it appear to be an exclamation that he made once for all, under a strong impulse or Divine inspiration, but we find in him throughout sentiments of the same character, worthy of a Prophet so esteemed. His answer to the princes, on the second time of their coming, was, "If Balak would give me his house full of silver and gold, I cannot go beyond the word of the Lord my God, to do less or more." What could better express a firm determination to do right? And on both occasions he would give no answer at all without first consulting God. And when he came to Balak, the king of Moab, how must all have been struck with the holiness of the Prophet, so entirely was he not his own, but under the hand of God. "Lo, I am come unto thee: have I now any power at all to say any thing? the word that God putteth in my mouth, that shall I speak." What more could any of us aspire to than this? "If any man speak, let him speak as the oracles of God," not his own words; but the words of God. And what words did he speak! what beauty and holiness is there in them! There is scarcely any thing to surpass them in all the Prophets of Israel. How does he describe the people of God? their goodliness and order as fairer than all things among men, "as gardens by the river's side, as the lign aloes which the Lord hath planted;" the invincible power that is in them, and the happiness in death of those whose strength is in the everlasting God. But this is not all, for it is given him to see the Saviour of the world, in Whom is all the might and glory of His people. "I shall see Him, but not now. . . . There shall come a Star out of Jacob, and a Sceptre shall rise out of Israel." So holy indeed were the sentiments expressed by him, that the Prophet Micah says, "Remember now what Balak, King of Moab, consulted, and what Balaam, the son of Beor, answered, That ye may know the righteousness of the Lord[1]." And what is this righteousness? It is, as the same Prophet goes on to explain, that which is truly good, that the essence of religion consists not in costly burnt offerings and sacrifices, but "in doing justly, and loving mercy, and walking humbly with God."

The expression then of the text, with its devout aspiration, was not a mere passing wish, but one that might characterize much of the life and the sayings of Balaam. Great was his knowledge and keen his sense of what was holy and good. His expressions to God, and to the Angel that met him by the way are almost like that of St. Paul, "Lord, what wouldst Thou have me to do?" I am ready to go or to turn back at Thy word. And yet, oh! the appalling perverseness of the human heart, this was all the while a bad man, self-deceiving, self-deceived, who lived and died in great wickedness! So that his good words on

[1] Micah vi. 5. 8.

the high places seem like those of evil spirits, who confessed Christ as the Holy One of God, and Son of the Most High, when there was scarce a man on earth who could have made such a declaration. For Balaam is referred to through the New Testament as the wicked Prophet, "who loved the wages of unrighteousness." He knew what was holy and good, and it may be that he loved it also, but he loved riches more; his knowledge was with God, his will was with Satan.

And now let us follow the course of his double mind, and the ways of God's dealings with him. When the messengers first came he asked of God, and was told, "Thou shalt not go," "thou shalt not curse the people, for they are blessed." But the second time, when he makes that strong protestation, if Balak should give him his house full of silver and gold, his heart was already beginning to give way; and if when he went again to ask of God, he had put his real thoughts into words, it would have been this, "though the people, as Thou hast said, are blessed, yet more honourable princes and greater rewards make me desirous to comply with their wish, that I may gain for myself both profit and honour." His hesitating, his wishing to ask God at all a second time was a sin. It was like the Prophet of Judah listening to the old Prophet of Samaria, who professed to bring another message from God. Second thoughts are often from the world, while the first are from God. But although God is displeased with him, yet He appears to go with him, and to allow him to proceed in the crooked ways of his covetousness. This is what we see in the ways of God's Providence. It is not unusual with God to grant, not only the desires of an holy and upright mind, but also our desires for inferior things, when the heart is set upon them in preference to

Himself. For instance, a man is on his guard against the dangers of wealth and station; but by degrees he thinks whether he cannot obtain them lawfully, and by and by he is engaged in the pursuit, and in such a case God gives the man usually that for which he craves. He seeks, he obtains; God seems to say, Go on. There is no greater danger than for God to answer a man according to the desires of his own heart; and therefore Job says, "If thou prepare thine heart, and stretch out thine hands towards Him; if iniquity be in thine hand, put it far away[2]." And in Ezekiel God says, if a man comes to inquire of Him with idols in his heart, and setting the stumbling-block of his iniquity before his face, He will answer him according to his idols, he will be taken in his own heart. "If that prophet be deceived," it is added in very remarkable words, "I the Lord have deceived him, and I will punish him[3]."

But yet in this case God does not give us up altogether. As when Israel asked for a king, He gave indeed what they desired—but He expostulated, He warned, He sent them a token of His displeasure. So will He show us by His Providence that He is displeased with us; in the way that we go, His angel with the sword in his hand will meet us, i.e. some calamity, some accident, some grief, is sure to cross our way to remind us from God that the way that we are going is not the way of holiness or of peace. And these are all calls from God, not at all the less so because when a man's eyes are blinded with worldly business and covetousness, he does not see them to be such. Balaam did not perceive the Angel, but the ass did; i.e. for the dullest natures in the world will see that God is in such visitations, in such impediments, as rise up before us, and stand in the way of temptation and sin; all will see except

[2] Job xi 14.   [3] Ezek. xiv. 4, 5. 9.

he who is blinded by his own mind, that it is God Himself Who says thereby, "I went out to withstand thee, because thy way is perverse before Me." And then for awhile he humbles himself, and offers to turn back; in the moment of alarm, from the depth of the heart, conscience will speak the truth, and he says, "I have sinned;" he knows it, though he is as if he knew it not. But he has leave still to proceed, as if in His dealings with us God still said, "Go on in the way your heart has chosen of riches and honour, but yet keep yourself therein from sin;" this is the way of Providence with mankind. The man proceeds, and says to himself, "I will be rich, but I will not sin against God;" and it is possible with God's grace that he might do so.

God is displeased because we love Him not as we should do; but still in His mercy He is ready to try us still in a second and inferior course. He lets us know that He is grieved, yet He bids us go on, as ready even again to accept us. As Samuel said unto the people, "Fear not; ye have done all this wickedness: yet turn not aside from following the Lord, but serve the Lord with all your heart, and turn ye not aside[4]." And thus it is possible that the Prophet even now might have proceeded without actual sin; it was, he might have thought, a great opportunity for good; he might speak the words of God, and bless them whom He would bless; he might be a witness of God. But in all this there was One Who knew him better than he knew his own heart which was hiding its own wickedness from itself. He wished to proceed together with God and Mammon; God on his lips, and Mammon in his heart. When he went to ask of God, there was one prayer which he could not have made, and that is, "Lead us not into

[4] 1 Sam. xii. 20.

temptation;" when a person puts himself in the way of temptation, he is already more than half gone, and in the toils of Satan. And when he allows such desires to mix with his prayers, he pollutes the very fountain of his life. "Come not to the Lord," says the Wise Man, "with a double heart[5]." And One far greater says, "If thine eye be single, thy whole body shall be full of light;" it is the double eye that makes the heart "full of darkness," and oh, "how great is that darkness!" It is for this reason that the Prophet says, "The heart is deceitful above all things, and desperately wicked[6]."

And now he has come to the high places, and seeks for enchantments in vain; and oh, how eloquent is he on the beauty of holiness, on the strength of God and His people! yet all the while his heart is set on the reward, and he is secretly devising to keep God's injunctions and yet obtain his purpose with Balak. As Ezekiel says of the Jews, "with their mouth they show much love, but their heart goeth after their covetousness. And lo, thou art unto them as a very lovely song of one that hath a pleasant voice, and can play well on an instrument: they hear, but they do not[7]." After this his description of the goodly tents, of the blessedness of the death of the righteous, of the Star out of Jacob, after he had said that God had not "beheld iniquity in Jacob, nor seen perverseness in Israel," and that therefore "his Lord God is with him," in the next chapter we read of the wrath of God having broken forth against His people, the plague among them, and a very great slaughter, on account of the Midianitish women: and a little further we find that all this was occasioned by the advice of this wicked Prophet Balaam. For knowing that nothing could overcome the children of Israel while

[5] Ecclus. i. 28.   [6] Jer. xvii. 9.   [7] Ezek. xxxiii. 31, 32.

faithful to their God, that there was "no enchantment against Jacob," instead of openly cursing them, he advises Balak to corrupt them by fornication and idolatry, in order that thus God might go from them and they might lose their great strength. "These," Midianitish women, it is said, "caused the children of Israel through the counsel of Balaam to commit trespass against the Lord[8]." It is almost impossible to conceive wickedness greater than this; it is being one with Satan, to cause God's people to sin in order that God might leave them and they be destroyed, and all this merely from his own avarice.

But we are not to suppose that Balaam now threw off the mask and became openly a bad man; it would appear that he still kept up his self-deceit and dissimulation; as if what he was doing was but lawful and right; so that he not only led them into practices of sin, but corrupted and perverted their principles also, persuading them that they might thus hold with God and yet with sin and the flesh. Thus he came, like others after, "with all deceivableness of unrighteousness in them that perish." For he is spoken of as having doctrines of wickedness. Thus Christ says in the Revelation to the Church in Pergamos "where Satan dwelleth," "Thou hast there them that hold the doctrine of Balaam, who taught Balac to cast a stumblingblock before the children of Israel, to eat things sacrificed to idols, and to commit fornication[9]." And St. Peter describing those who have "gone astray, following the way of Balaam," speaks of them as "sporting with their own deceivings," "having eyes full of adultery," and "an heart exercised with covetous practices," "beguiling unstable souls."

But to return to the text: did Balaam after all die the

[8] Num. xxxi. 16.   [9] Rev. ii. 14.

death of the righteous? No, death overtook him in the midst of these evil courses. For thinking that God's strength had now left His people, whom he himself had succeeded in corrupting, he proceeds together with Balak to fight against them; but in the meanwhile God had returned to Israel, having by the plague and the sword cut off the evil, and made an atonement for them, remembering His mercies in Christ; and thus Balaam, like Satan, was overreached by God's love to those that are in Christ. And now the same chapter that reveals the wickedness of Balaam mentions also his death: "They slew the kings of Midian," it is said, "Balaam also the son of Beor they slew with the sword[1]." "With the sword"! thus was the vision of the angel fulfilled, sent to warn him with the drawn sword: so wonderfully in that warning was there contained a mysterious intimation of his end.

Now what are we to think of such a wonderful history and character as this? Is it one that stands alone—out of the ordinary course of men in their ways? or is it a case that is not uncommon? It is to be feared that there is great danger of something of the kind wherever the knowledge of God is. This self-deceit, or danger of a double heart, is often alluded to in sayings and single expressions throughout the Scriptures; but here it is put forth at length in a narrative so striking, that it cannot but arrest the attention of all thoughtful persons. There are, no doubt, cases of the kind around us, those whose heart and life, if the veil were stripped aside by the all-knowing Searcher of hearts, would show a career no less awful and remarkable than this of the Prophet Balaam; but it is not my purpose to dwell on such, God only knows them; but

[1] Num. xxxi. 8. 16.

rather on this,—the instances of the same sort of self-deceit which any one of us by the aid of God's Holy Spirit, and a watchful desire to know his own heart, may detect in ourselves. It came forth so strongly when our Lord was upon earth, that those He most denounced, we may observe, He called "hypocrites." In the light of His Presence, in the holiness of God, it was this more than any thing else that appeared in its true colours—"hypocrisy," i.e. self-deceit: it consisted in eyes blinded and a heart darkened by the love of sin; it was found in the most holy places; it stood in the temple in the most honoured place there; it sat highest in the synagogues, and had the first room in assemblies; it was very particular in keeping the Sabbath, but without mercy and the love of God; it was very religious in outward washings, but passed over that saying of the Psalmist, "I will wash my hands in innocency, and so will I go to thine altar:" it made long prayers without drawing near to God with the heart; it went up to the Passover before the time in order to be purified, and to keep it aright, while the thoughts were wholly occupied in a determination to shed innocent blood: it was so full of a scrupulous conscience, that it would on no account enter into the judgment-hall of the Gentile lest it should be defiled; but without scruple or hesitation they could at the same time urge on people and a heathen governor, from envy and hatred of goodness, to crucify One they knew to be Innocent, the Holy One, the Lamb of God; and exult over His sufferings in death. Now that hypocrisy which came forth so strongly in Christ's Presence, and was so marked by Him, we may conclude is not uncommon in all generations. His own disciples were the most simple-minded of men, but He says to them, "Take heed of the leaven of the Pharisees which is hypocrisy."

Perhaps we may conclude from Scripture, that this self-deceit goes with covetousness more than with any other crime; thus we find that Judas Iscariot, though so very wicked a man, deceived others so thoroughly that no suspicion against him ever rose in the minds of the disciples with whom he was in the closest intercourse; he was probably deceiving himself as well as them; and this we find was the case with those Pharisees whose wickedness was so very great; they were as whited sepulchres, beautiful without, much esteemed for holiness and wisdom, deceiving themselves as well as others in a great degree; their blindness of heart was owing to covetousness and ambition. And hence we may observe that the deceivableness of riches is so much spoken of; the necessity of an undivided heart in approaching to God; we are warned against attempting to serve both God and mammon. Thus to take a better instance of this kind, in that Rich Young Man who came running and kneeling to Christ; what could be more holy than his wish to know what he might do to attain eternal life? it was like the desire of Balaam, that he might die the death of the righteous; but he knew not himself, till the great Searcher of hearts made it known to him—that there was something in his heart which he loved more than eternal life with God; and that was this present life and its advantages.

Oh that we might with all sincerity come to God with that prayer, "Try me, O God, and seek the ground of my heart: prove me, and examine my thoughts. Look well if there be any way of wickedness in me; and lead me in the way everlasting[2]." Oh that we might consider before

[2] Ps. cxxxix. 23, 24.

it be too late, His saying to us so often, in Scripture, in His Providence, by His Spirit, "Keep thy heart with all diligence; for out of it are the issues of life[3]."

There must always be much reason to fear something of this self-deceit where persons have such holy services and prayers as we have, as in the Psalms and Collects of the Church, and especially in the Lord's Prayer: to use such prayers we ought to be very good; and if we do not endeavour to be so there must be something of this insincerity. The danger besets us from our very childhood: children are taught to use holy prayers; but if their conduct is not watched by others and by themselves, they will come to "use vain repetitions," by not attempting to do what they pray for; and thus they will get into a habit of coming before God without singleness of mind. There are, again, some whose worldly interest and credit it is to appear good, as it was with Balaam, with Judas Iscariot, with the Scribes and Pharisees; it is so with all in some degree in a Christian country; this makes it necessary to be very strict with the thoughts and intentions; to bring before us continually the eye of God and the eternal Judgment.

Balaam was deceiving himself, but when he saw the sword in the angel's hand, his heart told him aright, "I have sinned;" and when at his death he saw, as it were, at the last the angel and the sword, if there had been time, his heart might again have said, "I have sinned." My brethren, the hour is fast approaching upon us all, when the veil shall drop from the eyes, and every one shall know his own heart: it will be at the sight of the Judgment, and of the angels, and of the sword that

[3] Prov. iv. 23.

shall cut asunder the hypocrite[4]: then the self-deceiving soul will know itself and say, "I have sinned;" "I will turn back;" but no, it is too late, there is now no turning back.

[4] St. Matt. xxiv. 51.

JOSHUA

And he gave Joshua the son of Nun a charge, and said, Be strong and of a good courage: for thou shalt bring the children of Israel into the land which I sware unto them: and I will be with thee.—
DEUTERONOMY xxxi. 23.

JOSHUA is represented to us as a warrior, one might say as nothing else; other soldiers in Scripture have strongly marked characters of their own, as David, as the Centurion in the Gospels, and Cornelius in the Acts. But in Joshua the character of the man is lost in the soldier. It is remarkable how repeatedly it is said to him, "Be strong and of a good courage." "Only be thou strong and very courageous; be not afraid." He was called upon for this courage; it was fulfilled in all his life; and at his death he gives the like injunction, saying to Israel, "Be ye therefore very courageous[1]."

But this in Joshua was a sacred courage, not that of the world, but of God; it was founded on faith. He was called upon to execute the purposes of God, and the call was ever accompanied with the promise, "I will be with thee;" and in that promise he trusted. It was always kept in view that his power was not in himself but of God; as when he overcame Amalek, by Moses interceding on the Mount[2]; by the angel meeting him when he entered

[1] Josh. xxiii. 6. [2] Exod. xvii.

Canaan, as "the Captain of the Lord's host;" by the Sun and Moon obeying his voice; by the hailstones from Heaven, and the hornets on earth[3]. And when it is said indeed that he was also "full of the spirit of wisdom," yet the reason is added, because Moses had laid his hands upon him[4] as the leader of his people.

Now the Church teaches us by her appointed lessons for the season, that Joshua's taking possession of the land of Canaan is the figure of our entering into the promised kingdom on the descent of the Holy Ghost. And we may observe that this character of Joshua had a sort of fulfilment at the Day of Pentecost, in the great "boldness of Peter and John," at which, it is said, the Jews "marvelled[5];" and in St. Stephen, and in St. Paul afterwards.

But the courage of Joshua speaks of something far more deep and extensive than this; as the Apostle in explaining Joshua and Canaan as the true rest to be found in Christ, adds, "Let us therefore come boldly unto the throne of grace, that we may obtain mercy, and find grace to help[6]."

It is not then of boldness in battle that God would teach us by Joshua, but it is altogether a figure of something else, of a brave courage in Christ; for "we wrestle not against flesh and blood," but against spiritual powers; our weapons are not carnal, but mighty through God; our armour "on the right hand and on the left," is the gift of grace. The Captain to whom we look hath the sword proceeding out of His mouth, and "a vesture dipped in blood;" but the armies that follow on white horses have no armour but the "righteousness of Saints,"

[3] Josh v. 13; x. 11. 13; xxiv. 12. [4] Deut. xxxiv. 9.
[5] Acts iv. 13. [6] Heb. iv. 16.

"clothed in fine linen, white and clean[7]." "Not by might nor by power, but by My Spirit, saith the Lord of hosts[8]." At the note of the true Sabbath of God—the trumpet-sound of the unarmed multitude of God—fall down all the walls of the enemy. And who is she that cometh forth from the accursed and doomed city, but the mother of the true Joshua, who "in righteousness doth make war," even the harlot Rahab, rich in faith, with the scarlet token of Him who is known as "red in His apparel," as "Mighty to save[9]"? "Gather together unto Me those that have made a covenant with Me with sacrifice." He goeth forth with the bow and the crown, "conquering and to conquer," for the destruction not of Jericho, but of that Jerusalem which slew His Apostles and Prophets, and is now in bondage with her children; but she that is set free is of the "Jerusalem which is above, the mother of us all." His army is clothed in righteousness, for the warfare in which we are engaged is one in which men are overcome, not by the sword of the enemy, but by the accursed thing hid in the tent, the forbidden treasure, the secret thing against God. In this war the powers of Heaven take part and fight for us; for there is "war in Heaven," and we partake in that war and victory, for we are with Michael, i.e. "Who is as God." Such is our Joshua, who hath taken upon Him not the nature of angels, but the seed of Abraham.

But as for all warfare the requisite is courage, so Joshua represents in particular that courage of heart which is a great ingredient in the "faith that overcometh the world," and in that "perfect love" which "casteth out fear." Hence it is that Christian faith is so often throughout the

[7] Rev. xix. 14, 15. [8] Zech. iv. 6.
[9] Isa. lxiii. 1. Rev. xix. 13.

Scriptures, and especially in the Psalms, armed with sword and shield, and clothed in circumstance of war, and speaks in terms of battle and victory. Such courage was the peculiar gift of the early Church, which is the going forth of the true Joshua; courage to give away all; courage to rejoice in tribulation; courage to take Christ at His word; and therefore it went forth on the white horse triumphant; courageous to trust, and in that trust mighty to conquer. Whereas that "faintness" of heart foretold of the Jew[1] is fulfilled in the weak Christian of the latter days, little of mind. In this warfare woe to the "fearful," for he shall have his lot with the unbelieving[2]. Woe to him that saith, "There is no hope;" to the faint-hearted who hath "lost patience:" "to the sinner that goeth two ways:" to him that is "afraid of a man that shall die, and forgetteth the Lord his Maker[3]."

Such then is to us the history and character of Joshua. It signifies that we who are entered into the privileges of the Gospel, must overcome every enemy to our full possession, every sin, every temptation; that we are in Christ called to this end: we are taught by Joshua of the necessity of faith in the eternal inheritance God has promised; in our power of obtaining it; in God's assurance that He will be with us; in sparing no hindrance to our rest in that kingdom; in allowing no bosom sin to escape and live. "The Lord your God," says Joshua, "is He that fighteth for you as He hath promised you. Take heed therefore to yourselves that ye love the Lord your God[4]." This is the standing still of the Sun and Moon: of strong walls falling down by miracle; of removing mountains. The history of Joshua sets before us that one great lesson of

---

[1] Lev. xxvi. 36.   [2] Rev. xxi. 8.
[3] Isa. li. 12.   [4] Josh. xxiii. 10, 11.

the Gospels, viz. the power we have in Christ by faith. "All things are possible to him that believeth."

To enforce this the more he bears the very name of God our Saviour; the type of Christ, not in His Priesthood as Melchizedeck; not in His kingdom as David; not in dying as Abel; not as the history of Joseph; or as the character of Moses; not in His death-passion as Hezekiah; not in life-long sorrows as Jeremiah; but in Joshua it is of victory. As our Lord Himself says, "Be of good cheer, I have overcome the world." And as St. John testifies to the same, "Who is he that overcometh the world but he that believeth that Jesus is the Son of God[5]?" And St. Paul, "I can do all things through Christ that strengtheneth me."

Now we observed that the characteristic of Joshua is a soldier's courage; other qualities are lost in this; his character is in a manner colourless, like the form of a statue rather than of a painting; like one sent from God, and bearing the name of God. "Behold, I send an angel before thee," says God, "to bring thee into the place which I have prepared. Beware of him;—for My Name is in him[6]." Who is this angel, says St. Augustine, in whom the name of God is but Joshua[7]; that is, "the true Jesus, the ruler and guide of His people into the inheritance of eternal life?" For it is not, he says, from the beginning of his life, but from this the change of his name that he becomes the leader of God's people.

The true Sabbath, the true Canaan, the true Joshua are, says the Epistle to the Hebrews, with us. We may observe that Joshua was with Moses in the Mount[8], and Christ was in the Law, but Moses departed and Joshua

[5] St. John v. 5.
[7] St. Aug. viii. 471.
[6] Exod. xxiii. 20, 21.
[8] Exod. xxiv. 13.

remained; the Law departed, but "grace and truth came by Jesus Christ[9]." Jesus remains. On the Mount of Transfiguration, when the kingdom of the regeneration had come, Peter would have made three tabernacles, one for Moses, and one for Elias, and one for Christ; but Moses and Elias, though they partook for a while of His glory, had gone, and when they looked around there was "no man, save Jesus only," and the voice from Heaven said, "Hear ye Him." Moses and Elias, the Law and the Prophets, bear witness to Him, and in so doing partake of His glory; but they depart and He remains. It is Jesus clothed with the glory of the Resurrection ready to lead us in alone. The Father bears witness to Him in the Voice, and the Spirit also in the Cloud, and then they are seen and heard no more; but in, and through, and by Him.

Thus St. Paul also in recounting that noble army of Patriarchs, Saints, and Martyrs, as partaking of His glory and seen as a cloud of witnesses, ends all by bidding us to fix our eyes on Him only; "looking," he says, the word means in the original, looking aside from all other things, "unto Jesus, the Author," or as in the Greek, the Captain, "and Finisher," or, as the word is sometimes rendered, the Arbiter and Rewarder, "of our faith." This therefore is the Joshua to whom we look, who speaks of power and of victory in God, and of nothing in man, but faith to take hold of that victory and power; in whose transparent character we see nothing but the Captain of our Salvation, inasmuch as man is lost in God.

It is then as St. Paul says, "Henceforth know we no man after the flesh; yea, though we have known Christ after the flesh, yet now know we Him no more[1]." And

---

[9] St. John i. 17. [1] 2 Cor. v. 16.

of himself, "I live, yet not I, but Christ liveth in me." Hence Joshua speaks not of human virtue and affection, but of power; not of man's disposition, but of victory in God. And what is this but of God in Jesus Christ? The one lesson therefore is that in all, and beyond all His Saints, we are to look to Jesus, remembering that He is God as well as man,—that it is altogether different to that of looking to the example of any man—on account of His Godhead, His Atonement, the gift of His Spirit; we look to Him and have power, we have power by looking; nay, by looking, as the Apostle says, we "are changed into the same Image even as by the Spirit of the Lord."

His example indeed seems in some sense to set us afar off; for He is all perfection, we full of imperfections. He is at such an infinite distance that we cannot approach Him. But the name of Joshua brings us near; for by that we know He has power to put His own mind into us, and to make us like Himself. And the reason of this is, because we can never look to Him merely as our Example, without remembering at the same time that He is in manifold ways unspeakably more. It is when we believe in Him as our God, that His example itself becomes profitable to us in a way perfectly different from any example of good men.

We are to "look to Jesus," because He is our God; to be "perfect" as "He is perfect;" "to be made like unto Him." Our ground of confidence in the Day of Judgment is, "because as He is, so are we in this world." Now all this is because He has enabled us of His power to do so. Oh, the wonderful Mystery of our great Exemplar! As man He sets us afar off by His infinite perfections; but as God and Man, by setting us afar He brings us near; by His Godhead He gives us power to approach and a will to do so. In following Him we are ever at an immeasurable distance; but, strange to speak, while He makes us to feel ourselves so far from Him, He brings us so intimately near as to be made one with Him by His infinite power and Godhead. He invites us to follow Him, and by inviting He draws; He commands, and by His commanding gives power to do. And all this is in the name of Joshua, or "the Lord the Saviour." His Name is a tower of strength; and therefore in this His Name is all our courage. For this His Name casteth out devils and all power of the enemy; this His Name is "the bundle of myrrh" on the breast, healing and restoring under every woe. His "Name," it is said, "is as ointment poured forth[2]." And what is this ointment but the anointing of the Holy One? The Law came by Moses, and is written in the lives of the Saints; but grace to perform and truth to enlighten is by Jesus Christ, Who leadeth into the kingdom. Our true inheritance, the rest of the meek, is in Him.

We "look to Jesus" as our Example because He is so infinitely more; He is not only the Way, but the Life also; He not only shows the truth, but gives us eyes to see it. As we look to Him our souls are cleansed, and we gain sight to behold Him more and more as He is, because He to Whom we look is Himself the true Light that lighteth every one.

Yet, further:—Our Joshua to whom we look is not only our wisdom, He is also our strength, as He Himself said, "He that abideth in Me, the same bringeth forth much fruit," and "Without Me ye can do nothing." So important is this great truth, that our victory over the world depends entirely on our rightly receiving it; for "this is the victory that overcometh the world, even our faith[3],"

[2] Song of Sol. i. 3, 4.   [3] 1 St. John v. 4.

our faith in Christ as God. Thus the example of our Joshua is different from the example of all His Saints, because of His Godhead. Powerful is the world around us, powerful is our own evil nature, and very powerful is the enemy of our souls to our destruction; and against these our own strength is but weakness, even as the chaff before the wind, or the leaf in the torrent. But mightier than all these is the strength of Christ, and we are strong by His strength when we endeavour to be like Him. By meekness, and mercy, and suffering, He overcame the world; and we in these things shall be strong in His strength, and partake in His victory, while by faith we look to Him.

Again, our Joshua is not only Light and Strength, but He is Love, He is Love Itself, in that He is God, for "God is Love." How do men imitate and delight in following one whom they love; they are conformed and changed, they know not how, by looking to one whom they love; his thoughts become their thoughts, his likings and dislikings theirs, his opinions theirs. For him they endure hardship, nor do they know any greater joy than in enduring hardship for his sake. Oh, how sweet and constraining is this power of love! And if it be so of earthly love, how much more of heavenly? If of man and in man, how much more of God? If love has power to create love, and we are inclined to love those who love us, how much more when we love God because He hath loved us? When He Who is Love, and hath implanted in our nature love for each other, fills our hearts with the love of Himself—gives us to partake of love as we partake of God.

This then is our Joshua, our courage, our victory; it is in this, the saving Name. Then it is that His Atonement works in us—then the wounded man is able to arise, and is strengthened for his journey; the Oil and Wine, the Spirit of God and the Blood of Christ, are poured into his wounds, and he has a strength which is not his own; to be sensible of his weakness becomes his strength; to know his sickness is his health.

Again, not only is He Whom we follow infinite Love, and by His Spirit works in us love also, but He sets before us Himself as the only object worthy of our love; which can fill and satisfy all the desires of our hearts, in that He is our God; Whom to love is the only end of our being; Whom to love is life. It is He Himself Who is seen by us enduring as Man all human suffering—our God in pain, in contempt, in sorrow; and all this for our sakes, and written that we may know it, that we may meditate on every part and see therein our God; and in every part remember ourselves also, beholding our own deservings in His burden. We see it all in our God, that humbling and hating ourselves, we may long in Him to be hidden, that we may lose ourselves and be found in God.

Such then is the adorable pattern set before us in our Joshua; He all light, we all darkness; He infinite strength, and we great weakness; He perfect holiness, and we full of sin and infirmity; that the more we contemplate Him the more conscious we may be of our own demerits. But in that He is God our Saviour, how may we notwithstanding rejoice in His goodness and be bold in His greatness, in that He may be in us and we in Him. And so far as this is so, well may we consider all the exhortations so repeated to Joshua as addressed to ourselves. "Be strong and of good courage, be not afraid," it is "the Lord your God that fighteth for you; take good heed therefore that ye love the Lord your God." "All things are yours, whether life, or death, or things present, or things to come; all are yours; and ye are Christ's; and Christ is God's[4]."

It is Thou, O God and Saviour, that leadest us into our true inheritance! In Thee alone, O Jesus, shall we find rest and peace! and no rest in Thee till every enemy which is in our old nature be overcome. But Thou art Almighty; in Thee is victory; Thou hast said unto my soul, "I am thy salvation:" "My grace is sufficient for thee." While we contend with Amalek our Advocate intercedeth for us; the Sun and Moon are yet waiting their going down, and our life is yet prolonged, that we may overcome before the night shall have overtaken us. "The stars in their courses fight for us," and we must have no peace till we are "more than conquerors through Him that loved us."

[4] 1 Cor. iii. 12—23.

SAMSON

And the woman bare a son, and called his name Samson; and the child grew, and the Lord blessed him.—JUDGES xiii. 24.

WE have seen in Joshua the great power we have in Jesus Christ to overcome every enemy and obtain perfect peace. And so it was with the early Christians; before them fell down all the strongholds of the enemy: but with us it is far otherwise. As with the Israelites after the death of Joshua, their enemies prevailed, and continued with them as "snares," as "scourges in their sides, and thorns in their eyes[1]." Yet God was so merciful, that, under the pressure of the evils which these brought, "He thought upon His covenant," and heard their prayers; "When they cried unto the Lord in their trouble He delivered them out of their distress[2]." He sent from time to time, when they cried unto Him, deliverers to their aid; such were Barak, Gideon, Samson, and others. Thus it is with us; our temptations, through the world, the flesh, and the devil, press us often sore. We have not overcome them with Joshua; when oppressed we call to God, are comforted and strengthened and, may be, overcome our enemies, though it be but for a time. The history of Israel, therefore, under the Judges, has a peculiar reference to the Church in the day of its weakness and the decay of faith.

[1] Josh. xxiii. 13.   [2] Ps. cvi. 42—44; cvii. 11—13.

But here arises the question, as these Deliverers raised of God were not blameless characters, how far they are intended to be examples for us to follow. And in this, as in explaining other parts of the Old Testament, we must remember the Apostle's words, "the letter killeth, but the spirit giveth life," and endeavour to ascertain under the letter the mind of the Spirit.

When St. Paul recounts the Saints of God, which by faith obtained a good report, he mentions "Gedeon, and Barak, and Samson." The history of Samson therefore is for our example. Yet in what? For he loved strange women, the daughters of the uncircumcised Philistine, so forbidden of God, nay, more, the harlot of Gaza; he was ensnared and entrapped by them, and died in their snares. No mention of repentance—no apparent consciousness of sin. As Solomon was gifted with wisdom, so was Samson with bodily strength; both for the Church of God; but it may be in neither for their own salvation; even as in the miraculous gifts of the early Church, when there might be faith such as to remove mountains, yet without charity, which alone faileth not; as they who at last will in Christ's Name have "done many wonderful works," but are not known of Him.

These Saints are set before us by St. Paul—but for what purpose? Not altogether as the objects of our imitation, but as witnesses of the power of faith; that we may look not to them, but rather off and from them, to Him of whose power they testify. "Wherefore seeing," he adds, "we are compassed about," not by examples, but "with so great a cloud of witnesses," let us look, he says, not to them, but to "the Author and Finisher of our faith." It is therefore of the power of this faith in Him that they bear witness to us; but if we have this faith it will be shown in overcoming, not wild beasts, but him who as a roaring lion walketh about seeking whom he may devour; not in rooting out Philistines, but besotting sins; accepting Christ as our pattern in all love and obedience. To us the example of Christ is manifested; the "bundle of myrrh" is laid open; the alabaster box is broken, and the perfume is abroad; faith in God implies Christ Crucified written on our hearts and lives by the finger of God; with them of old faith did not imply this; they knew of the power of God, and divined something of His goodness; but Christ's love was not spread out before them, with the "new law" of life. With the faith of Samson we shall have the power of Samson, not to destroy enemies, but to save them; and in death to overcome not them but ourselves.

Let us therefore endeavour so to take this remarkable history, that from thence may be derived meat for the soul's health, and out of the strong may come forth the sweetness of wisdom. Our consideration is particularly drawn to Samson, by the solemn circumstances which preceded his birth; they seem to say to us, "Put off thy shoes from off thy feet, for the place whereon thou standest is holy ground." Prepare thyself for some great manifestation of God's power and goodness, such as He will vouchsafe to all ages, when His people have undone themselves, and yet are at any time willing in their captivity and distress to look to Him Whom they have forgotten. For the account begins by saying that "the children of Israel had done evil," and the Lord had in consequence "delivered them into the hand of the Philistines forty years." Well might they ask where is our Joshua, and the victory, and the kingdom, and the power? It was then that the angel of the Lord appeared to the wife of Manoah, promising that to her, though barren, a child beyond nature should be given of God; but requiring the strict dedication of herself from that time, and of her son from his birth, as a Nazarite to God—one set apart and separate by a strict consecration to Himself. And as God is wont in Holy Scripture to repeat by a second admonition, or a second vision and manifestation, what He has strongly purposed for great ends; so at the prayer of Manoah this Angel again appears with circumstances fully detailed to arrest attention. They asked his name, but he told them not, for it was secret; clothed with a Divine terror was his countenance, and great the mystery of his appearance; he would not eat of the kid, but when it was offered in sacrifice to God he ascended on the flame; and they fell on their faces to the ground, and said, "We shall surely die, because we have seen God." And so indeed they would have died had they seen God otherwise than in Christ; but it was in Christ they beheld Him. And Manoah's wife said to her husband, "If the Lord were pleased to kill us, He would not have received a burnt offering at our hands." Thus then it was that Samson was wonderfully born, and as a child blessed of God, and moved by His Spirit, and made the instrument of His power, made to be as we may say of him as seen in Christ, "a light to lighten the Gentiles, and the glory of Thy people Israel."

Yet further, we must consider in Samson the peculiarity of his gifts. Of Joshua we read that by the hands of Moses he was filled with the Spirit of wisdom for his great leadership; but this was not the case with Samson; he was moved by the Spirit to great miracles of strength, but there was no wisdom to guide a nation, or indeed his own steps. Though in bodily power more than a man, he seems to have been like a child in understanding; and certainly with this there was much of the beauty of a childlike disposition, as in his constant reference to his parents, even in manhood. There was something childlike in that reserve which accompanies inspirations of God and the strong feelings of childhood, when he slew the lion, and afterwards took the honey from it; neither of which things he mentioned, it is said, even to his father or his mother, to whom yet he so looked up as a child. There is something childlike in not mentioning what greatly moves us. There is, moreover, something childlike in his great exploits:—as in carrying away the gates of Gaza to the hill of Hebron; in his device of destroying the corn with the foxes and the firebrands; in his slaying the thousand men with the jawbone; in the young lion that roared at him, which he slew as a kid; in eating the honey as he went; in the riddles, too, and the bonds. There is a childlike grandeur and sublimity in these wonderful works of God. To those who quailed before the giant sons of Anak, God showed by Samson with what weak instruments He could work such deeds of prowess, while one who had in himself the power of great armies, yet was as a child in his parents' hands, looking to them; and as a weak man in the hands of a woman. And in what was his great strength? not in himself, not in power of limb or arm—but hung in the hair of his head, as if to show how slight the gift.

What therefore are we to learn from Samson? His history of such romantic interest is no doubt in order to exhibit in a most lively manner the power of faith. There is something wild and sublime, and, at the same time, most simple and attractive in all that is recorded of him for this end; his life is all supernatural: unarmed with spear or shield, but armed of God, like David afterwards, in faith he stands alone as the great saviour of his people [3], or one whom God was willing to make so if they would but look to him. The very wildness and strangeness of his life but corresponded with that purpose of God, as to show what God was willing to do, but did not, on account of their unbelief. His course, wild and irregular as it might seem to be, is spoken of, in a singular degree, as under the influences of the Spirit "Who alone worketh great marvels." To this may be attributed much in explaining the conduct of Samson, for God can dispense with His own appointments. It is said on the first mention of him as a child, "And the Spirit of the Lord began to move him at times in the camp of Dan;" and when he slew the lion, "And the Spirit of the Lord came mightily upon him, and he rent him as he would have rent a kid." In like manner afterwards when he slew the thirty; and also when he brake his bonds and slew a thousand men, it is said, "And the Spirit of the Lord came mightily upon him [4]." These expressions raise his history into that which is quite beyond daily life.

And to this something may be attributed in explaining the conduct of Samson, of things which may have been done under a prophetic and Divine impulsion instigating or controlling him. Thus it is said that his parents "knew not it was of the Lord," that he took a wife of the Philistines. This expression indeed might signify as it is said in another place, "it was of the Lord to harden their hearts that He might destroy them [5];" implying that it was an evil permitted of God. Yet, in this case, it might have been an action, not evil but directed of God, who, for the carrying out of the great ends of His Providence, may suspend His own laws of separation between Israelite and Philistine; and like as when Hosea was com-

[3] Neh. ix. 27.   [4] Judg. xiv. 19; xv. 14.   [5] Josh. xi. 20.

manded to take "a wife of whoredom," that it was with some mystery and allegorical meaning under the instigation of God. For beside the immediate object it might have this further meaning, that it represented Christ our Deliverer taking His Church from among the Gentiles; and to the disobedient Israelites of that generation it might have implied that this their course of disobedience would lead to that consummation, the rejection of themselves, and the Gentiles being chosen in their stead. And indeed it is very evident, when the men of Judah afterwards bound Samson, and then delivered him bound into the hands of the Philistines, that this represented the Jews giving up Christ bound unto the Gentiles.

Yet at the same time to Samson himself those things might have had their own lesson of instruction from the evils they brought upon him. Thus at last in his blindness and sore bondage, the loss of bodily sight might seem a fit punishment for the want of wisdom to guide the ways of his life; darkness and chains in the midst of enemies, and the round of toilsome labour at the mill might, as St. Gregory has observed, represent the blindness and toilsome bondage of Satan's service[6]. His victory in death, mysterious and significant as it was, yet by his death accompanying that victory may indicate the punishment of a life that had not been without blame.

But God forsook him not,—and though he may not have acted well or wisely, yet may we not hope that the blessing which he had at the beginning when on the first mention of him as a child, it is said, "the Lord blessed him," returned to him at the last again? and that the self-sacrifice of his life, hallowed to excellent mysteries and granted to his prayer, in that mighty deed of heroic mar-

[6] St. Greg. In Job.

tyrdom was accepted? As He Whose name was "Wonderful[7]," appeared to his father, Manoah, and "did wonderously, as Manoah and his wife looked on," and ascended to Heaven on the flame from off the altar that "went up toward Heaven;" so we may hope it was with Samson in the end, and that at his death from that altar of sacrifice he ascended to God. Such a view indeed is to him charitable; to ourselves profitable; and most suitable to one of that army of martyrs who "through faith wrought righteousness, stopped the mouths of lions, out of weakness were made strong, waxed valiant in fight, turned to flight the armies of the aliens." For "these all," it is added, "obtained a good report through faith."

Moreover, many things in the history of Samson are, as in other Saints of God, sanctified to us as figures and types of Him on Whom shall rest "the Spirit of ghostly might," even of our Saviour Himself, appearing as weak in our weakness, tied by the bonds of our infirmities, Who among His own countrymen "did not many mighty works because of their unbelief[8];" of Whom it may be said now as it was of old, "O the hope of Israel, the Saviour thereof in time of trouble, why shouldest Thou be as a stranger in the land, and as a wayfaring man that turneth aside to tarry for a night? Why shouldest Thou be as a man astonied, as a mighty man that cannot save? Yet Thou, O Lord, art in the midst of us, and we are called by Thy Name[9]." Thus even in his discomfitures and failures Samson speaks to us of One Who should always be in our mind. And some points in his life may be dwelt upon more particularly as containing such spiritual instruction.

[7] Judg. xiii. 18, *margin. reading.*   [8] St. Matt. xiii. 58.
[9] Jer. xiv. 8, 9.

The first deed of prowess in his life seems to anticipate the end. For Our Lord is Himself called the Lion of Judah—and of Him came forth in death the life and food of His people; even that Word of life which is sweeter to the soul than honey and the honeycomb. From death "the eater" that devoureth all things hath come forth meat, even He who hath said, "My flesh is meat indeed." Wait awhile, and the multitude of the nations have gathered like a swarm in that death, and from thence derive life. But of that lion and its death, strange to say, Samson spake not, it is added, to his father or his mother. And still more strange of the honey, thence afterwards ensuing, Samson, it is said, told not his father or his mother. For thus was the death of Christ a mystery and a secret, and so were all the consolations thence derived, which Israel knew not, and could not understand. Nay, it was as a "riddle" for a long time—"to the Jews a stumbling-block, and to the Greeks foolishness,"—imparted only to and through her, who was taken to be the Church of God from the defiled nations of heathenism[1].

But more particularly in the death of Samson do we see our Lord and Saviour, when bound and set at nought, and blindfolded, and beaten in the hands of His enemies. He willingly gave up His life, and by His death overcame all the power of the enemy, and more than by His life subdued all the kingdoms of darkness. And a fulfilment of this there may be again, when the sun of this world shall go down, and the walls of the universe shall shake and fall. He says in the Psalms, "The earth is weak and all the inhabitants thereof, I bear up the pillars of it." But a time shall come when the faith shall fail and love shall wax cold, and He who is the great Deliverer of His people

---

[1] Judg. xiv. 12. 17.

shall be in darkness and in bonds; then when they shall say, "peace and all things are safe," the Strong Man shall awake, and suddenly there shall be a cry,—the earth is departing, the pillars of Heaven are shaken, and the Day is come.

In two points of view, therefore, is the example of Samson most profitable to us, first, in showing us the marvellous power of faith; and, secondly, in representing to us the great object of our faith, even Christ Himself,— the mysteries of His kingdom, His calling of the Gentiles, His victory in death itself; the weak instruments by which He will overcome the world; the childlike spirit of those that are strong in Christ as opposed to the wisdom and prudence of the world. It is, I am sure, thus that we are to read the characters of the Holy Scriptures, if the good Spirit will be pleased to interpret them unto us aright; and this to a childlike temper, which looks to Him in prayer, He assuredly will do.

But to return to what we first said of Samson, as the type of our strength irregular and broken in these latter days; when we spoke, on Sunday last, of Joshua, it seemed afar off, too high and heavenly: for Joshua spoke of Christ when the Church was in her "first love," when a bow was in His hand, to overcome, and a crown was given unto Him to reward, and He went forth on the white horse of triumph, "conquering and to conquer[a]." You cannot then, you think, overcome as Joshua, but yet you may as Samson; you have not gone forth victorious, but yielded, and are beset with manifold temptations, yet you may call to God in your affliction; and the lion that meets you by the way may through faith be overcome with ease; and yield you afterwards the sweetness of

[a] Rev. vi. 2.

divine consolation; though father and mother know not of it, those nearest you in the flesh may not know of your struggle, nor of your conquest, nor of your spiritual comforts thence derived. Yet you may have in yourself the power of Christ risen, and in that strength you may yet go on your way[a], and do great things. It may be that the Church of God is fallen upon evil days; no Joshua with the spirit of wisdom to lead, and direct, and conquer; but in Christ you may yet have power to work in faith even great marvels. "Thou shalt shew us wonderful things in Thy righteousness, O God of our Salvation."

Yet one word more in conclusion; the strength of Samson was in his hair, that which could least of all have any thing to do with means of strength; in order to show that his power was all of God; those unshorn locks were signs of his being a Nazarite, dedicated to God even before his birth; there was a power from that dedication which lasted all his life. "There hath not come a razor upon mine head; for I have been a Nazarite unto God from my mother's womb; if I be shaven, then my strength will go from me, and I shall become weak, and be like any other man." Thus with us our power is from our dedication to God at Baptism; water, the weakest of all things, could have nothing to do of itself with spiritual strength; but God has so appointed it as a sign and means; when we become defiled with sin, then is our strength gone from us; but after deep repentance and humiliation it may again return, and we at length may be so recovered, that when the last great trial comes we may in death prevail;—the strong man be cast out of his place by One Stronger than he; and in and through Christ "death be swallowed up in victory."

[a] Judg. xiv. 9.

SAMUEL

She bare a son, and called his name Samuel, saying, Because I have asked him of the Lord.—1 SAMUEL i. 20.

SAMUEL was the man of intercession; he might be called in more senses than one the child of prayer, even from his birth throughout unto the end. He was given as a child to his mother's prayers, and received his name from that circumstance, "the asked of God;" and his whole life was in harmony with this his name, for he was always as one asking of God.

We have seen lately how the circumstances which preceded the birth of Samson were significant and prophetic of his after-life; the same is remarkably the case with Samuel also. In the Scriptural account of the one there is the angel appearing to Manoah and his wife, with a "countenance very terrible," and "doing wonderously:" in that of the other we see a woman in very earnest prayer; and with circumstances which give a solemn and Divine character to that prayer; in the place of worship at Shiloh; with Eli the Priest on his throne, "by the post of the temple of the Lord," noting the earnestness of that prayer, and receiving it with his blessing; "Go in peace," he says to Hannah, "and the God of Israel grant thee thy petition that thou hast asked of Him." To which it is further added of both the parents, "And they rose up in the morning early, and worshipped before the Lord." Samuel also like Samson was to be a Nazarite; but Samson was so dedicated from the announcement of the angel; Samuel from his mother's vow in her prayer. Thus one spoke of the wonder-working God; the other of the signal prayer, the priest, the temple; and the prayer recorded, and the vow accepted of the Most High; and the name given on the fulfilment of the prayer. And then follows the solemn offering up of the child, and his mother's words to Eli. "I am the woman that stood by thee here, praying unto the Lord. For this child I prayed; and the Lord hath given me my petition which I asked of Him. Therefore also I have lent him to the Lord, as long as he liveth." And then to crown all is Hannah's memorable song of thanksgiving.

And the beginnings of life with the two Nazarites were in accordance with their birth; of Samson it is said, he grew as a child, blessed of God, "and the Spirit of the Lord began to move him at times in the camp of Dan." But Samuel we behold in the "House of Prayer;" clothed in the sacred garment of prayer; "he worshipped the Lord there," it is added; he "ministered before the Lord, being a child girded with a linen ephod." Such then was the institution of the child of Prayer; nor is this of itself a small matter, or one of little account with God and the Great Ones that are with Him, for the angels who see His face, watch over such little ones; and we know on Palm Sunday what the voice of acceptance was—" the children crying in the Temple, and saying, Hosannah to the Son of David;"—and the Lord of the Temple Himself acknowledging it as the most acceptable worship, and saying, " Yea, have ye never read, Out of the mouth of babes and sucklings Thou hast perfected praise[1]?"

[1] St. Matt. xxi. 16.

But the next circumstance in the history itself will tell us what the child of prayer is with God; for when about to bring in great changes and to substitute the New Priesthood in place of the old, not to Eli, the aged Priest, nor to any who might be great before men in station and authority does God reveal His judgments, but communicates the heavy tidings to the child in the Temple. The occasion may have part in our Lord's great thanksgiving, when He rejoiced in spirit and said, "I thank Thee, O Father, Lord of Heaven and earth, that Thou hast hid these things from the wise and prudent, and hast revealed them unto babes!" And how full of interest is the whole narrative; Samuel, the thrice called of God, the thrice chosen, thrice loved; as if, like as in the case of St. Peter afterwards, that repeated invocation of his name were a token of great things that were to be by him hereafter. And with what ready childlike obedience is the call heard! it was indeed receiving the kingdom of God as a little child. And we may notice the modesty of nature which there is about the child of prayer, he is as a child throughout in bearing this vision of God; he rises from sleep, he hastens to his Priest and Guide; and after all he lies down again in peace and quiet. How different to Saul, when it was said, "Is Saul also among the Prophets?" he "lay down naked all that day and all that night[3]," he was as it were not himself; but in Samuel the holier vision of God does not overturn, but sanctifies nature, humbles, quiets. There is nothing constrained, nothing unsuitable: for divine love "vaunteth not itself, is not puffed up, doth not behave itself unseemly:"—nor again willingly divulges what it receives from God; such is the natural simplicity of the child of prayer.

[3] 1 Sam. xix. 24.

And what is the next thing we read of Samuel? that God would "let none of his words fall to the ground:" his words partook of his communion with God. Now this is very important in those who are given to prayer: their words become after their degree and in a manner full of God; so that not with keen intellect, or learned education, or forcible eloquence, but with the man of prayer wisdom is to be found.

But this spirit of prayer in Samuel is but as yet as the "tree planted by the water side," replenished with the dews from above, and by the sun drawn upward towards Heaven; it has yet to spread forth branches laden with flowers and fruits, beautiful to behold and full of fragrance; "like a palm tree in En-gaddi, and as a rose plant in Jericho." For prayer is drinking into the soul the love of God; and thence in due season it shows itself in love to man; it embraces all around with tender sympathies, stretching forth branches of pleasant savour; "the mother of fair love, and knowledge, and holy hope[3]."

And thus we find that Samuel was reared for public station, for times of great difficulty, and humanly speaking attended with much disappointment, but hallowed by his prayers and intercessions. Such is that event which the history next mentions, that "the ark of the covenant of the Lord of Hosts which dwelleth between the cherubims[4]," was brought from Shiloh to be the strength of Israel in battle, but was taken by the Philistines. Now to the holy child from Ramah, ministering in Shiloh, and brought up apart in communion with God; who had no earthly home but the House of God, no hope in religion but connected with the visible ark of God's Presence, what greater calamity could have occurred? And what then did

[3] Ecclus. xxiv. 14. 18.   [4] 1 Sam. iv. 4.

Samuel? it is said, "Samuel spake to all the house of Israel, saying, If ye do return unto the Lord with all your hearts, and prepare your hearts unto the Lord;—He will deliver you." He speaks as with authority, as if inspired to do so in answer to prayer, for "God suffered not his words to fall to the ground;" to this it is added, "and Samuel said, Gather all Israel to Mizpeh, and I will pray for you unto the Lord." And such confidence was there in his prayer, that afterwards when the terror of the Philistines was upon them it is added, "And the children of Israel said to Samuel, Cease not to cry unto the Lord our God for us." And so powerful was his prayer, that as if he had been a warrior or an armed host or far more, it is added, "So the Philistines were subdued,—and the hand of the Lord was against them all the days of Samuel." So availing is the intercession of a righteous man; so full of healing and expiation that sacred ordinance of God; and so great the strength of one that had by habitual prayer made himself strong in God.

From this his tender regard for his people, as a father for his children, arises the next affliction of Samuel, on the signs of their unbelief in God in asking for a king; and here again is immediately specified the same never-failing remedy for his sorrow. "But the thing displeased Samuel, when they said, Give us a king to judge us. And Samuel prayed unto the Lord." And what does he then do with their murmurings and obstinate opposition? Did he tell it to his friends, or refer to counsellors for advice? No. "And Samuel," it is said, "heard all the words of the people, and he rehearsed them in the ears of the Lord[5]."

And after he has made them a king, the account of Samuel's dealings with them is very beautiful: he seems

[5] 1 Sam. viii. 6. 21.

by prayer, like Elijah afterwards, to hold as it were the elements—the thunder and the rain—in his hands, and this power he uses not to afflict them, or punish, but to warn; indeed his unfailing sympathies and great gentleness, and their confidence in his prayers, form the interesting and very soothing part of the history of those days and that hard people. So much so that he comes out strongly, as representing our Blessed Saviour Himself, standing a mediator between God and man with such a tender feeling for their infirmities. He expostulates—warns, yet at the same time comforts and encourages them, and they look to him. "And all the people said unto Samuel, Pray for thy servants unto the Lord thy God." ... "And Samuel said unto the people, Fear not; but serve the Lord with all your heart, for the Lord will not forsake His people." And then are these striking words, "Moreover, as for me, God forbid that I should sin against the Lord in ceasing to pray for you[6]." Here he shows that he held these continual intercessions for them so much as a part of his own duty, that to omit them would be a sin in him; that not only love to them, but duty to God was in his prayers.

And now in the history there awaits him a fresh occasion of sorrow; and it is met again by him in the same way, as if saying, "Is there not balm in Gilead for every wound?" "Is there any thing too hard for the Lord?" "Then came the word of the Lord unto Samuel, saying, It repenteth me that I have set up Saul to be king; for he is turned back from following Me." ... "And it grieved Samuel, and he cried unto the Lord all that night[7]."

In all these things there is in Samuel especially to be noticed, as always connected with the spirit of prayer, his

[6] 1 Sam. xii. 19. 23.   [7] 1 Sam. xv. 11.

great hopefulness: his readiness to hope the best even of those who are in sin; hoping even against hope; and no doubt having his prayers answered in some way, even in seeming disappointments, while he continued in the full confidence and assurance of prayer. Such hopefulness often brings about the very fulfilment of its most sanguine desires.

Further, a proof of this tender sympathizing spirit of the good Samuel, and the estimation in which he was held as a Protector and Divine shield, may be seen in the conduct of Saul towards him; the sad king clings as it were to the skirt of his mantle for refuge from his own evil self, and the evil spirits that haunted him; and even after Samuel's death, in his great distress, he still looks to and longs for Samuel. Throughout the compassions and parent-like pity of Samuel seem to have had an impression on his proud heart. He asks him not for his prayers, but clings to his protection, as if in Samuel himself resided the power of sheltering him.

And how affecting is that description of Samuel, when he "came no more to see Saul, until the day of his death;" that he "mourned for Saul," praying for him in secret, though he saw him no more, and continuing long to do so, till God said to him, "How long wilt thou mourn for Saul?" and told him that there was another answer to his prayers, in the man after God's own heart, not in Saul.

Such then was Samuel, so remarkable above all men for prayer, that the Psalmist singles him out as the chief among those that pray; "Moses and Aaron among His priests, and Samuel among such as call upon His Name[8]." And the Prophet Jeremiah places him with Moses as the two prevailing intercessors; "Then said the Lord unto

[8] Ps. xcix. 6.

me, Though Moses and Samuel stood before Me, yet My mind could not be toward this people[9]." They seem both here mentioned for the singular love they bore for the people over whom they were placed. Moses so earnestly interceded with God, that he was ready to die for them, "If Thou wilt forgive their sin; and if not, blot me, I pray Thee, out of Thy book[10]." And in like manner, his people were ever in the heart of Samuel, as the Urim and Thummim in the breastplate of judgment, with the names of the children of Israel on the breast of the High Priest when he stood before God[1]. His mind seems ever to have been as in those his words, "But God forbid that I should cease to pray for you." "For my love they are my adversaries: but I give myself unto prayer[2]."

Now there occur two observations which may be made on this interesting history of Samuel. First, that they were the troubles and sorrows of life which were the moving causes of his prayers; so that indeed the child of prayer could not have existed without them. So was it with his mother Hannah before his birth; we first read of the sore provocation with which she was tried, and how keenly her mind felt the trial. "She was in bitterness of soul, and prayed unto the Lord, and wept sore." "She continued praying before the Lord." She said to Eli, "I am a woman of a sorrowful spirit." "Out of the abundance of my complaint and grief have I spoken." Here we see that had it not been for this distress and sorrow, this prayer of faith would not have been made, nor would the child of prayer have been so born and named. And as was the birth of Samuel, so also was his life, nurtured as it were and sustained by drops from his Master's cup,

[9] Jer. xv. 1.
[1] Exod. xxviii. 29.
[10] Exod. xxxii. 33.
[2] Ps. cix. 4.

and crumbs from His table of sorrow. We have observed many occasions in which Samuel is spoken of as praying and interceding, and now every one of these was on account of some urgent distress and trouble; so that, as we read of his mother, she was "in bitterness of soul and prayed," so of Samuel, that "the thing displeased Samuel, and he prayed unto the Lord." And again, "And it grieved Samuel, and he cried unto the Lord all night." O blessed rod of affliction, when it thus turns the soul to Heaven and unites it to God! As the young bird when alarmed flies unto its parent's wing, so in trouble does the soul which He hath made fly unto God. It is said that "man is born to trouble, as the sparks fly upward;" and we may well see the reason for this, for it may be added, that as the sparks fly upward, so in trouble do the desires of a good man ascend to heaven.

Samuel's life was all affliction. As a child he was taken from home and parents, removed from the tender love of a mother; these were early trials that weaned the heart. Then the priestly guardian of his childhood was overwhelmed in ruin and misery. Samuel was unhappy in his children, in the people whom he had to govern, in the king of his anointing, so that over all these he had continually to mourn. Yet he was pre-eminently blessed of God, brought as it were near to His throne, which is the well of life and joy, there to intercede, not for himself, but for others; and this being brought near to God was through his prayers, and these prayers could not have been were it not for these occasions of sorrow. Every one became to him a step higher in that life which is with God. There are leaves and plants which give out their sweetness when pressed, bruised, and broken; so the soul under the pressure of misfortune yields her healing power and intercedes for others. It may be that Samuel's life was not marked with afflictions more than others, but we see in him the effect of such afflictions, as he was so much given to prayer. We see what God intends by them, and why the saints of God are usually more chastened than others, inasmuch as upon them such chastisements are not lost, but productive of much fruit. To those who will reflect on such things in their own hearts and lives, nothing will be found so wonderful as the dealings of God with the human soul, more so than all the marvels of nature and Providence in the world at large. We may yet further observe, that as trouble disposes the heart to prayer, so on the contrary every joy of the world, success, gain, any passion, or excitement, or self-indulgence, has its effect in withdrawing the heart from communion with God. However trivial it may be, it has this effect in its degree. It may be that we are pleased, and are at ease, and the day passes, passes on to eternity, there to be numbered with our appointed time. Or it may be we are vexed, saddened, darkened; and in consequence our comfort has been in prayer; and our prayers have been more real and earnest, and have been as wings strong enough to bear our heart and treasure to be with God.

The second observation I am about to make is this, that our having in various ways connexion with others becomes the continual occasion of intercession and prayer. It was his care for others, his charge whom he loved, whether the nation or the king, his deep and lively interest for those of whom he had the charge, whether Eli, or Israel, or Saul, which kept up in Samuel the spirit of prayer. His life of prayer was not in isolation or in contemplation, but an active, laborious life, as Priest at the altar, as Judge of Israel, and Prophet of God. All is for others—none for himself. As our Lord prayed on many occasions of establishing His kingdom,—before He called the Twelve, before He sent out the Seventy, before the confession of St. Peter, before His Transfiguration, before the Sermon on the Mount, and before giving the Lord's Prayer; so He has made in us our many responsibilities for others to be the constraining occasions of prayer. Prayer increases both love of God and love of man. Our family cares and interests, our sorrows and anxieties for dependents, children, and friends, these it is which bring us to lay aside such our troubles with Christ. Mary who had chosen the good part sat at Jesus' feet, but His eye and His heart is with Martha also, and by the many troubles of "much serving" He would bring her to be there also; and if this be not enough, by the sick bed and the dying of her brother Lazarus, He will even yet bring her to His feet, and she shall there confess, "Yea, Lord, I believe that Thou art the Christ, the Son of God, which should come into the world[3]." Now this saving faith is much brought about by anxieties and intercessions for others. Oh, what a sight it would be if the veil were uplifted, and we were to see all that is done by prayer!

[3] St. John xi. 27.

SAUL

But the Spirit of the Lord departed from Saul, and an evil spirit from the Lord troubled him.—I SAMUEL xvi. 14.

THE striking characters of Holy Scripture are set before us in conjunction with others, with whom they are most strongly seen by comparison or by contrast. Thus with Samuel the man of prayer, with David the man after God's own heart, with his son Jonathan, so lovely yet so truly great, comes to us the unhappy Saul. Thus we see in those that fall away, what they might have been if they had so willed; and how the grace of God hath moulded others to be as the stars that shine for ever. Saul might have prayed like Samuel, might have waited upon God as David did, might have loved with largeness of heart like Jonathan. We see, especially in the history of Saul, the awful progress of the soul, from the gradual changes that take place in him, while in his successive trials evil prevails over the Spirit of grace and opportunities of good. There is also a sort of natural goodness about him that rivets our interest; so that from the very feeling of a common nature, we are partly inclined to forget his crimes in his miseries.

Saul had every thing which the natural man could desire. Gifted in mind and body,—"See ye him," said Samuel, "whom the Lord hath chosen, that there is none like him." He was a "choice young man, and a goodly: and there was not among the children of Israel a goodlier person than he; from his shoulders and upward he was higher than any of the people[1]." The Spirit of God moreover was given him to fit him for his kingdom at that anointing. And the anointing was to him "the oil of gladness;" for the Prophet himself delighted in him; and God turned the hearts of the people towards him, so that, on the day of his institution, "Saul," it is said, "and all the people rejoiced greatly." The pride of the people—the chosen of God—and having in him qualities that even endeared him throughout to the wisest and best of men; but more than this, for even in those things in which he afterwards fell—disobedience and pride of heart,—he has at first the testimony of God for good; for the Lord says to Samuel, "Saul is turned back from following Me;" he had therefore once followed obediently the guidance of God. And Samuel says to him, "When thou wast little in thine own sight[2];" so that he once was humble of mind. But now he rejoices in himself, not in God; and there arises in him that self-elation which goes before a fall; "the beginning of pride is when one departeth from God;" "for pride is the beginning of sin[3]." The trial which comes does not occasion this self-confidence and rising of the heart against God, but brings out and proves that which was in the soul.

At the time of anointing him king, Samuel gave him the injunction to go down before him to Gilgal, and there to wait seven days till he himself should come to offer the sacrifices and burnt offerings. This, though he knew it not, was to be the proof of Saul's faith; this would show

[1] 1 Sam. x. 23; ix. 2.   [2] 1 Sam. xv. 11. 17.
[3] Ecclus. x. 12, 13.

whether he trusted in himself or in God, whether he could wait for God and upon God. What appeared an accidental urgency of circumstances was wisely calculated for this probation. The case seemed pressing; the appointed time just transpiring; the people were scattered; the Philistines were coming on; what could be more religious than Saul's anxiety at such a time for supplication and for sacrifice? Thus, as the Jews afterwards, he deceived himself with religion; but the heart and life of religion, faith, was wanting; for what was the use of supplication and sacrifice? were they not to obtain God's assistance? but could not God assist without them? " Stand still, and see the salvation of the Lord[4]," was the very pledge of deliverance given by Moses at the Red Sea. Thus Saul becomes a sign of the taking away of the kingdom from Israel. It is the opposite to the obedience of the Son of God. "Sacrifice and meat-offering Thou wouldest not; but Mine ears hast Thou opened." "Lo, I come to do Thy will, O God!" "Yea, Thy law is within My heart." "Thou hast done foolishly," said Samuel, "thou hast not kept the commandment of the Lord thy God. Thy kingdom shall not continue; the Lord hath sought Him a man after His own heart," even him whose saying is, "I waited patiently for the Lord." "My soul, wait thou still," i.e. calm and patient, "upon God."

"Woe unto them that have lost patience[5]." "Patient abiding," "possessing the soul in patience," "patient waiting for the Lord," are ever spoken of as the part of acceptable faith in the last days; when they that fall away shall say in their heart, as Saul did of Samuel, the prophet of God, "My Lord delayeth His coming."

[4] Exod. xiv. 13. [5] Ecclus. ii. 14.

Thus was he weighed in the balance and found wanting. As with Uzziah, that other king who invaded the Priest's office*, the secret leprosy of sin rose up to his forehead, and the subtle contagion of that pride filled all his body and clave to him to the last.

Then comes the second trial, when Samuel reminds him of his anointing, and sends him utterly to destroy Amalek; but Saul again is more merciful than the all-merciful God, more religious than the holy Samuel. He spares Agag, and he saves the best of the spoil to offer sacrifice to God; thus he blinds himself in his disobedience with a show of clemency and religion. "And Samuel said, Hath the Lord as great delight in burnt-offerings and sacrifices as in obeying the voice of the Lord? Behold, to obey is better than sacrifice." For obedience is the sacrifice of the soul itself to God, which is better than that of slain beasts; it is the offering up of the will itself. And here we may observe, as in the case of Ahab and Benhadad, the great anger of God with those who spare whom He would not spare, and His approval of those who execute His judgments, as Phineas, Joshua, and Jehu, warning us not to forget His judgments in His mercies.

But the state of Saul's heart appears still more strongly in his shadow of repentance than in his sin itself. He confesses, "I have sinned;" but this confession is not accompanied with humiliation before God, and in consequence a willingness to be humbled before men; on the contrary, he seeks his own honour, not that of God, with this confession on his lips. "I have sinned, yet honour me, I pray thee, before the elders of my people, and turn again with me, that I may worship the Lord." Here we have the very spirit of the Pharisees, loving the praise of

---

* 2 Chron. xxvi. 16. 19.

man more than the praise of God, and of the rejected Israel when the Gospel was preached. Even in the worship of God Saul seeks his own honour; whereas David in doing service to God says, "I will yet be more vile than this; and will be base in mine own sight[7]." David said, "I have sinned against the Lord;" and Nathan answered, "The Lord also hath put away thy sin[8]." Saul says, "I have sinned;" but "Samuel," it is added, "came no more to see Saul until the day of his death;" "and it repented the Lord that He had made Saul king over Israel."

From this commences a new phase in the history, as deeply impressive, as sadly affecting as any thing can be—the downward course of a man who hath departed from God in his heart. "Lo, this is the man that took not God for his strength;" yet for a while "I have seen him in great power, and flourishing like a green bay-tree." But now, in the awful words of the text, "The Spirit of the Lord departed from Saul, and an evil spirit from the Lord troubled him." And it is the harp of David that soothes the unhappy king. What a strange and solemn history; how divinely beautiful that harp; with what touching sweetness must it have lingered on the ears of the king, as it awakened for a time all the wisdom of his earlier life, and the promise of his youth! It must have been like a lost spirit listening to angelic strains in Heaven before its gates were closed against him for ever. "He was refreshed," it is added, "and was well, and the evil spirit departed from him." And yet more, he "greatly loved David," the minstrel. Here we have all the natural goodness of Saul, which renders his fall so awful and affecting. What great virtues had he shown had his heart

[7] 2 Sam. vi. 22.   [8] 2 Sam. xii. 13.

been but right with God! He had been generous to his enemies, who had refused allegiance to him[9]; he had been heroic-minded, yielding up his son Jonathan to die[1]. David's pathetic lamentation over him at his death shows that Saul was no ordinary character, to have engaged such love and kept it throughout. It required a voice from God Himself to awaken Samuel from his grief for one so loved and honoured; the kiss of love he had given at his anointing[2] continued in Samuel's affection to the end. And the "mountains of Gilboa" bore witness to the rare affection of a father and son, as "lovely in their lives," and "in their death not divided[3]."

And now the "evil spirit from the Lord" troubles him, and though driven away for a time, finds access into his heart, and brings with him all malice and misery. He had disobeyed God, obeying the people; he had listened to the people's voice, not to that of God; and therefore when another is in the praise of the people the evil spirit hath with envy filled his heart. "The women answered one another as they played, and said, Saul hath slain his thousands, and David his ten thousands. And Saul was very wroth, and the saying displeased him." "And Saul eyed David from that day and forward." David had been his aid in need; had subdued for him the Philistines; had comforted him from the evil spirit; but his love is turned into hate; the fire of Hell is kindled in his bosom, and makes visible the darkness of that heart wherein once was the light of God's countenance. Lo, he has become as Cain to Abel, "because his own works were evil and his brother's righteous." He becomes the type of him that

[9] 1 Sam. xi. 13.
[2] 1 Sam. x. 1.
[1] 1 Sam. xiv. 44.
[3] 2 Sam. i. 23.

is born after the flesh, and persecuteth him that is born after the Spirit.

Again and again he attempts to slay him: more than once by his own hand; and by means of his messengers; and through the Philistines. But all in vain, for he is fighting against God. And now all things around him that should have been otherwise his delight and glory, are turned to gall and wormwood, the poison of his soul. All his friends around him are hateful to him because they love one whom God loves. "All of you," he says, "have conspired against me." "There is none of you that is sorry for me." Doubtless all were grieved for him, but none could heal that malady which was in his own soul. Who can give peace to him who is not at peace with God? All the love which there is around him but adds to his own envy and misery; and that which charity would have made his delight and joy, has now become food for the never-dying worm which is in his bosom. God Himself hath set His love on the man after His own heart; Israel and Judah love him; his own daughter loves him; and his own son above all; and the priests of God favour him; and the consequence of this is, that Saul in all his prosperity is more distressed than Job in all his afflictions. Possessing all things, yet having nothing; while David in single-hearted faith is as having nothing, yet possessing all things. "The righteous shall hold on his way, and he that hath clean hands shall be stronger and stronger[4]."

How strange and impressive is now the narrative, while David with love answers the enmity and hate of Saul! And very striking is the description, when twice overcome by David's sparing his life when it was in his power, he relents and is softened for a time; but only for a time;

[4] Job xvii. 9.

for the evil spirit within him has become too powerful, has taken up his abode and will not be dislodged. "And it came to pass, when David had made an end of speaking these words unto Saul, that Saul said, Is this thy voice, my son David? And Saul lifted up his voice and wept. And he said to David, Thou art more righteous than I: for thou hast rewarded me good, whereas I have rewarded thee evil[5]." He even prays for him, "wherefore the Lord reward thee good for that thou hast done unto me this day." Who could have supposed that Saul after he had thus spoken, should yet again pursue David as he had done before; and should again have his life spared by him in the same manner, and make the like confession of his unreasonable hate and sin; and that yet notwithstanding, David's life should be no more safe with him than it had been before? "Behold," he says, "I have played the fool, and have erred exceedingly." "Blessed be thou, my son David: thou shalt do great things and still prevail[6]."

O miserable state, to be thus hunted and haunted by the evil which in his better moments he deplores! he is like two persons, his better self, and the evil one within him, contending and struggling together for awhile, till they become both one. And thus at length, while he yields to the evil spirit, he shuts up against himself the mercies and loving-kindness of God, and is cast out from His presence. For now the time of real distress and trouble comes upon him, and he feels the approach of the King of Terrors. "And when Saul saw the host of the Philistines he was afraid, and his heart greatly trembled. And when Saul inquired of the Lord, the Lord answered him not, neither by dreams, nor by Urim, nor

[5] 1 Sam. xxiv. 16, 17. [6] 1 Sam. xxvi. 21. 25.

by prophets." And now, O strange and sad reverse, the Anointed of God, the Hope of Israel, lies stretched on the ground in the witch's cave! Alas, indeed! it would seem as if the evil spirit were looking through his prison-bars and mocking him throughout with his false pretences to goodness, with semblances and counterparts of his former sins and inconsistencies. "Thou renewest Thy witnesses against me[7]." He that would spare the cruel Agag will not spare the merciful David; he that was so careful of sacrifice slays eighty and five innocent Priests of God in his wrath against David; he who saved the best from the Amalekites to sacrifice to the Lord his God, afterwards falls upon the priests; and "Nob, the city of the Priests, smote he with the edge of the sword, both men and women, children and sucklings, and oxen, and asses, and sheep, with the edge of the sword[8]." In "his zeal for Israel and Judah," he broke the covenant they had made, and slew the Gibeonites whom Joshua spared, till their blood called aloud to God[9]. He who would have the kingdom perpetuated in his own house, attempts to slay his own son on whom that house depended, because he loved the heir of the kingdom whom God had chosen. He who cared so much for the people's voice, now hates the sound of that voice because it is with David. He who in his zeal for God had put away all the witches from out of Israel, is now by her of Endor lifted up from the dust and comforted. Unseasonably and against God he spared the Amalekite, and by the hands of an Amalekite he himself dies.

Now to us all this lesson is very striking; Scripture always speaks to us in history and life what it enjoins us in word and precept; our Lord says, "Hold fast, that

[7] Job x. 17. [8] 1 Sam. xxii. 19. [9] 2 Sam. xxi. 1, 2.

no man take thy crown," and here before our eyes we see the choice and the crown transferred from one to another, and we see the reasons why—and the effect. May we consider it!

Let us not put away from us this account of Saul as belonging to another state of things, for whatever it may speak to kings and nations, it is full of a home lesson for the heart of each. For may not each of us in the home of his own heart have an evil spirit that troubleth him? It may be so with many in various degrees who think not of it. The cares which most suffer are from this source. What is envy, covetousness, impatience, the plague of the heart, but this, that a man has in some degree, perhaps in years long past, sinned in this way; and so, not having repented, given place to an evil spirit that troubles and keeps him from God? This may be the case, and yet for awhile he may have much comfort in religion, as Saul had in the harp of David; Church music may in like manner soothe him and raise him up as it were to Heaven; or it may be impressive sermons; or even the study of God's holy Word: so much so, that under the influence of these the evil spirit may depart, and he may be refreshed, nay, more, he may find rest in Christ. He may have soft passionate relentings, as Saul had, struck with the goodness of David, at the sight of which the Evil One may depart, as before from the heavenly music of David's harp. But this is not enough, unless he press forward earnestly, and give no place to such an inmate in his breast any more. "When thou goest with thine adversary, as thou art in the way, give diligence that thou be delivered from him [1]."

Scripture reveals to us that there is in such cases a

[1] St. Luke xii. 58.

spiritual being, a living person, who takes possession of the mind. And I would particularly call attention to the expression of the text, "an evil spirit from the Lord." Now although this is an awful and alarming expression, yet it is also full of instruction and comfort, as every thing must be which reminds us that we are in the hands of God; as we before noticed in the history of Pharaoh. When we trace in our very disquietudes and sorrows the indications of an evil spirit that troubles us, this teaches us where our health is. That this evil spirit is from God is no proof that we are given up of Him. For indeed even David himself when he numbered the people had an evil spirit from God, allowed to bring upon him that temptation and its consequent misery. He can touch no one but as permitted of God; and that permission may be for various reasons: he was allowed to tempt Job for his greater perfection; through the false prophets he deluded Ahab to bring upon him God's judgment; he troubled Saul with gloom and pride on his departing from God; he tempted Judas that he might go to his own place; he prompted David to sin from which he speedily recovered by repentance. In like manner he is allowed to tempt us; and it is indeed sometimes, as in the case of Saul and of David, a judgment upon us for some fault on our part, or some secret unbelief or pride of heart, but we are thus by this expression of the text taught to go to God for help. We cannot be too often urged in every way to do this. Why indeed is the account of our Lord's going about in the Gospels so vividly set before us, but to instruct us in this truth; the Apostle's description is, that He "went about healing all those that were oppressed of the devil;" and the same may be said at this day as He is seen by faith in His Church. When you find in yourself any ill-will, any worldly disappointment or envious sadness, go to Him at once in earnest prayer, entreating Him to remove from you the power and guilt of that sin which has allowed the evil spirit to disquiet you. When you have thus done all in your power, then again the lesson of Saul and David will come in for your guidance, warning you not to take things into your own hands from impatience and distrust of God, but to wait patiently upon Him. He will have the remedy and deliverance to be entirely His own doing. He only wants your faith and confidence in Himself. And His word is, "Be still then, and know that I am God[2]."

[2] Ps. xlvi. 10.

DAVID

To whom also He gave testimony, and said, I have found David the son of Jesse, a man after Mine own heart.—ACTS xiii. 22.

IN speaking of the Saints of God in the Old Testament, what shall we say of David? Of one who though he lived nearly three thousand years ago, yet whose thoughts and words are with us unto this day—nay, all the day long, our familiar companions by day and by night. We hardly know how to speak of him; it is like having to speak of a dear friend or relative, or of a saintly father and guardian, when we know not what to say, and had rather be silent. We cannot hold him apart and judge of him. We have him so deeply lodged within, like a part of our very souls, that we cannot take him out of ourselves, hold him up and look at him, as we would a picture, or judge of him as we would of another man. For such the use of the Psalms makes "the sweet Psalmist of Israel" to be to us. God has in an especial manner given unto us David as a friend.

But David is not only an inspired Teacher, he has a known history besides, and one of no little interest. Let us endeavour to consider him in that; for as if to teach us that something more is wanted in addition to good feelings and good words, God has been pleased together with the Psalms to give us an account of the life of him that wrote them; and that of one who was not only a minstrel, and a prophet, and a devout worshipper of God; but also a soldier, a shepherd, and a king; so as to be an example to every state and condition. We have of him in an especial manner the inner and the outer life as of no other man; and it is especially the life of faith.

Again; the history of his life is not only of itself so fully told and so engaging; but it has this remarkable circumstance connected with it; that we have in the different occasions of life the very thoughts they gave rise to, and the inner heart poured forth before God. It is not that he tells us what he did and what he thought, as when a person writes a narrative of himself, but much more—the same laid open at the time to the God of truth.

For instance; we read of his being chosen at an early age to play as a minstrel before Saul; the account is, "And it came to pass, when an evil spirit from God was upon Saul, that David took an harp, and played with his hand; so Saul was refreshed, and the evil spirit departed from him[1]." Here we might well inquire and wish to know what the wonderful strains might have been which the minstrel sung, that the evil spirit should depart, and the unhappy king find comfort in God. Now though we are not told the words and measures which he then played, yet in the Psalms we have the kind of subjects which were then upon the harp. It might for instance have been the shepherd's own song: "The Lord is my Shepherd, therefore can I lack nothing. He shall feed me in a green pasture. Yea, though I walk through the valley of the shadow of death I will fear no evil."

Again; all the circumstances of his contest while yet almost a child with the giant Philistine, derive a great interest from our having his own heart-words in the Psalms,

[1] 1 Sam. xvi. 23.

describing the spirit under which it was done. "It is not my sword that shall help me." "It is God that girdeth me with strength of war." "He maketh my feet like hart's feet." "He teacheth mine hands to fight." "Some put their trust in chariots, and some in horses; but we will remember the name of the Lord our God[2]."

Then next ensues the crowning part of David's life, his contest with Saul; the one adding injury to injury, evil to evil, hatred to hatred; and the other requiting all with forgiveness, with benefits and love; we read of his flying from cave to cave, with some few incidents the most beautiful in the history of mankind; but how does all this come forth in the Psalms—his struggles, his enemies, his faith in God? "In the Lord put I my trust; how say ye then to my soul, that she should flee as a bird unto the hill[3]?" "I will love Thee, O Lord, my strength; the Lord is my stony rock, and my defence[4]." Then follow his glorious and sublime exultations in God. History gives the picture; but in the Psalms the very picture is found to live; it is breathing full of expression; and the bloom of life is fresh upon it.

But the life of David is as yet high and prosperous; he goes forth before God with clean hands, trusting and rejoicing; and were this all, the Psalms would not be what they now are to the Christian,—for which of us has been thus? But the terrible blast of sin has to pass over him, in the bitterness of which he has to know the depth of man's wickedness: the blight and decay is on the leaf which was so full of promise; and from henceforth there is a deeper, sadder tone.

We read in the Scripture narrative of his repentance being accepted of God after his great sin; but it is through-

[2] Ps. xx. 7. [3] Ps. xi. 1. [4] Ps. xviii. 1.

out the Psalms that we find the depth and extent of that repentance. A dark heavy cloud had come for a time between him and his God; and though that cloud became lined with light, yet ever after he was as one brokenhearted to the end of his days; he walked near the ground mournfully and heavily, though comforted of God. Oh, how does he earnestly long, thirst, and faint for the light of God's countenance to an afflicted penitent soul! how does he forget all sorrows in the greatness of that sorrow that he had offended Him! how does he know no fear, but that God would take from him His Holy Spirit on account of his sin! "Make me a clean heart, O God; and renew a right spirit within me. Cast me not away from Thy presence; and take not Thy Holy Spirit from me."

In the anguish of his great sorrow he finds the hidden fount of consolation, to which he leads others as the chief of mourners, the prince of penitents. It is now we know him not as the sinner, not as the penitent, but as the forgiven penitent. It is this that renders him the pattern to the Christian, and the minstrel expressive of his hope. We see in him the beauty of Job's expression, who speaks of it as the attribute of God, "Who giveth songs in the night[b]."

And here it may be observed that faith in God, which was the great characteristic in David, was shown in the beginning of his life by his overcoming every enemy, but in the latter part by his repentance; which was so remarkable, so thorough and entire, that it evinced, it may be, even a greater faith than his youthful piety; as it required greater faith to rise and adhere to God, nor, let go His love, when overcome himself, than when he overcame others. For such repentance is more difficult, more

[b] Job xxxv. 10.

rare, and therefore more a proof of faith and love than innocence itself. Thousands and tens of thousands fall to one that thus rises after his fall. To fall and to rise again proves the Divine life even more than never to have fallen; to die and to be made alive is greater than the former life. Not that repentance is equal to innocence, but that to have been in the toils of Satan, to have been among the dead, and then to have escaped, is the greatest of miracles. To have been ill with a sickness in which most die, and to have recovered, is not so happy as not to have been sick at all, but it is a greater proof of strength. For the lust by which he fell was but a transient passion, says St. Augustine, not the abiding inmate of his bosom but a stranger; not as with Solomon the corruption of the heart[6]. And his repentance was as great and signal as was his sin; it went through his whole heart and life. It was then that he found out the depth of his own natural sinfulness, such as it had been even before his fall; he was set, as it were, to search out the dark corners of his heart, where such a serpent could have harboured, which before hid itself from God and from the light. "Behold," he says, "I was shapen in wickedness, and in sin hath my mother conceived me. But lo, Thou requirest truth in the inward parts." Yet his hope in God was equal to his grief, for he adds, "Thou shalt wash me."

Then comes all the tale of his outward afflictions; his grief for his child, a pattern for all mourners, fasting and praying while there was hope, and when that hope had ceased, resigned to God. And then his yet far more heavy cause for mourning. When he lost an innocent child he was comforted; but at the death of Absalom, he could find

[6] Vol. iii. pp. 94, 95.

no comfort but in the love of God. And then, "not in evil dejection," says St. Augustine, "but in pious humiliation, he accepted the chastening from the Lord; submitting to it as medicine; not returning evil for evil, but having a heart prepared to follow the will of God[7]."

The account of his grief for Absalom is indeed most affecting, but it has a most sacred interest in his own words in the Psalms, "Why art thou so heavy, O my soul, and why art thou so disquieted within me? O put thy trust in God: for I will yet thank Him, which is the help of my countenance, and my God[8]." But why in Scripture is heard that lamentable cry, so emphatically repeated, "O Absalom, my son, my son;" by the pen of inspiration engraven on the rock for ever? but that Christ's own voice was in that cry and His bitter cup, for His own Israel that had risen against Him, and sought His life.

Thus was David's repentance deepened, extended, perfected. Indeed it has been said that the expression of his being "a man after God's own heart[9]" arose from God's foreseeing the sincerity of his repentance, whereby he is in the number of those of whom he himself says, "Blessed is he whose unrighteousness is forgiven, and whose sin is covered[1]." Because it was the will of God to choose in Christ those that are sincerely penitent, there being none just before God. David was according to God's own heart as a pattern of this Evangelical repentance, and the humiliation of those that are accepted in the Beloved. This is set before us in the 51st Psalm.

By others[2] it has been supposed that David was the man

[7] In Ps. cxlii. vol. iv. p. 2263, and see vol. iii. pp. 94, 95.
[8] Ps. xlii. xliii.   [9] 1 Sam. xiii. 14; Acts xiii. 22.
[1] Ps. xxxii. 1, 2. See St. Aug. vol. vi. p. 234.
[2] As St. Hilary, St. Bernard.

after God's own heart, from his love of his enemies and forgiveness of injuries; and indeed we are told by our Lord Himself, that it is by this love more especially we bear the likeness of our Father which is in Heaven. But perhaps we should be wrong in limiting the character which God has given us of David either to this or to that; it was not in his repentance only, nor in his forgiveness of injuries, that he was the "man after God's own heart," but in something more extensive, of which these were but the parts. His love for his enemy was fulfilling the law of Christ before that law was given—for it was the "new commandment" which Christ brought with His Gospel; but it was a love secretly shed abroad in his heart by the love of God. Loving God, and feeling that he had need of His mercy, and also, as expressed throughout the Psalms, that he should obtain that mercy, he was disposed to love and forgiveness. He loved much because he had much hope of mercy; and loving much he felt he had much need of forgiveness. In the cases both of Saul and of Shimei his forgiveness is expressly connected with the love of God, and with his own trust of God's goodness to himself[3]. In these therefore he was after God's own heart as accepted in Christ.

But the foundation and the crown of all in David was his faith in God. All may be resolved into this; all the fruits were from this, or rather this was the fruit of all; begun and ended in deeper and yet deeper humiliation as he came more and more to know God's mercies in Christ. This faith it is that marks his first history, when he stands before the armies of Israel as the unarmed boy, the champion of God; and then it incidentally appears that this was but the progressive advancement of what

[3] See 1 Sam. xxvi. 24; 2 Sam. xvi. 12.

had already gone before; he had already proved his armour, his armour of faith in God. "Thy servant," he says, "slew both the lion and the bear." "And Saul," observes St. Augustine, "perceived that it was of God[4]."

It is remarkable throughout how this his great faith was in the keeping of humility, and how he studied to preserve it so; for we have no more beautiful description of this temper than in the 131st Psalm, "Lord, I am not high-minded; I have no proud looks; I refrain my soul and keep it low, like as a weaned child." Thus when Samuel first came to his father's house, he was forgotten and set aside by his own family as of no account. And afterwards when sent to his brothers in the army, great as he was in the sight of God, he was little amongst men; for how contemptuously does Eliab, his eldest brother, speak of him? Again, when afterwards his praise was in the mouth of all—the victorious soldier and the destined king—he overcomes Saul as much by his humility as by his forgiving charity. "After whom dost thou pursue?" he says; "after a dead dog, after a flea[5]?" In the service of God, he says to Michal, "I will be base in mine own sight[6]." Thus humility was preserved by his attributing every thing to God; the evil blast of pride touched not his spirit because it was strong in God; thus his slaying the lion, and the bear, and the Philistine, he assigns to God only. "Thou comest to me," he says, "with a sword and a shield; but I come to thee in the name of the Lord of hosts[7]." "He put his life in his hand," said Jonathan of him to his father Saul; it was no presumption, but a venturing all from holy confidence in God. And this will appear the more strongly by the temptation to the contrary

[4] Vol. v. p. 230.
[6] 2 Sam. vi. 22.
[5] 1 Sam. xxiv. 14.
[7] 1 Sam. xvii. 37. 45.

which assailed him in his latter years, when he numbered the people. How contrary was this thought to the usual grace of his character, and to what he had so often expressed in the Psalms, of all his strength being not in armies, but in God!

Such then is the meaning of the term, the "man after God's own heart," which is the testimony of God Himself to the character of David; one that thought as God thinks, willed as God wills; one therefore on whom was set the especial love of God: and he has through all generations the praise of God; the best thing found in the best of succeeding kings was that they should be as their father David. When we first behold him, he is as a shepherd boy amid his flock at Bethlehem, probably the same spot where the shepherds afterwards heard the Angelic song. By night and day, in Psalms and songs of praise, he exercised himself in the law of the Lord; like a tree by the water side, about to bring forth his fruit in due season. "With his whole heart," it is said, "he sang songs, and loved Him that made him[8]." Nor without toil and danger was his faith exercised, while he was thus trained in heavenly wisdom apart from the world. The eye of God was on his heart, and the remarkable expression concerning him is, "I have found David My servant." His eyes that are in every place, beholding the evil and the good, rested on one, found him out as we would a great treasure. And when Samuel came he was the one chosen of God, though little esteemed of his own, like Him of Whom it is said, "For neither did His brethren believe on Him." And then he comes forth as a pattern to the Christian of all time, in whom perfect love casteth out fear. He put off Saul's armour, which is, as it were,

[8] Ecclus. xlvii. 8.

the old law, and put on the new man, which is faith in Christ. He went forth "unarmed," says St. Ambrose, "in the sight of man, but armed with Godhead." The anointing of Samuel was stirred within him to this kingly prelude of power. He goes forth with the sling and the stone—like Him who by the Word of God overcomes the great enemy—like Him who says, "I looked and there was none to help, and I wondered that there was none to uphold. Therefore Mine own arm brought salvation[9]."

Thus no one can interpret the Psalms but He Who hath "the keys of David;" they that are in Him alone can understand "the Song of Moses and of the Lamb;" no man is worthy to open the Book and the seven seals, but "the Lion of Juda, the Root of David[1]." The anointing of the king hath overflown to the minstrel and the soldier; all these are found in Christ, and being in Him they partake of His anointing.

Thus then it is with the Christian, who is represented as a soldier, yet withal as prophet and priest; all war without, within the melody of the Spirit, speaking in Psalms and spiritual songs; without is sorrow, trouble, and danger, the lion and the bear, the giant Philistine, Saul, Doeg, Ahithophel, and Absalom: but within there is peace and joy in God, the oil of gladness, the light of God's presence, the sense of His nearness, the shield of faith, the sword of the Spirit, the good Shepherd leading to the waters of comfort.

Such is to us "the sweet Psalmist of Israel." And whom should God have chosen but the man after His own heart,—as one whose praises and prayers should be such as to convey the outpouring of the Christian soul

[9] Isa. xliii. 5.   [1] Rev. xv. 3; v. 5.

unto God? Nay, the Psalms are almost like the Prayer Book, if we may so speak, of our Blessed Saviour Himself. We have in the Psalms all the contests of the real life of David, as a minstrel, as a soldier, as a penitent, as an afflicted father; we have all his heart in the Psalms, and in and through all he is as the Anointed of God.

It is remarkable that when the anointing of David by the Prophet Samuel is first described, the account is immediately added of his minstrelsy. After the anointing it is said, " and the Spirit of the Lord came upon David from that day forward;" and then immediately is introduced, apparently out of the order of time, the mention of his playing upon the harp before Saul, and of the evil spirit departing from the unhappy king[a]. The mention of his music together with that of the Spirit being with him, seems to indicate that this his playing was of a Divine character; as the sound of the harp was to the Prophet Elisha; it partook of the anointing of God within, the expressiveness and the impressiveness of the Spirit of God that was upon his heart. This the first mention of David appears to be a sign and token of what he should hereafter be unto the end of the world; that in all the ills which the evil spirit raises against us without, or brings on our mind within, the Psalms should come to us as a fresh watery breeze in a desert. That to sing or chant the Psalms of David should be the delight of childhood, the protection of youth, the strength of manhood, the comfort of old age.

Happy is he who knows them best, says them over, and makes them the vehicles of his own thoughts continually to Heaven, so that the statutes of God become songs in the house of his pilgrimage. There is no com-

[a] 1 Sam. xvi. 13, 14. 23.

panion of a sick bed, no preparation for death equal to the Psalms of David; in the many troubles of life we find therein the soothing voice of the Great Comforter; when wars and dissensions are abroad, the heart is engaged by the description of them, in order that it may be led on to its true peace; all our temptations are entered into in order to show us a way to escape. "In the multitude of the sorrows" which are in the heart we are reminded that God numbers them all, and His comforts refresh the soul. There is no time, no occasion, no age, no condition, but will find herein a sympathizing friend, like an angelic guardian, or visitant from Heaven.

SOLOMON

Did not Solomon king of Israel sin by these things? yet among many nations was there no king like him, who was beloved of his God.—
NEHEMIAH xiii. 26.

THERE are three books in the Holy Scriptures written by Solomon, the Proverbs, Ecclesiastes, and the Song of Songs. It may appear remarkable that one who fell so grievously should contribute at all to the Book of God, nor is there any other instance of the kind: but his sad history adds a peculiar weight of warning to his words: nor are there any books more strongly marked by the Finger of God. The very order in which they occur is instructive[1]; and the three books together make up a perfect and impressive lesson.

In the Proverbs we have all practical wisdom taught us by one gifted beyond all men with understanding, as of all natural things, so especially of judgment in life and morals, the knowledge " to discern between good and evil[2]." To this is added the Ecclesiastes, of the vanity of all that is confined to this life alone; and then in an instructive order, after these two books, that which is spiritual and divine. Thus are we taught that to one first exercised in morals and prudence, and then learning in mortification of spirit that happiness is not to be found in this world,

[1] St. Bernard in Cant. Cant.   [2] 1 Kings iii. 9.

follows the Song of Solomon. "My beloved is mine, and I am His; He feedeth among the lilies," i. e. among the pure-hearted of the earth, "until the day break, and the shadows flee away[3]." Such is the Christian's course towards perfection; "He hath set my feet upon a rock and ordered my goings," and then "He hath put a new song in my mouth," the Song of Songs, which is as "a garden enclosed" and "a fountain sealed," to all but the pure in heart.

And who, even humanly speaking, from his own experience could have been so powerful a witness to declare unto us the vanity of life as this wise, and rich, and great king? He had given unto him abundantly all that the heart could desire of earthly good, and from the wonderful reach of his knowledge could look before and after to the bounds of human things, and yet felt within that aching void which nothing could fill but God. And then, considering the nature of those temptations by which he fell, how impressive becomes the Song of Solomon! He was ensnared by the love of strange women; and then—Oh, the wonderful love and the wonderful judgment of God!—in that the deep, dark emptiness and misery of heart which this occasioned, he speaks, as Job says, "wonderful things that he knew not;" he had infused into his understanding by the Spirit of God a sense that human love, even in its purest and best estate, was but an image of the union of the soul with God and of the pleasures which are at His right hand for evermore. It was given him to see "in a glass darkly," that which none but the pure in heart could know. For in that Song the Heavenly Bridegroom by earthly figures veils His face, as Moses did when he came from the Mount, so that none but they that are worthy

[3] Song of Sol. ii. 16, 17.

can behold. And indeed in the books of Solomon the Spirit of God speaks to us Christians; and therefore often with an intent and meaning far beyond what the writer himself could have known. In the very opening of the Proverbs, St. Augustine observes that Christ is spoken of. "My son, if sinners entice thee, saying, Let us lie in wait for blood, consent thou not[4]." And when passages from the Proverbs are referred to in the New Testament, a new light and a new sense is often given them.

There is also another great dignity attached to Solomon in the Church of God, that he is an especial type and figure of Christ; as the promised Son of David, the King of the Jews, on the throne of his father, the Builder of the Temple, the Prince of Peace; for the name Solomon signifies "the Peaceable." "I will give him rest," said God to David, "from all his enemies round about; for his name shall be Solomon; and I will give peace unto Israel in his days[5]." All such promises to Solomon, as throughout the 72nd Psalm, have their true fulfilment in One greater than Solomon, in Christ alone[6]. Our Lord pointed out to the Jews that He Himself was both the Son of David and the Son of God. He is "the Peaceable," for there is no peace but in Him; He is our peace; it is He that gives peace, peace in this world in anticipation of that perfect peace when the last enemy shall be destroyed, and nothing more shall disturb that peace. He is the true Solomon to Whom judgment is given, and Who searcheth the hearts to know what true love is. He is the Framer of that true Temple whose Builder and Maker is God; building up living stones into that spiritual House, without

---

[4] Prov. i. 2.   [5] 1 Chron. xxii. 9.
[6] St. Aug. Civitas Dei. vol. vii. p. 768; vol. iv. p. 1061. Enarr. in Ps. lxxii.

noise, all fitted and prepared, each one for his place, to make an habitation meet for the indwelling of God. For all this is being fulfilled in His visible Church, since that time when at His Resurrection He sat down on the right hand of God, according to the promise made to David in the 110th Psalm, "Sit Thou on My right hand, until I make Thine enemies Thy footstool." From that time **He** is our Peace amidst the wars and troubles of this world, Himself our Rest, extending His kingdom "from the flood," the Jordan of His Baptism, as St. Augustine explains it, "unto the world's end[7]."

To this must be added one sad reflection; that as Solomon sets forth in figure the visible Church of God, and the wisdom of the world, its riches, and honour, and power flowing into it, and all the kingdoms of the earth, the Queen of the South, the Kings of Arabia and Saba bringing gifts; so does Solomon seem to represent to us its falling away in these latter times; the visible Church, when it has become great and established, falling into idolatries, ensnared by the many arts and temptations of wealth, the "seducing spirits" of the last days; and thus by the righteous judgment of God becoming broken and divided, as the kingdom of Solomon was on account of his "heart being turned away from God[8]."

It was beholding this, the corruption of the Church, that St. John in the Apocalypse "wondered," he says, "with a great astonishment." And early writers, though they saw a figure of the Church's increase in the peace and prosperity of Solomon's kingdom, yet did not thus anticipate a resemblance in its decay and fall; it has been the sad experience of after ages which has added this.

Thus Israel which was trained by temporal promises,

[7] Ps. lxxii. 8.   [8] 1 Kings xi. 9—11.

was given to see that the highest pinnacle and crown of all that the world esteems is not all, as shown in their one great chosen king, the heir of the temporal promises; something more was needed. As St. Augustine has observed, the Jews were thus taught that this was not that true Son of David, that they might look forward to another Solomon in whom the promises were fulfilled, and something higher and better in the Heir of the kingdom. Thus, like the false mother in the Judgment of Solomon, Israel after the flesh overwhelmed with her own weight and killed her own son while she negligently slumbered[9], and then claimed for herself the Son of the true mother, and says in envy, Divide it with the sword that it be not thine nor mine; but the true Israel, that which beholds God, as the name imports, in losing her own Son hath received Him again as alive from the dead. Love is ever the sign of the true mother, the true Church[1]; the false church is for herself, is full of envy and self-seeking; the true Church anxious only for the salvation of the children of God, willing with Moses and St. Paul for herself to perish rather than they. And alas; in Solomon himself, for want of that true love, how was Christ divided? For "what agreement hath the Temple of God with idols?"

And now let us take home to ourselves the sad history and example of Solomon. He was chosen of God, and afterwards rejected as Saul had been; he was full of wisdom and understanding, and what is far more, of holiness and goodness. There is perhaps no one of whom the early promise of good seemed so decisive: when first mentioned it is said, "And the Lord loved him[2]," which seems to indicate an early growing in grace as in God's

---

[9] 1 Kings iii. 19.   [1] St. Aug. Serm. x. vol. v. pp. 92—100.
[2] 2 Sam. xii. 24.

favour. And after he came to the throne: "And Solomon loved the Lord, walking in the statutes of David his father[3]." "And the Lord his God was with him, and magnified him exceedingly[4]." And then follows his prayer for wisdom, and that with all humility; for he says as his plea, "I am but a little child; I know not how to go out or come in[5]." And the wisdom for which he asks is not the knowledge of the stars or of the secrets of nature, but "an understanding heart to judge Thy people; that I may discern between good and bad." As the same is elsewhere expressed by him, "Give me wisdom that sitteth by Thy throne," "that I may know what is pleasing unto Thee" . . . "for she shall lead me soberly in my doings," "so shall my works be acceptable[6]." And even for a higher wisdom than this, "the things that are in Heaven, who hath searched out . . . except Thou give wisdom, and send Thy Holy Spirit from above?" Thus was it the very best wisdom for which he sought, and he sought for it in the very best way, not by study, but by prayer, as the especial gift of God. For it is "a point of wisdom," he says, "to know whose gift she was[7]." What can be higher than the account of wisdom which he himself gives in the third chapter of Proverbs? "All the things that thou canst desire are not to be compared unto her. Length of days is in her right hand; and in her left riches and honour. Her ways are ways of pleasantness, and all her paths are peace. She is a tree of life to them that lay hold on her." It is evidently of religion itself that he speaks; and his actions and words indicate holiness as well as wisdom; instance his care in the building of God's House, of all the appointments connected with it; and the great holiness of

[3] 1 Kings iii. 3. [4] 2 Chron. i. 1. [5] 1 Kings iii. 7.
[6] Wisd. ix. [7] Wisd. viii. 21.

his prayers in the dedication of it[8]. And the acceptance and express approval of all by Almighty God.

Add to which, of the Queen of the South our Lord speaks, as if from a desire of holiness and goodness she came from the ends of the earth "to hear the wisdom of Solomon," attracted by their report: and it was by his worship and the ordering of his people in religion that she was overcome with a devout wonder and astonishment[9]. Indeed, he was given not only to set forth the fulness of love, but also the fulness of knowledge, which is to be laid up in the Church of God; "there came of all people to hear his wisdom from all kings of the earth;" "for God gave him wisdom and understanding exceeding much, and largeness of heart, even as the sand that is on the sea-shore. And Solomon's wisdom excelled the wisdom of the children of the east country, and all the wisdom of Egypt." And the wise of the world are mentioned as not to be compared with him. "For he was wiser than all men; than Ethan the Ezrahite, and Heman, and Chalcol, and Darda, the sons of Mahol[1]." Thus as Daniel was wiser than the astrologers of Babylon, and Moses than the magicians of Egypt, so Solomon in his largeness of understanding beyond Egypt and the children of the East seems to indicate "the treasures of wisdom and knowledge which are hid in Christ," the deep things of the Spirit of God; that those mysteries beyond all understanding which are revealed of God in His Church, surpass all the marvels of physical science, and the discoveries made by its advances, when in the latter days "many shall run to and fro, and knowledge shall increase," "and none of the wicked shall understand, but the wise shall understand;" and "some of them of

[8] As 1 Kings viii. 27.   [9] St. Luke xi. 31; 1 Kings x. 1—9.
[1] 1.Kings iv. 30, 31.

understanding shall fall[2]." Wisdom so expressly given of God must have been true wisdom.

To what then are we to attribute the great change in Solomon? It has been said, as by St. Augustine, that he was more injured by prosperity than profited by wisdom. Yet we may observe, that his falling away is not in Scripture attributed to his wealth, his power, and honour. And perhaps we may consider that as these were given him by Almighty God, not of his own seeking, but as a reward for his prayer for wisdom, that God, who reserves to Himself[3] the power to counteract the evils of wealth, did by his great wisdom preserve in him an antidote for these great temptations, the gold of Ophir, the admiration of the Queen of Sheba, and of all the kings of the earth, the subjection of all his kingdoms. One express cause is assigned for it: "But king Solomon loved many strange women." "Many," that was against the Law; and "strange," that was against the Law[4]: and this perverted his heart to idols. It was as the sin of Adam, of Samson, of David. His very wisdom, and the light he had received from God aggravated his condemnation. "And the Lord was angry with Solomon, because his heart was turned from the Lord, which had appeared unto him twice, and had commanded him concerning this thing[5]." Solomon was very highly favoured; he comes before us almost like one of the saints of God in his earlier years: but he needed the great mark of Christ. Solomon was not afflicted. Great is the holiness expressed in his prayers; "Behold, heaven and the heaven of heavens cannot contain Thee; how much less this house which I have built[6]!" but there is no humiliation and confession

---

[2] Dan. xi. 35; xii. 10.   [3] St. Matt. xix. 26.
[4] Deut. xviii. 17.   [5] 1 Kings xi. 9.   [6] 2 Chron. vi 18.

of sins, as in Job, in Daniel, in David. There is a secret knowledge which is hid from the wise and revealed by the Father unto babes; and this is the mystery of the Cross; it is made known to Christ's little ones; of whom as clothed with His righteousness it may be said, that "Solomon in all his glory was not arrayed like one of these."

Alas! how like is it to the case of that rich young man in the Gospels, of whom it is said that our Lord "looked upon him" and "loved him." He had kept the commandments from his youth, but laden with possessions he was not willing to take up the Cross; he was too big for the narrow door of life. And what a warning to ourselves, that we take not the many signs of God's love which we find about us, nor even the bright light of His countenance within the soul, for any sure indication of our final perseverance and acceptance. All his wisdom, all his greatness and power, nay, all his holiness and good deeds pass away "as the dew of Hermon," or the morning rays that lit up the hill of Sion; and are but as a sad history to add force to those words;—" What shall it profit a man, if he gain the whole world and lose his own soul?"

We cannot indeed conclude that Solomon himself did not at last repent; but this has always been considered by the Church as very doubtful, to say the least. All we know is, that Scripture has fully made known to us his falling away from God, but has said nothing of his repentance. The very silence is awful and impressive. And what has he left on record? He to whom the wisest of the world yield the palm of wisdom, before whom "the children of the East," the mighty names of the sages of old pale away and hide their lights? He has left to all the world treasures of Divine wisdom, and with them the warning of his own folly.

"They that be wise shall shine as the brightness of the firmament;" but he seems as a star fallen from Heaven, or as a "wandering star" which has lost its course; and become the fearful token of sadness and dismay.

How shall we speak of Solomon? We too from the utmost parts of the earth, like the Queen of Sheba, are drawn to him, our hearts and affections are moved towards one of whom we learn so much, whose Divine sayings are in our heart of hearts, whose wisdom is our guide. We cannot bear to think that he should have fallen. We are moved by it as by the loss of a friend or instructor, and are disposed to leave it in silence with God, saying, in those touching words spoken over the prophet that delivered the witness of God, and then himself disobeyed,—"Alas, my brother!"

What more melancholy than the fall of one so great—so wise? What words could have been spoken to him more powerful than his own? What eloquence could describe his fall with more feeling and beauty than his own words? What could more powerfully paint the loveliness of that holiness from which he fell? What the overpowering sweetness of that Divine love which he was contented to give up to feed on ashes? Who can describe the temptations to those very sins by which he was ensnared in a more searching manner than he has done? Who can express as he has done the vanity of all things else but the one thing needful, which is keeping the commandments of God? Hath he not taught us unto the end of time how "the path of the just is as the shining light, that shineth more and more unto the perfect day"? How hath he "forsaken the guide of his youth, and forgotten the covenant of his God[7]"! How hath he "gone to the house that inclineth unto death, and her paths unto the dead[8]"! How hath he been as one that "knoweth not that the dead are there; and that her guests are in the depths of hell[9]"! How hath he been "holden with the cords of his sins," till "his own iniquities" have taken him away[1]! Yea, the fools themselves of his own Book of Proverbs shall take up a taunting proverb against him and say, "Art thou also become weak as we? art thou become like unto us[2]?" How must his own sweet and divine words sound to him like music of Paradise to the lost spirits, yea, as songs of Heaven would come back to fallen angels in sad remembrance; of "the eyes of the Lord pondering the ways of men[3]," of doing with our might our appointed task, "for there is no work, nor knowledge, nor wisdom, in the grave;" of "God bringing every work into judgment[4]."

It is very awful to think how God may use men as instruments of good, that His Spirit may teach them, and through them teach others, and guide them to the living fountains of waters, yet they themselves at last fail of the prize of their high calling. What a warning for fear; yet even so it was that St. Paul himself, who had been taken up into the third Heaven and there heard unspeakable words, might have left us those treasures of Divine wisdom, yet been himself a cast-away; and so it would have been if he had not kept his body in subjection.

[7] Prov. ii. 17. [8] Prov. ii. 17, 18. [9] Prov. ix. 18.
[1] Prov. v. 22. [2] Isa. xiv. 10. [3] Prov. v. 21.
[4] Eccles. ix. 10; xii. 14.

ELIJAH

Elias was a man subject to like passions as we are.—ST. JAMES v. 17.

THERE is something very wonderful about the history and character of Elijah: it seems hardly like that of other men: his being sustained by ravens; his travelling forty days without food, after the cake given him by an angel; his being carried to Heaven in a whirlwind; his appearing again at the Transfiguration; the intimations of his being the messenger of Christ's coming; his appearing and disappearing amongst men, like an angel with messages from God, according to that apprehension expressed by Obadiah, "as soon as I am gone from thee, the Spirit of the Lord shall carry thee whither I know not;" his very name, more like that of the angels—as Michael, Gabriel, and Raphael,—Elijah, or God the Lord; the expression he applies to himself almost like that of a ministering spirit, "the Lord of Hosts, before whom I stand[1];" his shutting up the Heavens over a whole country, so that trees languished, beasts perished, birds drooped, men looked up in desolation, at the voice of a man; his again opening the skies and raining down joy and gladness; the mode of his treating mankind, as if the man were lost in the messenger of the Most High—as to the widow of Zarephath who was dying of hunger, he said, "Go, and make me a cake first,"

[1] 1 Kings xviii. 12. 15.

thus exercising and calling forth her extraordinary faith and charity, like our Lord Himself was wont to do in those for whom He wrought miracles. His standing forth and claiming deference as a man of God, even such, that to lay hands on him was to rise against God; "If I be a man of God, then let fire come down[2]," as did that avenging fire on the two companies that came to take him from king Ahaziah, the son of Ahab; his having mercy on the third, sparing him and being gracious to him. Add too his casting his mantle on Elisha, his acceptance of him and his words, "If thou see me when I am taken from thee, it shall be so unto thee." All these things, and his very manner of speaking, are like those of one whose individual character is lost in the messenger of the Most High. And thus it is said of him in the Apocryphal Scriptures, Elias "stood up as fire, and his word burned as a lamp." An expression like that used respecting angels, that He maketh His "Ministers as a flame of fire;" not to allude to that of God Himself that He is "a consuming fire[3]." "Blessed are they," it is added, "that saw thee and slept in" love[4].

Thus then was there something, as it were, angel-like and Divine about one of whom St. James says, "he was a man subject to like passions as we are;" the word is the same in the original as that which St. Paul uses to those who would offer sacrifices to him as if he were a god; "we also are men of like passions with you[5]." Even this Elijah then was like ourselves, clothed about with this soul of human passions in the regulation of which lies our mysterious probation; he was tried as we are, even as you and I have been: thus by the circumstances of mortal life his faith was exercised, tried, perfected; he might have

---

[2] 2 Kings i. 10.
[3] Heb. i. 7; xii. 9.
[4] Ecclus. xlviii. 1.
[5] ὁμοιοπαθεῖς, Acts xiv. 15.

become like many others have done, might have become as an evil spirit among men, a tempter, an apostate, a seducer, a Balaam, a Gehazi, a Judas; but by faith he became what he was, till like as he changed at last the garment of hair for the clothing of fire and the whirlwind, so his earthly passions became Divine graces, wrapping him around with Divine affections as with the whirlwind and fiery chariot of the Spirit of God, which lifted up his soul toward Heaven. If therefore he was of like passions with ourselves, in like condition of trial, let us ask what that his character was.

The first mention of him is this, "And Elijah the Tishbite, who was of the inhabitants of Gilead;" thus he comes before us as a man like ourselves, he was one of the inhabitants of that country, of Mount Gilead, he was but as one among them; no external difference to put him apart. As the potter is at work forming many vessels of the like clay, but one turns out at last very different from others; thus it is in any country or neighbourhood, the hand of God is at work, the Spirit is moulding souls[6], one turns out a chosen vessel for use or honour, while another is rejected.

But we wish to know something more particular respecting him,—what was his early life, his disposition, his circumstances. Of these nothing is told us; but in this silence of Scripture respecting Elias we may have this clue to guide our inquiries. So much is said of Elias being as it were one with John the Baptist, that we may reasonably infer that in their whole course there was something similar, and perhaps in their natural character also; and this, as far as it goes, is borne out by the history; the outlines of both are alike, and what is

[6] Jer. xviii. 6.

wanting for the filling up of one may be supplied by the other. Thus we hear nothing of the birth and childhood of Elijah; but we may infer that he was as the Baptist, like one set apart; that in the wilderness, "the mountain of Gilead," he was reared until his "showing forth unto Israel;" there is a like solitude about his appearance as a prophet; no father or mother are mentioned, no child, or friend; whereas even Elisha had his yoke of oxen, a father and mother to bid adieu to, a servant Gehazi in attendance on him, the sons of the prophets in converse with him; but the mention of Elijah is at intervals, as one appearing in peopled neighbourhoods, no one knew from whence; not as Jeremiah, not as Moses, Samuel, and others; but in the desert, on the hill-top—seen and recognized as by surprise in the hairy garment of the prophet, the solitary of God, as one without scrip or purse, even, it may be, as He who had "not where to lay His head," having food to eat which man wot not of. Thus it may have been, that in the wilderness, in trials known to himself only, by the secret communings of the Spirit of God was his faith formed and nourished.

And again in character;—there appears in Elijah something of that which is so peculiar in the holy Baptist; reared in severity, mortified and separate from the world, —and therefore so calculated to witness against it,—yet there appears in John a singular gentleness to others; accommodating to their modes of life with a considerable fellow-feeling for their infirmities and temptations. Thus with Herod what sweetness was there mixed with sternness, so that "he heard him gladly," and "did many things" because of that very Saint whom he shut up in prison. Thus Ahab spoke of Elijah as "hast thou found me, O mine enemy?" yet he complied at his warnings,

P

made a show of repentance, and "did many things because of him." And if the Baptist from the wilderness is found in the palace of the king; so Elijah girded himself as an attendant before the chariot of Ahab, and hastened before him as the messenger of gladness unto the city of Jezreel. And in like manner he went without fear even into the palace of Ahaziah.

Thus was there in both the remarkable example of perfect love that casteth out fear. In both the same hatred of hypocrisy; the same impatience of wickedness in high places. And in the voice of the Baptist,—saying to the Pharisees, "O generation of vipers, who hath warned you to flee from the wrath to come?"—we may discern that great Prophet who slew the Priests of Baal by the brook Kishon. On one occasion indeed we find in Elijah that which seems especially to mark one "of like passions with ourselves," when the countenance of God seemed withdrawn and he was troubled. We may not conclude that there was any faltering of human infirmity in the Baptist, when about to meet death from Herodias, he sent, saying, "Art Thou the Christ?" yet in outward appearance the occasion might seem not very unlike that of Elijah when he complained of Jezebel, "I only am left, and she seeketh my life." But to say nothing of this, certainly the general impression we have of both is of a wonderful combination of severity or self-mortification with compassionate goodness; as of the Law and the Gospel meeting together, for both of them are as the Gospel veiled in the Law.

But the question is, in what respect Elijah is to be an example to ourselves, so that although there may be something in his history unlike that of other men, yet he is set before us as one of like passions with ourselves.

Now there is one point in which he is not to be imitated by us; for when James and John wished to bring down "fire from Heaven as Elias did" on a city of the Samaritans, because they received not their Lord, He reproved them for so doing, telling them that they knew not "what manner of spirit" they were of [7].

But we are not to consider that the act referred to was any fault in Elijah himself, for under the Law such acts of zeal were highly commended of God; as St. Basil observes, speaking of Elijah, that "Moses the meekest of men, in condemning the idolatry of the golden calf, armed the Levites to slay their brethren; Phineas slew the fornicators, Samuel hewed in pieces the king of Amalek, and Elijah in like manner slew the eight hundred and fifty priests [8]." And we may add that this is sanctioned in the Revelation, where it is said of God's chosen Witnesses of the last days, "If any man will hurt them, fire proceedeth out of their mouth, and devoureth their enemies [9]." Moreover it may be noticed, that as Elias is the great forerunner of Christ, and Christ's comings are of two kinds, one in salvation, the other in judgment, so in Elijah are set forth the judgments of God in things not to be imitated by us, as in his bringing the famine, in slaying the Prophets of Baal, in his causing fire to come down from Heaven when Ahaziah the son of Ahab sent to take him. All these things in him were most righteous and good, but they are rather of the whirlwind, the earthquake, and the fire going before, than of that "still small voice" which afterwards spoke of Christ: they are as it were streaks of fire that speak of His last coming, they partake of the terrors of Mount Sinai more than of the law of Pentecost

[7] St. Luke ix. 55.   [8] St. Bas. Hom. xx. De irâ.   [9] Rev. xi. 5.

written in our hearts by the finger of God in the blood of Christ Crucified; for we are to be of the like spirit with Him Who has now come, not to judge, but to save the world.

There is also another point in the history of Elijah, in which he is an example of something not to be imitated but corrected by us; when despairing of Israel he requested that he might die, failing as it were in that charity which "hopeth all things," for God had more in Israel than the Prophet knew of [1].

But the one great point in which Elijah is our example is that adduced by St. James. "Pray one for another that ye may be healed. The effectual fervent prayer of a righteous man availeth much. Elias was a man subject to like passions as we are, and he prayed earnestly." The one important lesson then from the history of Elijah is prayer, effectual fervent prayer for others, others in sin, that they may be saved. To this we must add all our Lord's own promises and pledges to us Christians, to whom the Spirit of supplications is in Baptism given by Him who worketh great marvels,—promises of effects which are no less than what was miraculously shown in Elijah, that the prayer of faith shall remove mountains, shall move the sycamore tree from its place, that nothing shall be impossible to it, that it shall do greater things than the miracles recorded in the Gospels themselves. And the very thing is stated of the Christian Witnesses in these latter days, "These have power to shut Heaven that it rain not [2]." We are not to shrink from this duty, as persons of another kind from Elijah—we, we Christians here this day are those to whom this appeal is made—we are to be as Elijah in prayer; not

[1] Kings xi. 4. 14. 18.   [2] Rev. xi. 6.

for destroying sinners, but for their repentance, for bringing down on their cold hearts the fire of the Holy Ghost, the dews of restoration on the withered land. For thus did Elias set forth in type more than he knew of, the sacrifice of Christ, the prayers of the Church, the outpourings of the Spirit. We are not to despair for others, but to pray without misgiving, without fainting, till the hand shall at length appear arising from the sea of this troublous life, and the little hand shall become a great cloud, and the great cloud shall fall in blessing[a].

Of Elias's prayer that it might not rain we have St. James's account that "he prayed earnestly." Of his prayer that the heavens might be again opened we have the history itself. How strong in faith was that prayer, when he said, "I hear the sound of abundance of rain," before any token of rain had appeared! And then at the sacrifice, and at the Mount Carmel, how importunate, how persevering, how humble was his prayer! "he cast himself upon the earth" in his humiliation, "he put his face between his knees," he continued in prayer till his servant had gone and returned seven times. He prayed and doubted not, and for this reason and for the miracles thus wrought by his prayers, he is to be the object of our especial imitation.

In voluntary, but extreme poverty, wandering solitary without either food or raiment, he was so rich in the power of prayer as to have in his hands, as it were, the keys of Providence. For this purpose, like the Apostles themselves in our Lord's lifetime, he was supernaturally supported. "I have commanded the ravens," "I have commanded the widow woman," said God, "to sustain thee."

[a] See St. Aug. De Heliâ. Serm. de Temp. 201.

When he prayed for the famine he despaired not; when he slew the priests of Baal he despaired not; when he called down fire on the two captains and their companies he despaired not; in all these cases God was glorified, and there followed repentance and mercy on His judgments; but when he fled from Jezebel, and said that he only was left, he then despaired. For this he was reproved. As was the case with many of the saints of Scripture, his failure was in that very point in which he was for the most part singularly great and gifted of God. Thus by his strength and by his weakness, by praise and by reproof, he inculcates alike this one lesson, to pray and faint not; however perplexed, not to despair, in praying for our friends, and especially for the Church of God,—whatever appearances may be, not to give over. Effectual fervent prayer availeth much.

AHAB

But there was none like unto Ahab, which did sell himself to work wickedness in the sight of the Lord, whom Jezebel his wife stirred up.—1 KINGS xxi. 25.

WE may be sure that Scripture has some wise purpose in holding up so much to our notice an account of the wicked Ahab, that there is something in it calculated to teach us the knowledge of ourselves and of the human heart, and set before us in the person of a king, in order to arrest our more particular attention. The mercies of God shown to Ahab, and signal warnings, chastenings intended for his correction, and prosperities to call forth his thankfulness, the knowledge which he had of the true God, his understanding and feeling of what was right, the memorials of good which were given him in living examples, all these things make the character one of great weight with regard to ourselves. He had Elijah, one of the greatest of Prophets, living in his time and country, and sent to deal especially with himself; we find incidentally that he had even at his right hand a witness of God in the faithful Obadiah; like as his counterpart Herod had of his own household, and his own Steward's wife one that ministered to our Lord. And by this Obadiah numerous Prophets of God were protected. Add to which, there was Jehoshaphat, the king of Judah, who gave him wise counsel and good example. There was therefore no want of better knowledge on the part of Ahab. There were signal miracles wrought for his especial benefit. And even at last one Prophet of God, Micaiah, the son of Imlah, had so often warned him as to have incurred his settled hate as a messenger of evil to him. Often reproved, he hardened his neck till destruction came upon him without remedy. He went on from bad to worse, he opened his heart more and more to the returns of the evil spirit, till that evil spirit entered in with seven others, and took his permanent abode within him.

The scene as it proceeds becomes crowded as it were with living agents, for and against his soul; with Satan also in the background promising life where God had warned of death; obtaining leave to deceive where he wished to be deceived, filling the mouths of the false prophets to his ruin. Jerusalem on the one side; Tyre and Zidon on the other; and behind the veil Heaven and Hell.

Ahab too himself was one in whose soul there was a contest between good and evil. He was not as one that neither knew nor cared any thing for God, like Jezebel; as one that feared neither God nor man; but he had his misgivings; his miserable upbraidings of conscience. It is more than once said of him, that he "went to his house heavy and displeased," till the gloom of his dark soul, like the groves in which he worshipped, became the resort of wicked spirits; there was the wish to do evil even when he had not the courage to do it; conscience enough to make him wretched, not enough to do what is right; so that it is said of him repeatedly that he "sold himself," that is, that he gave up his better self in exchange for the wages of wickedness. And what paved the way to his soul's ruin was what is usual with such persons, that he associated with others more wicked than himself; so that part of the description of him is "whom Jezebel his wife stirred up:" by the company of the evil wickedness became familiar to him; his "way was made plain with stones, while the end thereof was the pit of hell[1]." Yet the care of God never left him, although that care he never ceased to frustrate and make void.

Let us then more particularly consider his history. He comes before us as a king of Israel. Now Israel had already fallen from God, and given up the purer worship at Jerusalem, following "Jeroboam, the son of Nebat, who taught Israel to sin," and proceeding on that high road of declension; the kings of Israel were in consequence worse than the kings of Judah; in this respect then Ahab the more strongly represents the great body of people among ourselves, who by the sins of their forefathers or their own have fallen from the highest and best privileges of grace; yet they have sufficient knowledge of God to rise, and not to fall lower; but they are for the most part content with this state, and to be no better than others before them and around them; and this necessarily leads to their being worse. Thus we find it was with Ahab; the kings of Israel had fallen from God, yet they knew far better than the heathen, but they went downward in their course and united themselves to them. Thus the first thing we are told of Ahab is this, "as if it had been a light thing for him to walk in the sins of Jeroboam, he took to wife Jezebel, the daughter of Ethbaal, king of the Zidonians[2]." Now this was a splendid and rich alliance; Zidon was one of the best known cities then in the world for its wealth and merchandise; like Tyre, its merchants were

[1] Ecclus. xxi. 10.   [2] 1 Kings xvi. 31.

princes, the sea and all its riches were theirs. What therefore follows from this union? He married Jezebel, "and went," it is added, "and served Baal, and worshipped him." She came in with all the spirit and power of the false gods, multiplied her priests through all the land of Israel, made it to become even as the heathen, and worse, for the knowledge of the true God existed with the service of devils throughout the kingdom.

Now take away the outward circumstances by which the trial of human souls is clothed, and the case is not uncommon. Men who know God make themselves one with people of the world on account of wealth, station, or some worldly advantages, and thus the course of their own souls becomes downward, and is made easy. But though they are doing all they can to forget God, He is not forgetting them; He calls to them, makes them to see His hand in mercy and judgment, and visits them with fatherly chastisements.

Thus the next thing we read of in the history of Ahab, is the famine brought on the land through the prayers of Elijah on account of their idolatry; and this continued for three years and a half, the very space of time in which our Lord went about teaching, and inviting the afflicted, seeking fruit for three years of that tree, for which He interceded that it might yet be spared, while He dug about its roots. "I spake unto thee in thy prosperity; but thou saidst, I will not hear;" but in adversity they will consider. "Is Ephraim my dear son? For since I spake against him, I do earnestly remember him still[3]." Then follows the long account of Elijah appearing before Ahab, telling him the whole truth, summoning the priests of Baal, making that solemn appeal to Heaven, and bringing down fire on

[3] Jer. xxiii. 21; xxxi. 20.

the sacrifice. Ahab is so much relenting that he acquiesces in all this; he appears as it were to take part in it; he is, one might almost think, reconciled to Elijah; the Heavens are opened, the Prophet is acknowledged, all is rejoicing, all forgiveness and mercy. Ahab is gone up to eat and drink; his chariot is ready; Elijah himself attends him, and he enters Jezreel.

And now one might suppose that there is hope for Ahab; that his heart, as the dry land, will not receive the grace of God in vain; that there will be no more halting between two opinions, between Baal and the true God; and so it might have been, were it not for his evil marriage, and that he had taken a serpent to his bosom. The account proceeds, "And Ahab told Jezebel all that Elijah had done, and withal how he had slain all the prophets with the sword[4]." Thus does his heart turn back again to her and her gods; he does not protect Elijah from her fury, who had done for him so great things; whom he had seen with his own eyes to be God's own miraculous messenger.

But Ahab is not cast off of God; He has yet other mercies in store for him; as if saying, "Surely he will repent and turn." The human soul is very dear to God. Ahab's heart is set on human greatness: well, that also he shall have; peradventure even yet he may be won, that God may be gracious unto him. Look on the map of Israel, there you will see Zidon on the one side, with that he is married; but on the other side is Damascus, there is Benhadad, his powerful enemy and the enemy of God. The hand of that king of Syria is heavy on him, and his insulting boasts are against Israel and Israel's God: and Ahab is chosen by God to the high privilege of avenging

[4] 1 Kings xix. 1.

His cause. And Ahab knew full well that the faithfulness of the kings and people of God was shown in cutting off those whom they were commissioned to destroy. But he has made friends for his own interest with the enemy of God; the King of Syria, whom he has overcome, is sitting up with him in his own chariot; as it was, "Jezebel my wife;" so it is now, "My brother Benhadad."

But now Ahab, by the mercies of God who is good to the unthankful, is made rich; the cities of Israel which his father had lost are restored; Damascus itself owns his power. And with prosperity comes hardness of heart, and covetousness, and next we read of the vineyard of Naboth, and a deed known to all generations. At Jezreel, to which he was once led by the Prophet of God amidst the miraculous blessings of rain, in this very Jezreel Elijah must meet him again, while Ahab receives him with the words, "Hast thou found me, O mine enemy?"

However great may be his gains or possessions, it is often for a trifling matter that a covetous man forfeits his soul; as if Satan did it to mock him; Eve for an apple; Judas for thirty pieces of silver; Esau his birthright for a morsel of meat; the rich king Ahab for a garden of herbs. Possessing palaces and cities, yet for a little spot of ground which could not lawfully be his, he pined away in heaviness and displeasure, and fasted; till he took part in the great wickedness of his wife; as Adam in the sin of Eve; and the words of God met him in the garden, "Hast thou killed and also taken possession?" But oh the unspeakable forbearance and graciousness of God! even on the poor show of an imperfect repentance, He puts off from him the evil day and withholds the rod.

At length we come to the final scene of this miserable man: he was as Saul in his latter days when God had gone from him; he fears to ask counsel of the prophet of God, as knowing what his conscience foreboded of evil; and in consequence makes himself the prey of seducing spirits: and thus we find him in going forth to his last battle in company with Jehoshaphat the king of Judah, deluding himself with the multitude of false prophets, and avoiding the voice of the true Micaiah the son of Imlah. Thus the word of God becomes hated when it bears witness against us. "For every one that doeth evil hateth the light, neither cometh to the light, lest his deeds should be reproved."

Indeed, one thing is observable in the history of Ahab throughout, how much a self-deceiving conscience seems at work in it all; his sin is ever as a serpent that hides its head: it has some cloke or shelter, rather than being of that open and bold character which defies God: "heavy and displeased," he broods over sinful wishes; and is glad to reap fruits of that wickedness which he did not dare by himself to commit. If the worship of Baal was introduced it was Jezebel's doing, he might say, not his own; if the prophets of God were slain, if Elijah was persecuted unto the death, it was his wife, and not Ahab; if Naboth was slain by false witnesses, and under the pretence of a religious fast, it was Jezebel's deed. If he goes forth to the battle at Ramoth-Gilead, there is the same self-deceiving hypocrisy; he sits on his throne with the king of Judah, and in a solemn and religious manner has brought before him the prophets to consult them; but there is one prophet that he avoids, and only at the requirement of the king of Judah will he meet him, or face the Eye of God. But the character of Ahab is not at all excused by all this; this double dealing with his own soul is the very thing which Scripture condemns, as proving that there is not in the heart the love of God. And what is the Scriptural account of him? "There was none like unto Ahab, which did sell himself to work wickedness:"—"he did more to provoke the Lord God of Israel to anger than all that were before him[5]."

Now in considering the character of Ahab, it may be thought that he was so entangled in sin by having Jezebel for his wife, that he might have had great difficulty in setting himself free and acting better; and the like may be said of Israel itself in its subjection to her and her prophets of Baal; but this miserable state, and the perplexities of sin, had been brought upon themselves; and after in vain waiting for their repentance God will judge them for it. This sadly instructive page of history is a glass held up to ourselves. If we receive not the love of the truth, we shall become the prey of seducing spirits more and more; it will be no excuse for us that we have added to our own temptations, and made a net for our own feet. All this case is carried down to ourselves by our Lord Himself in the Revelation of St. John, "These things saith the Son of God, Who hath His eyes like unto a flame of fire: because thou sufferest that woman Jezebel, who calleth herself a prophetess, to teach and to seduce My servants; behold, I will cast them that commit adultery with her into great tribulation, except they repent of their deeds; and all the Churches shall know that I am He which searcheth the reins and hearts[6]."

Be infinitely careful of the dealings of God with your soul; associate not with the wicked, for what fellowship hath the temple of God with idols? seek not flatteries; but open your heart to the prophet of God; his prayer may avail you much; remember how forbearing God has been

[5] 1 Kings xvi. 33; xxi. 25.   [6] Rev. ii. 18–23.

to you on your weak shadows of repentance, and what will He then be to you, if you repent with your whole heart? sell not that which it hath cost the blood of Christ to purchase for you; for what will it avail, if you gain the whole world, and lose your own soul?

Further: we may notice that God never leaves men in sin without a witness; as God to Adam in Paradise; as Enoch and Noah before the flood; as Lot to Sodom; as Melchizedeck was to the Canaanites; as Moses to Pharaoh; as Samuel to Saul; as Nathan and Gad to David in his sins; as Isaiah to Hezekiah; as Elijah and Micaiah to Ahab; as the prophets to Jerusalem before the captivity; as Daniel to Babylon; as John the Baptist to Herod; as our Lord and His Holy Spirit to Jerusalem before its last destruction; as the Christian Martyrs to Heathen Rome; so to this land now is the Church of God; so to every soul in every place there are witnesses and calls of God. And thus on the Last Great Day "all the Churches shall know" that Christ is "He which searcheth the reins and hearts.'

ELISHA

And Elisha said, I pray thee, let a double portion of thy spirit be upon me. And he said, Thou hast asked a hard thing; nevertheless, if thou see me when I am taken from thee, it shall be so unto thee.—2 KINGS ii. 9, 10.

THESE words of the prophet Elijah and the fulfilment of them may be considered as containing all the history of Elisha; great as was Elijah in power of miracles, far greater was his successor Elisha whom we ever associate with him. But the occasion on which the words were spoken, and the circumstances connected with it seem to lead our thoughts to some further figurative meaning in all that occurred to Elisha. Elijah's being taken up to Heaven is an obvious sign of our Lord's Ascension, by His own indwelling Godhead; and before departing our Lord declared to His disciples that if they believed in Him after He had gone from them, if they saw Him risen, they should have greater power than He had manifested already among them: "greater works than these shall he do, because I go unto My Father;" "it is expedient for you that I go" that the Comforter may come. "He shall glorify Me, for He shall receive of Mine." Elisha then, with the mantle of Elijah, seems to represent to us what our Lord would be to those who live in the power of faith after His Ascension; what His Spirit is to us; what He is to us in His Church. The sons of the prophets were still searching for Elijah on earth, but Elisha saw him, it is said, ascended.

This will explain much to us. It appears that when the temporal Israel was breaking down and failing, as the Prophets such as Isaiah and Jeremiah were sent to speak of the Gospel; so two successive prophets in their life and actions were made to be full of signification and Divine meaning, and then given at the same time to represent Christ in His miraculous doings in His Church both before and after His Ascension; and in the latter case, in Elisha, with a striking fulness of significancy and power; his very actions were made to be figures of Christ and to exhibit the spiritual things of His kingdom.

Thus immediately after the ascension of Elijah, one of Elisha's first acts is that of healing the waters by casting salt into them, that "there shall be no more death or barren land," which seems at once to intimate that after our Lord's Ascension, on the descent of the Holy Spirit, by the preaching of the Word which is the salt of the earth, and the waters of Baptism, the curse of Adam, and the effect of the fall is removed. The same may afford some explanation of a mysterious circumstance which is mentioned shortly after in the same chapter, that of the forty and two children destroyed for mocking Elisha. For thus when the Church was strengthened by a greater power, by the Holy Ghost, immediately we read of the awful deaths of Ananias and Sapphira at the word of St. Peter; and of Elymas the sorcerer being struck blind[1]; forcibly reminding us, that whosoever speaketh against the Son of Man, i. e. of Christ seen in the flesh and not known to be

[1] Acts v. 10; xiii. 11.

God, it should be forgiven him; but whosoever should speak against the Holy Ghost, it should not be forgiven him. For these children may represent to us those that have been admitted into Christ's kingdom. It was in the idolatrous Bethel, and these children no doubt spoke the spirit and mind of their parents; for they were the "children of those that slew the prophets." And their expression "Go up," and "Go up," might allude in mockery to Elijah's having gone up to Heaven, as if deriding not Elisha only, but Elijah; as he that speaketh against the Holy Ghost speaketh against Christ, as seen no longer as the Son of Man only, but ascended into Heaven. These then are " the scoffers that shall come in the last days;"— "*cursed children,*" as St. Peter calls them, "who have forsaken the right way[2];"—children of Bethel, having fallen from the true faith, and being therefore under the curse of the Law.

Thus the life of Elisha may be considered by us as a parable containing the Gospel; his history itself is like a prophecy. All his actions seem to contain Christ in mystery; but some of the more obvious may perhaps be mentioned. Who, for instance, does not at once understand the cleansing of Naaman, as exhibiting in a living manner the Gentile world coming to the Israel of God for Christian Baptism? Our Lord Himself in speaking of the call of the Gentiles refers to it; and in this light how full of instruction are all its circumstances! We see the simplicity of the rite in the words of the Syrian servants, "if the prophet had bid thee do some great thing, wouldest thou not have done it? how much rather then, when he saith to thee, Wash and be clean;" in the flesh as a little child out of leprosy, the type of sin, we recognize the new birth;

[2] 2 Pet. ii. 14.

and in Gehazi, the leprosy of the Gentile cleaving to the covetous Jew and his "seed for ever;" while in the very unworthiness of the messenger, we are not without a sad warning for the Christian minister.

Again; take the restoration of the dead child; the explanation given of old commends itself to one at once; first he sends his messenger with the staff; thus our Lord before He came by his servant sent the Law, but it "could not give life;" then He came Himself "in the likeness of sinful flesh[3]," made conformable unto death; the living to the dead; He made Himself small, He contracted as it were His limbs to the limbs of the child of Adam; full of sympathies and compassions for us; He breathed seven times with the breath of His seven-fold Spirit; until the dead limbs became warm by His life and revived[4].

We may add, what a beautiful allegory of Christian love is there in that multiplying of the widow's oil; the widow being the Church of Christ; the prophet's injunction for the performance of the miracle, "When thou art come in, shut the door upon thee," is like our Lord's own command, that in faith we enter into the closet, and shut to the door, and look to the eye of God in secret, the true Fountain of Love; the oil while it abode alone sufficed not for herself only, but wasted away and the debt increased; but when poured into the empty vessels of all the neighbours it continued to increase ever more and more; the more it is expended on others, the more is itself augmented; thus as love increases the debt grows small. For loving much hath much forgiven. Of this kind is the explanation of St. Augustine[5].

[3] Rom. viii. 3.
[4] See St. Aug. vol. v. Serm. xxvi. and cxxxvi. And St. Greg. on Job ix. 35.   [5] Serm. de Temp. 206.

With regard to the double portion of the spirit of Elijah which was, according to the promise, to rest on Elisha, it is observable, not only that the miracles recorded of Elisha are double in number those of Elijah; there being twelve of Elijah and twenty-four of Elisha; but there is a greatness, a majesty about them; a facility manifested in their performance, an absence of effort; they are often through the instrumentality of others: he is among the companies of the prophets; they "bow themselves to the ground before him [6]," he sends them on his embassies of power and mercy. Elijah anoints Hazael king, but Elisha sends one of the children of the prophets to anoint Jehu. He speaks too with more authority, as in his message to Naaman the Syrian Captain; and in his stern address to the King of Israel. "And Elisha said unto the King of Israel, What have I to do with thee? Get thee to the prophets of thy father, and to the prophets of thy mother." ... "As the Lord of hosts liveth before whom I stand, surely, were it not that I regard the presence of Jehoshaphat, the King of Judah, I would not look toward thee nor see thee [7]." And then a minstrel plays before him and he prophesies. He had ministered unto Elijah [8], but others minister to him. Thus in multiplying the widow's oil the miracle is like that of Elijah, but he is not like Elijah, a poor suppliant, himself having no where to lay his head. Still more so is it in raising the dead child; the same miracle is performed by both in the same manner, but there is the like difference of character. The rich Shunammite "bows herself to the ground" before Elisha. "He said to Gehazi his servant, Call this Shunammite. And when he had called her, she stood before him. And he said unto him, Say unto her,

[6] 2 Kings ii. 15. [7] 2 Kings iii. 14. [8] 1 Kings xix. 21.

wouldest thou be spoken for to the king, or to the captain of the host?"

Moreover he exemplified the boldness which was seen in Peter and John and all the Apostles after the day of Pentecost, so unlike what they had been before when St. Peter had trembled at a woman; as Elijah in fleeing from Jezebel. Thus it is said of him in the Apocryphal Scriptures, "Eliseus was filled with the spirit of Elias; whilst he lived, he was not moved with the presence of any prince; no word could overcome him[9]."

And again, there was set forth in Elisha a kind of spiritual knowledge, which seems to express the Spirit of Christ in His Church, the heart-searching God. Thus he says to Gehazi, "went not my heart with thee?" And thus it is said to the king of Syria, "Elisha the prophet that is in Israel, telleth the words that thou speakest in thy bedchamber[10]." So likewise does he speak to Hazael the Syrian Captain as knowing his "thoughts long before;" for the prophet knew his designs before he knew them himself[1].

Further; these considerations will illustrate a sort of resemblance which is observable between some of the miracles of Elisha and those of Elijah. "The works that I do," says our Lord, "shall he do also; and greater works than these shall he do, because I go unto My Father[2]." Now this is what we find shadowed forth and represented in Elisha; his works are greater than those of Elijah, as our Lord in His Church does greater things than He did before His Ascension; and not only this, but at the same time there is a sort of resemblance between them; as if exemplifying those our Lord's words, "the works that

[9] Ecclus. xlviii. 12.
[1] 2 Kings viii. 13.
[10] 2 Kings vi. 12.
[2] St. John xiv. 12.

I do shall he do also." By both there is a dead child raised to life; by both a poor widow is supernaturally sustained; in the case of both there is a sore famine on Israel relieved by a great and sudden change. Thus Elijah and Elisha resembled each other.

And as Elisha is so remarkable a type or figure of our Lord in His Church, so it would appear as if some circumstances in his history were intended to remind us of Christ by their resemblance to things recorded of Him. For instance, do we not see like a preparation for our Lord's two miracles of the loaves in this? Barley loaves were brought to Elisha; "and he said, Give unto the people that they may eat. And his servitor said, What, should I set this before an hundred men? He said again, Give the people that they may eat. So he set it before them, and they did eat, and left thereof." And so likewise his restoring the dead child represents, says St. Augustine, our Lord Himself in mystery. Nor did this resemblance cease with his life. As it is said in Ecclesiasticus of Elisha, "And after his death his body prophesied[3];" that is, was made full of a Divine significance. For the dead man, who was cast into his grave, coming again to life on his touching the dead bones of Elisha sets forth very strongly that, "all in Christ shall be made alive." "Together with My dead body shall they arise."

Another remarkable incident may be mentioned in the life of Elisha. Our Lord wept over Jerusalem at the thought of the time when her enemies should cast a trench about her and lay her even with the ground; and how much it resembles this account of Elisha. "The man of God wept. And Hazael said, Why weepeth my lord? And he answered, Because I know the evil that

[3] Ecclus. xlviii. 13.

thou wilt do unto the children of Israel: their strongholds wilt thou set on fire, and their young men wilt thou slay with the sword[4]." This tenderness too in Elisha marks him as of one and the same spirit with Elijah;—to say nothing of that common bond of strong affection between the two, as seen in Elisha's cleaving to Elijah so that he would not let him go, and his lament at his loss.

Now, my Christian brethren, what a beautiful significancy is there in all this! not only do the Prophets prophesy of Christ, and the Psalms sing of Him, but His saints also by their very lives are made to speak of Him. Not only has our Lord condescended to take upon Him our nature, and to be as it were one of us, but also to make other men to be like Himself in the incidents of their lives, and thus likewise to preach His Spirit and power amongst men. Like Elijah is Christ gone up to Heaven; like Elisha He is with us still with a double power. And yet in one sense is He in both alike, for both are made to resemble each other; our Lord in the synagogue at Nazareth speaks of both of them together as prefiguring Himself in calling the Gentiles; He reminded them that Elijah was sent to the widow of Sarepta; to Elisha came Naaman the Syrian[5]. And we may observe that of both Prophets alike at their departure the same remarkable words are used, "My father, my father, the chariot of Israel, and the horsemen thereof[6]." Thus as a branch on a tree sometimes represents the form and structure of the tree itself on which it grows, so do individuals that are in Christ exhibit Christ Himself.

On some occasions indeed Elisha seems like as if he were acting a visible representation, or drama, of some-

[4] 2 Kings viii. 12.   [5] St. Luke iv. 26, 27.
[6] 2 Kings ii. 12; xiii. 14.

thing that is to be a living Christian truth by the power of faith. As for instance, when surrounded by an armed host he opened his servant's eyes. "And his servant said unto him, Alas, my master! how shall we do? And he answered, Fear not: for they that be with us are more than they that be with them. And Elisha prayed, and said, Lord, I pray Thee, open his eyes that he may see. And the Lord opened the eyes of the young man, and he saw: and, behold, the mountain was full of horses and chariots of fire round about Elisha⁷." What was this but setting before our eyes that engaging Christian truth that, as St. Paul says, we "are come unto Mount Sion, and an innumerable company of angels;" that as twelve legions of angels were ready to aid Christ when His enemies approached, "the angel of the Lord encampeth round about them that fear Him"? And then immediately afterwards the enemies are made blind and led by the Prophet into the midst of Samaria; and when thus taken captive, not destroyed nor injured, but their eyes are opened, and they are received with welcome and with provision of bread. What a lively teaching of Christ is there in all this! Of Him Who hath come "that they which see not might see; and that they which see might be made blind;" Who hath received us Gentiles walking by faith and not by sight; Who when we were enemies by wicked works, hath not punished, but laden us with the abundance of His house, and received us as guests at His table.

Thus in the histories of Elijah and Elisha are our thoughts raised above the common things of this our daily life, and led to the contemplation of the wonderful things of Christ, to the wonders that He doeth for those that live by faith, to realities of more lively interest than

⁷ 2 Kings vi. 15—17.

all our highest hopes and aspirations. And in Elisha especially, who sets forth the double portion, we see our Lord Himself, speaking to us in all that is recorded in one of His prophets of old; as if thereby saying, "If ye see Me ascended, if in heart and mind ye are ascended with Me, ye shall partake of My power at the right hand of God; in My Church which is united in love is My mantle without seam, in it ye shall do greater things than ye have seen Me do, and nothing shall be impossible to you."

Now this marvellous history of Elisha is such as is full of interest for a child; like a tale of great wonders; and we learn from Scripture that the wisdom of children is often nearer the wisdom of God than that of grown men; and we have often, as we grow older, to go back and learn of childhood. We are brought by the Gospel into a spiritual world which is full of things great and wonderful beyond conception, such as eye hath not seen nor ear heard. To these we have to raise our minds continually; no imaginings of a child can reach these realities of God; but it opens the way to that childlike faith which makes things to be true which it believes. Divine childlike love "hopeth all things and believeth all things," and can do all things through Christ strengthening. But it must ever be accompanied with reverence and godly fear, or, like the children who mocked at the Prophet "going up," instead of seeing him ascend in faith, it will bring down its own destruction, not a double portion of blessings.

HEZEKIAH

He trusted in the Lord God of Israel; so that after him was none like him among all the kings of Judah, nor any that were before him.—2 KINGS xviii. 5.

THERE is much to make us thoughtful in what we read of the good king Hezekiah. Succeeding his father Ahaz and coming before his son Manasseh, both of them among the most wicked of the kings of Judah, he himself has the especial praise of God; and his life exemplifies wherein the safety lies, and wherein the dangers of good men. In the first month of his reign he commenced opening and repairing the house of God, and from thence he proceeded to the extirpation of idolatry throughout his kingdom; and all this so earnestly and sincerely that it is said of him, that "in every work that he began in the service of the house of God, and in the Law, and in the commandments to seek his God, he did it with all his heart[1]." Thus becoming "strong in the" strength of "the Lord," as his name imports, he prospers in all his ways, and casts off the yoke of the king of Assyria. But some years after this same Sennacherib, Israel being now carried away captive, and all the fenced cities of Judah being taken, comes against Jerusalem, and Hezekiah by a great ransom, for which he spoils the house of God, and cuts off

[1] 2 Chron. xxxi. 21.

the gold from the doors and pillars of the temple, purchases peace. But this hollow truce, while it renders apparent the weakness of king Hezekiah, does not succeed; for shortly after Sennacherib makes that great and memorable invasion to besiege Jerusalem. And here, as in contrast to the former human means which he had taken, Hezekiah has recourse to God. "Be not afraid," are his words, "for the king of Assyria, nor for all the multitude that is with him." "With him is an arm of flesh; but with us is the Lord our God[2]."

It has been often observed that man's helplessness is God's opportunity; that when things are humanly speaking most hopeless God interferes. The reason of this may be in great measure owing to the power of prayer, which is wont to be most importunate, persevering, and earnest in the season of such need, when man has nothing in himself to trust to. It is not distress merely, but the prayer of distress which brings God so near. And now the faith of king Hezekiah, confirmed and nourished by all his former works of religion in restoring the pure worship of God, was to be tried. It is one of those signal instances recorded in Scripture of faith strengthening itself by seeing the Invisible; hoping against hope, and trusting in God for that which nothing but Almighty power could bring about. Instead of the costly ransom as before, or numbering of armies, we read "Hezekiah received the letter of the hand of the messengers and read it; and Hezekiah went up into the house of the Lord and spread it before the Lord[3]." Another more brief account is this; "Hezekiah the king and the prophet Isaiah prayed and cried to Heaven[4]." And the result is, "Then the angel of the

[2] 2 Chron. xxxii.   [3] 2 Kings xix. 14.
[4] 2 Chron. xxxii. 20.

Lord went forth, and smote in the camp of the Assyrians a hundred and fourscore and five thousand."

This remarkable deliverance is one of the most extraordinary events in the history of the world; and is related in three distinct places of Scripture, in the Kings, and the Chronicles, and in the prophet Isaiah; recorded for the example of all ages, when the need of assistance is great, and all human help fails. Such is ever the case with the human soul; besieged by the armies of darkness and warring with the principalities and powers in high places; when there is no salvation but that which is of God, and such deliverance brought about by faith and earnest prayer.

The other circumstance most memorable in the history of Hezekiah was the lengthening of his life, and the sign that was given him of the sun going back, in consequence of his prayer; when humanly speaking and without a miracle, according to the word of the prophet Isaiah, he would have died. The sign indeed of the sun going back in his course may appear the greatest miracle of the two; but thus was it shown that as "the sun knoweth his going down," so man also, as the suns and days of this world, hath his appointed time; both are alike in the hand of God; both are but the shadows of that true life which is with Him, the light that goes not down.

Here arises a question, how far it would be right, if we were apparently at the point of death, to pray that our life might be prolonged; and so also when those who are dear to us are in immediate danger of death; how far is it wise to pray that they may live? Certainly such a prayer should only be made with great caution, and submission to the Divine will, lest it might be that we love our own life, or the life of our friends more than the will of God;

and so in our human infirmity we should bring evil upon us and not good; or derive a less blessing instead of a greater one which God in His love had designed for us; that life may be granted to our prayers, when it would have been better for us to die. Thus we may observe in our own Prayer Book, in the Visitation of the Sick, there is no prayer for the prolonging of life. In the case of the good king Hezekiah we see the wonderful power of the effectual prayer of faith. This is a lesson to us of infinite value. But there is in the whole circumstance something mysterious which we cannot fully explain, and we are not told that the object of that prayer was altogether acceptable or the best. The account is this, " In those days was Hezekiah sick unto death. And Isaiah the prophet, the son of Amos, came unto him, and said unto him, Thus saith the Lord, Set thine house in order; for thou shalt die, and not live. Then Hezekiah turned his face toward the wall, and prayed unto the Lord." To which it is added, "Then came the word of the Lord to Isaiah, saying, Go and say to Hezekiah, Thus saith the Lord, I have heard thy prayer, I have seen thy tears; I will add unto thy days fifteen years[5]." It would appear then that it would have been God's will that he should have died at that time, had it not been for that prayer; and God may have so determined it in consequence of foreseeing some evil approaching, or some danger that would arise to the good king Hezekiah from the lengthening of his days. And although these evils may have been in some way lessened by the Almighty power of God, and turned into good, yet they may not have been altogether averted. For instance; the great misery which hangs over the memory of the good Hezekiah is this, that he was the father of that wicked

[5] Isa. xxxviii. 1—5.

king, Manasseh, who beyond all others provoked God to anger, and overwhelmed Jerusalem in destruction. But now it appears that this his son Manasseh was not born till three years after King Hezekiah recovered from that sickness. If then he had died at that time it would have saved him from this great calamity.

Nor is this all; for it was after that sickness, and apparently in consequence of his recovery from it, that Hezekiah fell into that sin which brought upon him the judgments of God. It is thus spoken of in the Book of the Chronicles in connexion with that his miraculous restoration. "In those days Hezekiah was sick to the death, and prayed unto the Lord; and He spake unto him, and He gave him a sign. But Hezekiah rendered not again according to the benefit done unto him: for his heart was lifted up; therefore there was wrath upon him, and upon Judah and Jerusalem[6]."

It is indeed a very sad truth that persons are seldom rendered better by sickness; and even miracles do not change the heart. Out of ten lepers that were cleansed at our Lord's word, one only returned to give thanks to his Deliverer. For it was soon after Hezekiah's sickness that there came ambassadors from the King of Babylon to congratulate him on his recovery; the Babylonians, or Chaldeans, being great observers of the stars, they came it appears also to inquire respecting the miraculous sign which had occurred of the sun going back ten degrees. As it is said, "Howbeit in the business of the ambassadors of the princes of Babylon, who sent unto him to inquire of the wonder that was done in the land, God left him, to try him, that He might know all that was in his heart[7]." Like David when he numbered the people, glorying in

[6] 2 Chron. xxxii. 24, 25.   [7] 2 Chron. xxxii. 31.

the multitude of his armies, so Hezekiah showed them all his treasures. The strength of Hezekiah like that of David had been his trust in God; but now it is in his own riches. "For God," it is said, "had given him substance very much." He "had exceeding much riches and honour." Oh, how miserable is the glory of this world! Oh, how poor are the best things it has to bestow, so that it were far better for us not to have them at all, unless in having them we are as if we had them not! For then came by the Prophet Isaiah the heavy burden of God's judgment, that all those his treasures and his children should be carried captive to Babylon.

But it is full of the deepest interest, and very consolatory to observe in the failings of good men, that they continue not in sin, but immediately and thoroughly repent. So was it with the royal Penitent, who on the prophet Nathan coming unto him said, "I have sinned;" so with him who, when he saw his Lord's look, "went out and wept bitterly;" so now with king Hezekiah. "Notwithstanding," says the account, "Hezekiah humbled himself for the pride of his heart[8]." And in the prophet Jeremiah it is referred to as a signal instance of humiliation on being reproved. "Did not Hezekiah king of Judah fear the Lord, and besought the Lord, and the Lord repented Him of the evil which He had pronounced[9]?" The very words of the good king on receiving the terrible tidings of woe are extremely touching and beautiful. "Then said Hezekiah unto Isaiah, Good is the word of the Lord which thou hast spoken. And he said, Is it not good, if peace and truth be in my days[1]?" As Job, on seeing the extremity of his distress, arose and said, "Blessed be the

[8] 2 Chron. xxxii. 26.   [9] Jer. xxvi. 19.   [1] 2 Kings xx. 19.

Name of the Lord!" As Eli on hearing the awful sentence which Samuel had feared to tell him, said, "It is the Lord; let Him do what seemeth Him good." So now does the good Hezekiah in like manner love that hand which was stretched out to punish him; and in seeing and loving God has more joy in that severe chastening than worldly men have in their prosperity.

And here let us again pause to reflect on this interesting history. How wonderfully do all things work together for good for them that love God! "O the depth of the riches both of the wisdom and knowledge of God! How unsearchable are His judgments, and His ways past finding out[2]!" We might have supposed that all this great evil had been brought on Hezekiah when God by His Prophet had said he should die, and he prayed for longer life; yet who shall say that the evil outweighed and counterbalanced the good? Who shall say that a good man by his prayers could make a net for his own feet? it may be so, yet God, in delivering him from the same, may strengthen him yet the more, set his feet upon a rock and order his goings, and put a new song into his mouth, even the song of the Lamb. "Thy right hand shall hold me up, and Thy loving correction shall make me great[3]."

If we have in our hearts desires and prayers that are not after God, we have reason to fear lest God should answer us according to those our desires and prayers. But His mercies are so great, that He has compassion on these our infirmities, and answers us not according to our own desires, but according to His own love. For it is indeed most pleasing to Him that we should pray to Him for all things, not only for the highest and best, such as our

[2] Rom. xi. 33.   [3] Ps. xviii. 35.

own eternal happiness and the life with God; but also for
the lower wants of our human life and the objects of our
natural desires; and so great is His goodness that He is
often pleased with such prayers, and in answer to them
gives not merely the precise objects we pray for, but
something better instead, something that we shall in the
end value infinitely more. But at the same time if we
pray for human things God may give them to us, when it
would have been His wish that we should have loved and
prayed for objects more worthy. Yet to turn to Him
always is good; He sees us seeking other things than
Himself, and pities us, and gives us even these weak
desires that they may become to us greater good. How
good is God! May He give us to desire and pray for
what is best; or, may He answer our prayers not according to our own desires, but according to His own
great goodness. Or He may blend them both together
and convert our own weak human desires to His own
high purposes infinitely great and good. Thus was it
with the prayer of Hezekiah; if the wicked King
Manasseh was born to him because he asked for the
lengthening of his days; yet also by the same means may
it have been brought about that Christ should be born of
his lineage; for Hezekiah, together with his son Manasseh,
is numbered among the fathers of Christ according to the
flesh[4].

Moreover, if after his sickness Hezekiah fell into sin, yet,
as we have seen, his humiliation and repentance was great;
and his faith thereby strengthened to do great things by
the power of prayer. He was taught by bitter experience
not to trust in himself but in the Living God; and
thus not only to be numbered among the Saints of

---

[4] According to the lineage in St. Matthew. See St. Matt. i. 10.

God; but also with those great penitents, as his father David, and St. Peter the chief of Apostles, and St. Paul of Christian teachers; to whom it was given to know that there is no true life but in the atoning Blood of Christ.

When Hezekiah with the riches of the temple bought off Sennacherib, and when he showed his treasures to the ambassadors from Babylon, the fault in him that needed correction may have been the same, that he relied on such things more than a good man ought to do. His faith in God required correcting, purifying, enlarging. And it is to be observed that although in the Bible the account of the destruction of Sennacherib's army is given before the sickness of Hezekiah, yet in point of time it is supposed by some to have occurred afterwards. And if so, that prayer of faith which overwhelmed the Assyrian armies was after his humiliation.

And it may be that the mystery of that circumstance, sentence of death having gone forth from God, and then recalled by his prayer, consisted in this, that therein is signified the death of Christ and His resurrection; that the strength of this good man was owing to his thus being by a sort of figure and resemblance united with Christ crucified; he had done much in restoring the worship of God, he spoke of the good he had done, but at the door of death he had a lesson to learn of greater perfection than any to which he had attained, and this was granted to his prayers. It was the power of Christ's resurrection which he had to learn. "I will hear thee in the time of trouble, and thou shalt praise Me." It was that which St. Paul had to practise daily. "We had sentence of death in ourselves that we should not trust in ourselves, but in God which raiseth the dead[5]."

[5] 2 Chron. i. 9.

O blessed wisdom of the grave, to be learned by being with Him "Who offered up prayers with strong crying and tears unto Him that was able to save Him from death, and was heard in that He feared[6]." "I have walked," said Hezekiah, "before Thee with a perfect heart[7]," but in that confession there was no peace, no rest; and the sentence of death was upon him; for he knew not as yet that there was no perfection in man but in deeper humiliation at beholding the Crucified; but in that after and second life, when "on the third day he went up unto the House of the Lord," in that new covenant respited from the second death, he came to understand how weak is man and how strong is God. "After two days," saith the prophet Hosea, "will He revive us: in the third day He will raise us up, and we shall live in His sight. Then shall we know, if we follow on to know the Lord[8]." Oh, let not the pride of life, nor the riches of this passing world, nor apparent security, wrest away the heart again or lead it to forget that hour when eternity knocked at the door! Alas, that aught again should loosen that hope, the anchor of the soul; should dim that vision of peace, which in the sun that is stayed in its going down hath the pledge of redeemed life. O blessed lesson, to unlearn this life, and to learn that better life which is with God! And happy the penitent who as one alive from the dead is at the feet of his Deliverer, of Him Who hath the keys of death and of hell! Yet a little while, and "thy sun shall no more go down, neither shall thy moon withdraw itself; for the Lord shall be thine everlasting light, and the days of thy mourning shall be ended[9]."

[6] Heb. v. 7.
[8] Hosea vi. 2, 3.
[7] Isa. xxxviii. 3.
[9] Isa. lx. 20.

JOSIAH

Because thine heart was tender, and thou didst humble thyself before God, when thou heardest His words against this place, and against the inhabitants thereof, and humbledst thyself before Me, and didst rend thy clothes, and weep before Me; I have even heard thee also, saith the Lord.—2 CHRONICLES xxxiv. 27.

WHEN the ten tribes of Israel had been carried away captive, and the like judgments were drawing on upon Jerusalem, there were two remarkable kings, Hezekiah and Josiah, both described in much the same language as walking in the ways of their father David, both as pre-eminent above all other kings before and after. We read of both labouring to restore the worship of God, to destroy idolatry, both keeping a great passover, both accepted of God, but unable to avert His coming wrath from Jerusalem. But in Josiah there is something peculiarly affecting: his early youth, for "in the eighth year of his reign, while he was yet young," i. e. but sixteen years of age, "he began to seek after the God of David his father[1]:" the extreme ignorance and darkness which had overwhelmed the nation; for the finding of the Book of the Law in the temple seems to have been a great discovery as of something altogether forgotten and lost; his exceeding zeal and earnestness in instantly doing with

[1] 2 Chron. xxxiv. 3.

whole heart whatever he knew to be right; but in all and above all his singular tenderness of spirit. Such is seen in his consternation on learning the contents of the book of Moses that was found; and his sending in consequence to inquire not of priest, or prophet, or scribe, for he seems to have known of none to send to, but to "Huldah the prophetess, the wife of Shallum, the keeper of his wardrobe." A woman, the youthful king, and her answer to himself from God in the words of the text are very expressive; and may serve to afford us a sad description of the state of the age in which they were spoken; and they also furnish us briefly with the whole character of Josiah. He was so tender of heart, that he humbled himself and rent his clothes and wept—not for his own sins—but for those of his forefathers and his people; he thus humbled himself and wept before God, and trembled on account of God's words. O beautiful spirit of sacred sorrow, so richly fraught with the blessing of them that mourn!

In strong contrast to this we have a circumstance mentioned of his son Jehoiakim, in the prophet Jeremiah; the word of God was sent to him by the prophet, "So the king sent Jehudi to fetch the roll. And Jehudi read it in the ears of the king. And when he had read three or four leaves the king cut it with the penknife and cast it into the fire that was on the hearth, until all the roll was consumed in the fire that was on the hearth. Yet they were not afraid, nor rent their garments, neither the king nor any of his servants that heard all these words[2]." In this remarkable instance there was a sure token of God's heaviest judgments coming on because they feared not His words; and so likewise in the case of this good King Josiah, because he feared when he heard the words of

[2] Jer. xxxvi. 21—24.

God, and took them home to his heart with such grief and humility, he was gathered into the sure protection and mercy of Almighty God.

These words which he heard were those of Moses,—the Book which he commanded to be placed in " the ark of the covenant" to be " a witness against them[a],"—words which we ourselves hear, and have heard; they speak to us as much as they did to him; they speak with the light of the Gospel filling every letter, so that the very characters are fire and light: we are to bind them about us so as to clothe as it were every part of us; to be a witness against us if we do evil. Do we hear them with a like awe and humiliation? Alas, is it not the very character of our age that without fear it takes on itself to judge God's word, rather than be judged by it?

But now it must be observed that all this goodness of King Josiah and that of Hezekiah before him did not prevent the destruction of Jerusalem; they may have delayed it, relieved it, and perhaps the remembrance of these good kings, and of that repentance which they brought about, may have been connected with the restoration of Jerusalem after the captivity; for the kingdom of Israel where there were no such kings was never restored. But to all appearance God's threatened judgment came on Jerusalem notwithstanding all the intercessions and labours of the good King Josiah. And not only this, but under a sense of that coming judgment and in that state of things in which he was born, Josiah had to sustain a heavy burden all his days. And even too unto his death, for although God had promised him this one thing only, that he would gather him to his grave in peace; yet that did not save him from dying a violent death, a death indeed in its circumstances

[a] See Deut. xxxi. 26.

very much like that of the wicked Ahab. For in an unsuccessful battle with the king of Egypt at Megiddo, he was wounded as it were by an accidental hand, for he had disguised himself in the battle, and was carried home and died[4]. So that even in that which came especially under God's promise, as the Preacher says, "there is one event to the righteous, and to the wicked[5]."

Yet who could be in greater favour with God than this good King Josiah, tender-hearted and humble, of such a temper as the Holy Spirit chooses above all others for His own; of that meek spirit which is of great price with God; how could He not set on him the seal of His especial favour and love? Some indeed consider his very name to signify the "sacrifice of God." Such a character is meet beyond any to be a sacrifice and a victim; and as such in some faint way to resemble Christ; Who was a "man of sorrows," as "a root out of a dry ground;" Whose days were "cut off out of the land of the living;" Who made "His grave with the wicked:" Who wept over that destruction coming on Jerusalem, which all His calls to repentance and all His intercessions averted not; Who was eaten up by a zeal for God's house. Nay, we are reminded of the day of Judgment itself in the good King Josiah, when he came to Bethel, where the idolatrous calves had been, but which now had long departed together with that guilty nation itself that worshipped them. He came and had the graves opened, and men's bones burnt on the altar; and in those their graves made a distinction between the righteous and the wicked. He had been called of God for this purpose three hundred years before; and the burden of this judgment was laid upon him before he was born[6]. As Cyrus

[4] 2 Chron. xxxv. 22. 24.   [5] Eccles. ix. 2.
[6] 1 Kings xiii. 2.

designated by name in prophecy as the "Shepherd'" of God's people, for the restoration of the dry bones of Judah, so was Josiah to execute His judgments, and even as it were anointed and sanctified by His Spirit for this awful type of the great Judgment. "I the Lord have called thee in righteousness, and will hold thine hand, and will help thee⁸." "I have called thee by thy name, thou art Mine."

Thus did this blameless king labour to restore his people, and they were willing "for a season to rejoice in his light." Yea, thus did he strive to undo what was done, and to expiate the evil of Israel even as it were beyond the grave; even the sins of Solomon⁹, and the sins of Jeroboam; yet as to himself did it appear as if his candle were put out in obscure darkness; by a Pharaoh of Egypt slain, and by a Pharaoh of Egypt his throne given away. The very Scripture that describes all his goodness, after declaring that there was none like him, "that turned to the Lord with all his heart," yet adds to the account, "Notwithstanding the Lord turned not from the fierceness of His great wrath."

Now a consideration of this, the holy and sweet, yet awful and sad life of Josiah, may much correct our view of human things; God declares that He visits the sins of fathers upon their children; it is so throughout the Scriptures; last Sunday[1] we read of the seventy sons of Ahab slain by Jehu, as if they had been guilty of some great crime, because they were the sons of Ahab: we see it is so in the world; and if so it must be God's doing, because it is His world. What is much more, we see righteous men born to a sad inheritance of woe; kings blameless and holy,

---

⁷ Isa. xliv. 28.   ⁸ Isa. xlii. 6.   ⁹ 2 Kings xxiii. 13.
[1] Preached on the Thirteenth Sunday after Trinity.

weighed down all their days by the sins of their forefathers; and again princes suffering for their people's sins, and people for the sins of their princes. Yea, more, the meekness and holiness of kings have made them the more meet victims of suffering: they have been made on that very account to bear the heavy burden. It may be that Satan sees upon them the mark of Christ; and therefore directs against them all his assaults, but God through the Cross turns all to good. Because they are holy they suffer; and because they suffer they are made the more holy. Their light indeed is put out; and the world goes on as it did before. But shall we say that they have lived in vain; for themselves, for their people, for their God? Surely this cannot be so. We know that the only strength of the world is Christ; and this the apparent failure of good men, bears a resemblance to Christ. He also bore the sins of others, not His own. He, the Beloved of God, the strength of God, the Life of the world, appeared as in weakness, and sorrow, and cut off before His time prematurely as one that had failed of his mission. It was said of good King Josiah that he should go down to his grave in peace, yet in one sense it was not peace, but a sword. Yet when we put this by the side of Christ Crucified, we may say surely that good king died in peace. By dying he entered into peace, a peace-maker with God, reconciling Him to His people, the sacrifice of peace. He was taken from the evil to come; he died in peace; and while nothing but trouble and anguish was on his people, he himself was with God. "In the sight of the unwise they seemed to die; and their departure is taken for misery; but they are in peace[2]."

"The righteous perisheth," saith the prophet, "and merciful men are taken away, none considering that the

[2] Wisd. iii. 2, 3.

righteous is taken away from the evil to come. He shall enter into peace[3]." And his memory was blessed. "The remembrance of Josiah," it is said, "is sweet as honey in all mouths, and as music at a banquet of wine[4]." A solemn lamentation was written of him by the Prophet Jeremiah, and singing men and women commemorated and spoke of Josiah[5]. Nor is this all that connects it with Christ Crucified; for in that memorable prophecy in Zechariah, where he speaks of Jerusalem "looking upon Him Whom they have pierced, and mourning as for an only son, every family apart," he says that this shall be as the mourning for Josiah "in the valley of Megiddon." The mourning for Christ Crucified is as the mourning for Josiah slain. The shadow of that all-atoning death covers him.

We must not think then that Josiah failed, or that such as he could fail in their life or in their death. On the contrary, we are hereby taught with awe and wonder to raise our minds to the greatness of their crown, their strength that is among men, and their reward that is with God. For of them the world is not worthy; they are the salt of the earth which preserves it from corruption; they are the light set on a hill which cannot be hid; they shine like stars for ever and ever giving light unto the world. The doctrine of Christ Crucified will teach us not to judge of the success of such men by what appeared in their lives; it may be more precious and lasting than man can judge of. Even in their temporal failure there may have been a life and restoration from the dead in that for which they laboured. "Thy work shall be rewarded, saith the Lord; and they shall come again from the land of the enemy; and there is hope in thine end[6]." In the destruc-

[3] Isa. lvii. 1, 2.
[5] 2 Chron. xxxv. 15.
[4] Ecclus. xlix. 1.
[6] Jer. xxxi. 16, 17.

tion of Judah there is hope, but not in that of the nations. In like manner with regard to ourselves, who can tell whether our having the Church among us here at this day may not be owing to some good king of this nation, who may have lived and died as a martyr to the faith of Christ?

Nor is the crown and the blessing of God which awaits good men like King Josiah such as this world can take account of: it is far too great and good for that; for their reward is with God; such as eye hath not seen, nor ear heard, nor heart of man imagined. Their end and their beginning is with Christ in God. Through apparent failure they are purified and strengthened to obtain that crown. And thus we may see in the account of Josiah; he humbled himself and wept at the words found in the Book of God; and when on sending to Huldah the prophetess she entirely confirmed those words, by saying that the judgments therein threatened on Jerusalem should not be averted, but should in their awful fulness come on that people;—the good king did not on that account slacken his zeal and exertions or sit down in despair; but immediately "with all his heart and with all his soul" brought all his people into covenant with God. He said not, It is in vain to serve the Lord, for He has and He will cast us off. But he wrought a thorough and entire repentance through all his kingdom, both of Judah and of Israel too, and left the issue with God.

And observe what was the praise of God which marks this good king; perhaps no one in any age or nation ever made so entire a reformation, and that at so youthful an age as Josiah, both in the house and worship of God in His Temple, and also through all that nation, cutting off every root and branch that remained of idolatry and profaneness, restoring all as far as in him lay to obedience. Yet it is not this which is mentioned as rendering him so acceptable in the judgment of God; but—" because thine heart was tender, and thou didst humble thyself before God, when thou heardest His words, and didst rend thy clothes and weep." For it is not the outward actions which God weighs, but the heart from which they proceed. It is not so difficult to find works of religion and charity, as to find a humble spirit that fears God's words. A contrite heart that reverences His word is with God the best sacrifice; and as it is of such price with God it is so very rare amongst men. Measuring himself not by what he had done, but by what he would have wished to do, and by that love which is infinite as the nature of God, he speaks not of his doings, but oppressed with a sense of his shortcomings, he puts his hand on his mouth and is silent, or says, God be merciful to me a sinner!

If any one might glory in works it were the good Josiah; for his works were especially those of religion, such as had a direct reference to the service of God, the restoring His temple and worship, and this not for mere external service, but accompanied with deep calls to repentance, of which he himself set the most lively example; if therefore any had works on which to rest his claim for Divine favour it was this righteous king. It is not service that God requires, but servants;—not service, for what can our service be to Him?—but servants whom He may love in Christ, on whom He may bestow His love; and they that tremble at His word, who look to Him in tenderness of spirit, these are the servants in whom He delights, as ready for His service, and meet to receive His love.

In the history of all His saints He writes that no flesh

shall glory in His presence; and in holding them up for our example He reminds us of this, for there is no one without fault either in life or condition. To say nothing of the earlier patriarchs, Moses was not altogether accepted; Job, though a perfect man, is known for his afflictions; Samuel had to mourn; David was bowed to earth with his repentance; Solomon grievously sinned; Hezekiah was not without blame; and Josiah's praise is that he humbled himself and rent his clothes, and not this only, but his "sun went down while it was yet day," and a night of sorrow came on its close.

One observation more. What light does the history of Josiah afford us in our present perplexities? The revival of religion which has taken place in these days, the restoration of the Houses of God, and care of His worship, together with calls to repentance and to the ancient paths, and this too after a deep sleep and much corruption and decay of faith, all this so far turns our eyes to that pause in the declension of Judah. Such a call may not be responded to, or may be responded to for a time, and then the light go out; on all this it were needless and presumptuous to speculate; but even if it were fruitless, and to end in darkness yet worse than before, we are taught by the history of this good king not to despair, not to give over; but it may correct and purify our views to know what to look to. We are not then to congratulate ourselves overmuch on the restoration of external worship as if it were any worthy end or object in itself, but rather to look to tenderness and humiliation of heart before God; let the other follow if it will, it is of no value without this, but this of itself without that is of value inestimable. Moreover, we see in this history that no temporal prosperity, no personal or national success, no setting up or saving of kingdoms, can serve as a test of God's acceptance: the matter is of far too great importance for this;—it is of eternity, of Heaven and Hell, of dwelling for ever with God or with His enemies; of being united in life and in death with One Whose life and death was in human eyes covered with sorrow and shame.

JEREMIAH

Oh that my head were waters, and mine eyes a fountain of tears, that I might weep day and night for the slain of the daughter of my people! Oh that I had in the wilderness a lodging place of wayfaring men; that I might leave my people and go from them!—
JEREMIAH ix. 1, 2.

I HAVE chosen these words of the text as expressing the character itself and life of the prophet Jeremiah. He lived in the time of the good king Josiah; both were as children called of God; and engaged in the same work of reformation before the judgments came on Jerusalem. The one sets forth the kingly, and the other the prophetic office, which were both found combined in Christ.

But Jeremiah not only represents Christ as a prophet, but that peculiar designation of Him as such which is expressed by Moses: "The Lord thy God will raise up unto thee a prophet from the midst of thee, of thy brethren, like unto me[1]." "Of thy brethren," one peculiarly full of brotherly affections and "from the midst of thee," i.e. "the Son of man," nay, the "man of sorrows," one in Himself all humanity; and yet more, "like unto me," even as the meekest of men, as if to mark yet more strongly this characteristic. Our Blessed Saviour was

[1] Deut. xviii. 15.

beyond all men full of human tenderness, compassionate, such as was represented by the living Body stretched upon the dead; with limb answering to limb; the feeling with the unfeeling; the warm with the cold; thus was He full of sympathy with our infirmities, as alive in every part with a fellow-feeling for us. He was clothed all over, and compassed about on every side with pity, such as one most tender-hearted amongst mankind feels in the most intimate relations of life; as a mother, as a brother, as an husband. And this rendered Him as a victim so full of sorrow and "acquainted with grief," when He came to a people about to be overwhelmed with the consequences of their sins. "In all their affliction He was afflicted." In a manner most intimate, deep, and penetrative, "He hath borne our griefs and carried our sorrows." We might conceive it otherwise; God might have executed His judgments, as a stern Judge, Himself unmoved. But it is not so; the Judge Himself bears the heavy burden; and has made Himself one with us that He might carry our griefs. Now all this speaks to us through Jeremiah; his natural character was peculiarly suited for this; he was chosen and sanctified from his mother's womb for this purpose. So that there was more meaning in it than they knew who, when they saw our Lord's sufferings and compassions, said it was "Jeremiah[2]." Not only that it was "one of the prophets," arisen from the dead, but especially mentioning Jeremiah.

It was, I observe, founded in the natural disposition of Jeremiah, hallowed of God for this end before his birth. "Before I formed thee in the belly," said God, "and before thou camest forth out of the womb I sanctified thee, and ordained thee a prophet[3]." Hence his writings are

[2] St. Matt. xvi. 14.   [3] Jer. i. 5.

marked especially with this character throughout. For though these prophecies are the Word of God speaking to us thereby; yet they partake throughout of the prophet's own natural mind. Like as the light of the sun falling through a painted window; it is still the light of the sun though it partakes of the colour through which it passes to us. Thus Jeremiah is considered by the ancients to be, in the words of one of them, "the most inclined to pity of all the prophets[4]."

The times in which he lived were exceedingly sad; his whole life was intimately connected with the ruin and breaking down of the people of Israel, filling up the measure of their iniquities, adding sin to sin, and with it increasing their miseries and sorrows to the last. The good king was cut off as too good for that people, but the prophet remained. Jeremiah continued with them throughout even to the last remnant that was left in Israel, and afterwards with that remnant doomed to judgment in Egypt. The King of Babylon would have done him honour, and kept him in safety and peace: but he stayed behind, as if to the last dregs drinking with them of their cup of sorrows. This was of itself very mournful and distressing; but it was that heart in Jeremiah so full of tender sympathies which increased the intensity of his sufferings. It is therefore in this respect that he so especially brings home to us the sorrows of Christ: as the good Samaritan, stopping to take care of the wounded man, and putting him on his own beast; as suffering with us and for us. He says in the Lamentations, "I am the man that hath seen affliction by the rod of His wrath[5]." This is spoken by the Prophet of himself, and of Christ; it is spoken of them both in their suffering with the

[4] St. Greg. Naz. Orat. xvii.   [5] Lam. iii. 1.

suffering Israel of God. And this may be seen throughout the Lamentations of Jeremiah. When it is there said, "Is it nothing to you, all ye that pass by? behold, and see if there be any sorrow like unto my sorrow⁶:"—then we see at once that it is spoken of Him who "bare them and carried them all the days of old⁷." Nor is all this any thing that is passed and gone. It is to every human soul that the Word of God speaks in Jeremiah; speaks of the compassions of God towards him in Christ; it speaks of Christ: and at the same time it is Christ Himself therein speaking to each one; and drawing out His expressions of infinite concern and mercy.

Our Lord is represented in a well-known picture as the good Shepherd taking a lost sheep out of the thorns; and Himself in so doing as wearing a crown of thorns with a bleeding countenance. It is this throughout that speaks in the prophet Jeremiah. It is the bleeding Shepherd extricating His lost sheep from among the thorns of the world. It is purposely so ordered of God; the penitent of all ages and countries in studying the Bible in order to know God and himself, does naturally read the Prophet Jeremiah under this impression; whether he stops to contemplate the fact or no, so it is; the feeling with which a devout person looks on that representation of Christ, of which I am speaking, is like that which the reverential reader experiences when hearing in Jeremiah the voice of the good Shepherd.

Nor is this all, for Jeremiah was in the meanwhile made also like unto Christ in suffering himself from others, while he suffered with them and for them; for as a witness of God he was hated, smitten, imprisoned, and at last, it is supposed, stoned to death. Indeed, that he should have

⁶ Lam. i. 12.   ⁷ Isa. lxiii. 9.

lived so long among them was like a continual miracle vouchsafed to him of God, Who gave him this promise. "Gird up thy loins, and arise and speak unto them—be not dismayed at their faces—for behold I have made thee a defenced city, and an iron pillar, and brazen walls against the whole land: . . . and they shall fight against thee, but they shall not prevail[8]." This was repeated to him more than once. Thus he was made to suffer, and preserved in life that he might suffer, in bearing the heavy burden of God; to exhibit unto us our Lord Himself. For instance, how like as of Christ Himself are these words, "I was like a lamb or an ox that is brought to the slaughter; and I knew not that they had devised devices against me, saying, Let us destroy the tree with the fruit thereof, and let us cut him off from the land of the living," . . . "but, O Lord of hosts, that judgest righteously, . . . unto Thee have I revealed my cause." And this was said by the prophet of the men of Anathoth, the prophet's own native place, who were seeking his life[9]. And in like manner it was the men of Nazareth, His own city, who first attempted our Lord's life. "He came unto His own, but His own received Him not." Now it is then this home relation, this tenderness of human pity, these the motherly compassions of Him that was born of woman, not of man, this love of Christ compassing about the soul of man, that Jeremiah speaks throughout. The very first mention of him is of this character. As Josiah was but a child on coming to the throne, and when he sent to Huldah the prophetess; so Jeremiah when called to his high office says, "Ah, Lord God, behold, I cannot speak: for I am a child." Thus was represented the Gospel, strong in weakness. It speaks of the times in which, as the prophet

[8] Jer. i. 17, 18; xv. 19, 20.   [9] Jer. xi. 19. 21.

Isaiah describes, a little "child shall lead them[1];"—when a little child was set in the midst of Apostles, as their example, and as the greatest in the kingdom of Heaven.

And then after the Prophet Jeremiah is thus called and strengthened with the promised protection of God, what an exceeding tenderness is there in the first words which he delivers from God to His people, how do they serve to express the character of all his prophecies which follow! "Go and cry in the ears of Jerusalem, saying, Thus saith the Lord, I remember thee, the kindness of thy youth, the love of thine espousals, when thou wentest after Me in the wilderness." "What iniquity have your fathers found in Me, that they are gone far from Me[2]?" Wonderful to say, it is God that thus speaks, and not man, but so full of human affections, that we hear Him in His prophet while His prophet himself speaks. And sometimes the prophet turns himself to God, as it were in surprise at these messages of God which he has to bear. "Ah, Lord God," he says, "Thou showest loving-kindness unto thousands," "the Great, the Mighty God, the Lord of hosts is His Name[3]."

But more particularly,—with regard to that expression, "I remember thee, the kindness of thy youth, the love of thine espousals,"—it is this figurative allusion to lost affection, and to the remembrances of "first love," which is so common in this prophet. And that usual image under which the grief of Christ is expressed by him, is that of all the most bitter, most intimately reaching the affections of the human heart, that of an husband bewailing an unfaithful wife. "Can a maid forget her ornaments, or a bride her attire? yet My people have forgotten Me days without number. Why trimmest thou thy way to

[1] Isa. xi. 6.   [2] Jer. ii. 2. 5.   [3] Jer. xxxii. 18.

seek love?" "Why gaddest thou about so much to change thy way⁴?" And again, "What hath My beloved to do in Mine house, seeing she hath wrought lewdness with many⁵?" "Turn, O backsliding children, for I am married unto you." And further on; "Surely as a wife treacherously departeth from her husband, so have ye dealt treacherously with Me, O house of Israel, saith the Lord." "Return, ye backsliding children, and I will heal your backslidings⁶." Now all this is typical and expressive of the dealings of Christ with a human soul, His intimate relation to it, His tender, unwearied love. It speaks in every part of a life nourished by the death of Christ, which has its existence in His flesh and blood; and cannot be sustained but in Him; the Bride taken as it were from His bleeding side in death. And alas! it speaks also of the unfaithfulness which we are to expect even in the members of His Body.

Frequent also in this prophet are expressions drawn from another most tender of human relationships, that of a parent. "Wilt thou not from this time cry unto Me, My Father, Thou art the guide of my youth?" And again, "But I said, How shall I put thee among the children, and give thee a pleasant land?" "And I said, Thou shalt call Me, My Father; and shalt not turn away from Me⁷." The full force, too, of this figure can only be known in that new relationship into which we Christians have been brought as children of God, saying by the Spirit, Abba, Father. It anticipates those appeals to us in our Lord's Sermon on the Mount on God's more than fatherly love; throughout the whole of which we are addressed as the children of our Father which is in Heaven.

⁴ Jer. ii. 32. 36.
⁶ Jer. iii. 14. 20. 22.
⁵ Jer. xi. 15.
⁷ Jer. iii. 4. 19.

But even when these figures of natural affection are not used, and the prophet speaks in his own person, it is of a like spirit and character of tender-hearted compassion, even unto death. "When I would comfort myself against sorrow, my heart is faint in me[8]." "But if ye will not hear it, my soul shall weep in secret places for your pride; and mine eyes shall weep sore[9]." Must we not think that this opens to us some intimation of our Lord's own secret sorrows; of the heavy untold anguish which was in the bitterness of that cup which He drank? of His "sighs," of His "groaning deeply in spirit," of His "strong crying and tears"? And from expostulating with his people, the prophet turns in a like strain to expostulate with God Himself in their behalf, making himself one with that sinful people. "O Lord, though our iniquities testify against us; for we have sinned against Thee." "O the hope of Israel, the Saviour thereof in time of trouble, why shouldest Thou be a stranger in the land, and as a wayfaring man that turneth aside to tarry for a night? Why shouldest Thou be as a man astonied, as a mighty man that cannot save? Yet thou, O Lord, art in the midst of us, and we are called by Thy name; leave us not[1]."

There is indeed in this prophet great sadness, almost verging on despair, for had he not reason for despair? "Can the Ethiopian," says he, "change his skin, or the leopard his spots? then may ye also do good, that are accustomed to do evil." Sinking under the heavy burden, he curses the day wherein he was born[2]. Yet it is not all of this character, very much the reverse.

As our Lord, when His hour was come, and the night of His great sorrow, spake so much of comfort to His

[8] Jer. viii. 18.   [9] Jer. xiii. 17.
[1] Jer. xiv. 7. 9.   [2] Jer. xiii. 23; xx. 14.

disciples; and looking beyond the cloud rejoiced under that great tribulation, and spake more than ever of peace; so this His prophet, who speaks so much of His sorrows, turns also at last to the consolations that are in Christ; and descries the morning of Resurrection illumining the night of the grave. He sees no longer the captivity, but the restoration beyond it, and in that restoration the pledges and types of the Gospel; "Fear thou not, O Jacob My servant, saith the Lord; for I am with thee; for I will make a full end of all the nations whither I have driven thee; but I will not make a full end of thee[3]." Strange that there is no part of Scripture so full of comfort as those chapters in St. John's Gospel on the saddest of all sad nights, when our Lord, under the sense of that coming agony, gave His Body and Blood to His disciples. So full is all the account of joy and thanksgiving, and yet at the same time of unspeakable sorrow. In like manner, perhaps, there are no passages in Scripture, unless it be those our Lord's last Eucharistic discourses, so eloquent of love and consolations as the 31st chapter of Jeremiah,—and we may add the 33rd also. No words can be found in any language of more touching beauty than all that strain. And indeed so similar in tone is it to those passages I have spoken of in the Gospel, that it is chosen by our Church for the Evening Lesson of that Thursday night in the Holy Week. The prophet, in bearing the good tidings, speaks as one awakening after a deliverance from some terrible affliction. For he had said, "Woe unto us; for the day goeth away; for the shadows of evening are stretched out." He had said, "I am black; astonishment hath taken hold on me[4]." But now, in the 31st chapter, he says, "Upon this I awaked, and beheld, and my sleep

[3] Jer. xlvi. 28.   [4] Jer. vi. 4; viii. 21.

was sweet unto me." All is changed, the very tenderness of his former woes adds to the intensity of the expressions of joy. "Rachel weeping for her children" is comforted, and they are come again from death. Ephraim is again remembered as a dear son, and received with the overflowing compassions of a father. The virgin of Israel hath come again. In their heart is written holiness by the finger of God, and their sins are remembered no more. With weeping and supplications do they come, but they shall sorrow no more at all. "I have loved thee with an everlasting love; therefore with loving-kindness have I drawn thee." Nay, yet more than this, "the nations of the earth shall hear all the good that I do," "they shall fear and tremble for all the goodness." The voice of joy, the voice of the Bridegroom, and the voice of the Bride shall be heard, and of them that say, "Praise the Lord, for He is good[s]." Such are but allusions to that outpouring strain of consolation and joy with which this prophet speaks in the desolations of Judah.

The Prophet Jeremiah is much to be considered in days like the present, when "the overflowings of ungodliness make us afraid" of what is coming on; and by means of the Press, "the fiery darts of the wicked one" are weekly and daily spread abroad, encompass us on all sides, and forcibly bring before us the character of the days in which we live. In these the tenderness of Jeremiah, the hatred of evil together with so much compassion, such appeals to God, and from God to man, such prayers for those who pray not for themselves, are most seasonable. He will teach us sorrow rather than anger; expostulation instead of desponding silence. But this, after all, is but a secondary study of this prophet. It is as setting forth the com-

[s] Jer. xxxiii.

passions of Christ towards ourselves, His love for the Christian soul which He has so dearly purchased, His intimate knowledge of it and regard for it. And as arising out of this, we learn from him in the second place, the compassion we ourselves ought to have for others, and especially in reproving and correcting them. For in this all God's people in one sense are prophets; in that by the Spirit of God they ought to improve and reform each other. And this can never be done effectually, unless it is with much charity, and in the fear of God.

A Christian must be in the world, like his Master, a "man of sorrows," not merely on account of his own personal sufferings, but because he is in a sinful world; and the more holy he becomes, the more must he be "acquainted with grief;" for as Heaven is the abode of happiness because of holiness; so this earth must be the abode of sorrow because of sin; the servant of Christ must live in a world of his own, apart from that which is without, in the thoughts of his heart; if the world hates him because he is not of the world, but is born of God, so likewise must he hate the world; and this implies desolation of heart and mourning; and the more this mourning is, the more will his consolation abound. Thus not mourning only, but joy and peace are his portion. For the Christian's life is in itself as a great contradiction; his religion is made up of contradictions, because Holy Scripture is full of the same; and his course, as it advances onward, harmonizes them all, and out of such discords forms the everlasting concord of heaven. If joy is the mark of sonship, yet this his very acceptableness depends on his sorrow. It is those that lament the sins that are around them on whom is set the seal of

God⁶. "They that fear the Lord," and "speak often to one another" in sympathies of sacred sorrow are the jewels valued of God⁷. In some days there is scarce any stronger token of holiness; as in the good Josiah, because he wept and his heart was tender; and in this prophet when he says, "if ye will not hear it, my soul shall weep in secret⁸."

In this respect then is Jeremiah the Christian's study, as therein he studies his Master's own life, and the mind which was in Christ. To look on the prophets only as foretelling things to come, is but a partial and limited mode of taking them; nor are they only as "preachers of righteousness," but likewise real living characters in which Christ Himself is speaking by His Spirit. Where Christ is, there must His servants behold Him. They live on earth that they may learn to love, and they learn to love that they may live,—that true life which is with Christ in God.

⁶ Ezek. ix. 4.   ⁷ Mal. iii. 17.   ⁸ Jer. xiii. 17.

EZEKIEL

And, lo, thou art unto them as a very lovely song of one that hath a pleasant voice, and can play well on an instrument: for they hear thy words, but they do them not.—EZEKIEL xxxiii. 32.

THESE words are spoken of the Prophet Ezekiel; he is as the lovely song, as the pleasant voice, as the instrument of music, all this even to the worldly mind; yet we might have thought otherwise; so full is he of woe, of the wrath of God; and how dark and obscure are his visions! Should we not say of him rather as of his Divine Master, who "speaks by the prophets," he is "without form or comeliness," "there is no beauty that we should desire him"? Yet so it is, very beautiful is the lightning though it be a messenger of wrath, and the breaking forth of the burning mountain. Thus they made much of this prophet, as if there were something attractive about him; they come to him, they assemble at his house, they ask for his revelations, and sit before him[1]. Let us consider what there is in his history and in his prophecies that will account for this.

The great prophets came for the most part in succession; when one departed another arose, as watchmen in the dark days; they passed on the lamp one to another; for God left not His Church without witness; but now when His

[1] Ezek. xiv. 3; xx. 1; xxxiii. 31.

people were divided, some being still left in Jerusalem before its destruction, while others were carried captive to Babylon, the light becomes twofold; Jeremiah and Ezekiel both prophesy together; but the one in Jerusalem, the other at the same time by the river Chebar in the captivity of Babylon; for Ezekiel had been taken there among the captives eleven years before Jerusalem was destroyed. It is said[2] that his prophecies were also carried from thence at the same time to Jerusalem; and those of Jeremiah were brought to Babylon: thus these two great prophets united as it were their lights together; though vast distances intervened, they mingled their tears.

How great a change must have come over the mind of an Israelite who had been carried away to Babylon; the great city of wonders; the seat of Oriental magnificence,—of the wisdom of the ancients; where the Chaldeans watched the stars in the broad expanse of Eastern plains; the country whence Egypt itself derived its language of mystery, making "living creatures" to represent the spiritual and Divine! Like St. Paul at Rome, he is a captive; but "the Spirit of God is not bound;" nay, is more free in chains. And now to speak to captive Israel, he takes up his parable from Babylon; and applies the new imagery and scenes of the East. The God of Abraham, Isaac, and Jacob is henceforth known by a new name, as "the Lord of Hosts," the God of those armies of Heaven whom the Babylonians ignorantly worshipped. With new language does the Spirit clothe itself, and one meet for that language is chosen; the earthen vessel is moulded by the Divine hand for this use. As the Gospel comes to us in the garb of Greek and Roman simplicity; these prophets speak with the wonderful visions and symbols

[2] By St. Jerome.

of the East: each with its appropriate adaptation of God.

Nay, not only the images by which God speaks, but scenes and events themselves are changed; the Children walking in the fire; the Saint in the lions' den; the Hand of fire writing on the wall; these are things of a new character; they are of Babylon, not of Jerusalem; or rather they are of Jerusalem in Babylon. The coming of Christ is foretold in a new manner; in Daniel, one like the Son of God is seen with His faithful ones walking in the midst of the flames. In the Prophet Ezekiel the Incarnation is set forth in a vision of four living creatures where the throne of God is; the living fire is there; the face of a Man; the Lion to speak His kingdom and strength; the Ox the sacrifice of His death; the Eagle His Resurrection and Godhead. Now these considerations will account for the peculiar character of Ezekiel; and why in the prophet of the captivity more than in any other it was fulfilled, "I will incline mine ear to the parable: and show my dark speech upon the harp[s]." When they sat down by the waters of Babylon, and remembered Zion and wept, in shadowy and sublime outline they saw in its dark waters the reflection of the spiritual Zion, and through the visions of Assyrian allegory spake to them the mysterious wisdom of God.

But before entering further into the subject, let us consider what it is in Christ Himself which is peculiarly to be found in Ezekiel? for as our Lord spake by the prophets, so in the prophets severally seems set forth something in His own ministry. Now, in addition to many expressions which remind us of our Lord's own words, I think we may hear His voice in those heavy denunciations which Ezekiel

[s] Ps. xlix. 4.

declares against the Jews. In the Gospels are the terrible Woes pronounced against the Pharisees after their day of visitation was past, and their "house left unto them desolate;" so in Ezekiel, when the sentence of condemnation was already gone forth, we hear the awful Voice by the prophet, "thou shalt speak unto them whether they will hear or whether they will forbear," "for they are most rebellious:" such is his commission: his "face is made strong" as adamant against their faces; "thorns and briers" are with him, as with Christ, when He wore His crown of thorns; and he also "has his dwelling among scorpions [a]," that same "generation of vipers," of whom our Lord Himself speaks.

It might then at first sight appear inconsistent with this, that the Prophet Ezekiel should in style be considered so engaging, that even to those to whom he was sent with heavy tidings he should be as one that had a "pleasant voice;" in like manner, that although the roll which is given him is "written within and without," "with lamentations and mourning and woe," yet it should be in the mouth of the prophet, that is, to the natural man, " as honey for sweetness [b]."

Yet this is in accordance with much we find in Scripture; for instance, what could be more sternly severe and full of reproof than St. Stephen's speech at his death? But on that occasion, "looking stedfastly on him, they saw his face as it had been the face of an angel." Thus God arrested their minds till His martyr should speak to them all his burden of sad admonition. In like manner there is something of deep interest and beauty in the visions, the similitudes, and the images which Ezekiel uses, and unwilling minds are held by them till they have heard all his

[a] Ch. ii. 6, 7.   [b] Ch. ii. 10; iii. 3.

warnings; not only thus, but they continue with them unforgotten, and such as will not be put by. Thus our Lord's own warnings of the terrible day of Judgment have mostly come to us under the dress of most striking parables and figures. Who does not listen with interest to the parable of the Ten Virgins; of the Householder taking account with His servants; of the King coming in at the Marriage Supper; of the net which the angels are emptying and sorting on the shore; of the Shepherd dividing His sheep from the goats? These will be always remembered by those who would be most willing to forget the Day of Judgment itself. In like manner the solemn prophecies of St. John in the Revelation, from the types and symbols in which they are expressed, engage the attention of the natural mind, and so carry on and hold up to every age the witness of God.

For these reasons then we need not wonder if the prophet most commissioned to declare messages of judgment, should be found in language most figurative, most picture-like of inspired writers; that the watchman and the witness for the captives should be apparelled, not in the sublimity of the Prophet Isaiah, nor the tenderness of Jeremiah, but in the oriental imagery of Ezekiel.

Again, such types and figures have a life such as no mere words of themselves can have, they clothe themselves with form and spirit, and continue. Thus the images of Ezekiel not only speak of themselves in the place where they are found; but they come up again and are of frequent occurrence in the Apocalypse, as if still waiting for their fulfilment. Thus indeed, much that is in Ezekiel is also in St. John; things which already have been in some sense fulfilled; but even now are fulfilling themselves, and yet to be more largely and worthily fulfilled. The vision of the four living creatures for instance, in Ezekiel, is found again in St. John; it is still before us; still new; we know much of what it means, but we have much more yet to learn. The glory of the Lord coming from the East; His voice like the noise of many waters; the earth shining with His glory⁶; these and many such things in Ezekiel are reproduced in St. John. In both, the angels of judgment are represented as waiting till the children of God are sealed with His "mark upon their forehead." Gog and Magog with their armies are both alike in Ezekiel and in St. John as about to come forth in the times of the end. The assembling of the fowls to the great sacrifice is in both. And especially that subject of many chapters in Ezekiel, the measuring of the Temple and the vision of the Holy City, is marked in both as yet to be. As Joseph said to Pharaoh, the vision is repeated, because it is established of God, and soon to be fulfilled by Him⁷. Thus things in Ezekiel over which the tide of ages seems to have rolled, come up in St. John; all as showing that it shall be perfected in measure, in number and weight; that, notwithstanding the confusion that prevails, there is a secret order incomparable in beauty, and every gem hath its place assigned of God. The memorable vision too of the dry bones has been more than once fulfilled in some sense, but still awaits its last completion.

Now I have said that one effect of types and similitudes such as these is, that they may not die away and be forgotten; thus if we look to those subjects of Holy Writ which arrest at this day most attention in the world, we shall find it is such figurative prophecies; every age, nay, every scene of popular interest, has its interpreters and their readers, who apply such things to passing events; in a manner indeed

⁶ Ezek. xliii. Rev. vii. 2.   Gen. xli. 32.

very inadequate, and perhaps unprofitable and vain; yet, however mistaken, they serve to keep alive the knowledge of them; God will not have them hidden and lost; every time that a conspicuous enemy, real or supposed, springs up, there are interpreters that cry out, and many that hear them, saying, This is the Antichrist that is to be. So that in this way, people are made to know and remember that the great enemy of God has been foretold, is to be always expected, and at any time may be at the door.

Such are some reasons for the symbolic language of Ezekiel; it is a language suited for all times and countries, that never grows out of date, or loses its power. Add to which it may be naturally accounted for by the character and circumstances of the prophet, and the heavy tidings he had to bear. Strong feeling does always naturally express itself in figures and similitudes; it gives vent to itself in burning words that take form and are full of life. Thus the Psalmist first says, "My heart shall muse of understanding," and it is to this he adds of opening his ear to the parable, and showing his dark speech upon the harp. Now Ezekiel was in delivering his prophecies thus eaten up as it were by a burning fire within. "I went," he says[s], "in bitterness, in the heat of my spirit; but the hand of the Lord was strong upon me." For seven days he sat among his people as one astonished ere he opened his mouth. Moreover, he himself was made to drink deeply of the cup of affliction in his prophecies: he was made to them a sign and a terror from the heaviness of his burden, to add weight to his words, "Thou shalt bear thy burden in the twilight, thou shalt cover thy face that thou see not the ground, for I have set thee for a sign to the house of Israel." His wife, the desire of his eyes, was

[s] Ch. iii. 14.

taken from him at a stroke, and he was forbidden to mourn[2]; he had to eat of bread foully polluted that he might so speak the more powerfully[1]: he had to lie on his side in fasting and bonds for many days, to bear the iniquity of the house of Israel and of Judah. "Sigh therefore," it is said to him, "thou son of man, with the breaking of thy loins; and with bitterness sigh before their eyes," in order that they may ask, "Wherefore sighest thou[2]?" Thus it is that in reading the Gospels, we, my brethren, are made to ask, why our blessed Saviour sighs. As St. Paul, lest he should be puffed up by the abundance of the revelations that were made to him, had an angel of Satan sent to buffet him, and had laid on him a multitude of sorrows: so had Ezekiel the like mark of Christ; that his words might have weight as one that bore about in the body the dying of the Lord Jesus. Ezekiel is peculiarly addressed as "the Son of Man," and it is observed by an ancient writer, St. Gregory[3], that it is whenever he is called to the vision of things heavenly he is thus designated by that name in which our Lord Himself ever delighted, when He went about in the power of His Godhead. Thus as a plant which when crushed gives forth its sweetness, as from the grape trodden under foot is the Wine of God; and from the corn thrashed and ground is the Bread of Life: so was Ezekiel stricken of God that he might speak the more powerfully in the likeness of Christ. And O the blessedness of that suffering, the inestimable value of that affliction which gives us power to speak the words of God! And well did he need visions and words of power, for nothing else would reach the hearts of those to whom he was sent. As our Lord

[2] Ch. xxiv. 16.
[2] Ch. xxi. 6, 7.
[1] Ch. iv. 15.
[3] In Ezek. ch. xi.

Himself so often repeated the words, "he that hath ears to hear, let him hear;" so God says by Ezekiel, "He that heareth, let him hear; and he that forbeareth, let him forbear[4]." "Whether they will hear, or whether they will forbear; thou shalt speak My words[5]." "Son of Man, thou dwellest in the midst of a rebellious house, which have eyes to see and see not; they have ears to hear and hear not[6]."

For these reasons the prophecies of Ezekiel, like our Lord's own miracles and parables, present things more to the eye than to the ear; for thus they more powerfully reach the mind. Hence the whole style and character of Ezekiel; where another prophet persuades, Ezekiel sees a sign or symbol and leaves that to speak. This might be shown in instances out of number. Thus Isaiah says, "the law shall go forth from Mount Sion, and the word of the Lord from Jerusalem[7];" but Ezekiel instead of this sees the vision of waters going forth from the threshold of the Temple to the four quarters of the world. He sees, and describes at great length as he sees, the Shepherd and the sheep, the dark mountains, "the cloudy and dark day," and quiet waters[8]. He sees the burning forest, while they cry out in mockery, "Ah, Lord God, doth he not speak parables[9]?" But the end of God is answered by their attention being thus arrested by his visions, for it is added, "then shall they know that there hath been a prophet among them[1]."

He is raised in visions by the Spirit far above; he is among angels and the secret providences of God before they go forth on earth; he sees and hears as it were un-

[4] Ch. iii. 27.
[5] Ch. ii. 7.
[6] Ch. xii. 2.
[7] Isa. ii. 3.
[8] Ch. xxxiv. 12.
[9] Ch. xx. 49.
[1] Ch. xxxiii. 33; ii. 5.

speakable words which it is not for man to utter; and therefore he is called the "Son of Man:" he walks near to the ground and mourns; with a fire within that drinks up his spirit. He sees deeply into the spiritual nature of God's judgments; and that although in things temporal children are punished for their fathers; yet in very deed before God none bears but his own burden, as he explains throughout the 18th chapter; and that amidst temporal judgments which are dark and inscrutable all things work together for good to those that love God. He is set as a watchman to watch for the morning, and descries its light from afar, while fires as of Mount Sinai blend with the milder radiance of Pentecost. He is the prophet of Christ's second coming no less than of His first. As in the Day of Judgment amidst sights and signs the most sublime and terrible, will be manifested wonderful depths of God's wisdom, the reach of His Providences, and the scales of eternal justice; so throughout this Prophet amidst visions and imagery, great, striking, and awful, there occur full and clear enunciations of God's mercy and truth, the rising of His temple, the sublime and wonderful but most beautiful order of His ways on earth, bearing onward the throne of the Incarnate Son of God. Such is the style and the course of this the great seer of Eastern captivity, while amidst all this we hear from him as his one great message the first words of our Prayer Book, "When the wicked man turneth away from his wickedness, he shall save his soul."

Thus then it is that the prophet Ezekiel being so intimately connected with our Lord's own teaching in the Gospels, and being bound up more than any other prophet in the Revelation of St. John, comes especially home to us Christians, the Israel of God in the Babylon of the world;

to them that are for awhile in the furnace of affliction that they may come forth purified; hewn out and broken and fitted by His hand that they may be living stones for His temple that is to be; a remnant ever found in the ruins of the visible Church. "Although I have scattered them among the countries, yet will I be to them as a little sanctuary, saith the Lord God[2]."

One of the Christian fathers, St. Jerome, says that he was used when young to go on the Lord's day into the caves at Rome, where the Apostles and Martyrs were buried; and there in silence and darkness amid the chambers of the dead to meditate on the visions of Ezekiel; and that thus he learned to approach them with awe and reverence, not with idle curiosity, and so in some measure to understand them; seeing light, he says, as in the dubious obscure, and exclaiming, "I have found Him whom my soul loveth, I will hold Him fast and will not let Him go[3]." Thus, "in the cloudy and dark day," in the times of affliction, we may understand Him better than now we do. There is no doubt that the prophet Ezekiel and the Revelation of St. John are especially intended for the edification and comfort of Christians in the last days, those of "the great tribulation." And here I would observe that those who are singled out by the seal of God in their forehead to be safe under those His judgments, are not described as those who have done any great thing, but such as "sigh and cry for all the abominations that are done in the midst of the sanctuary[4]."

One word more of caution; a holy Bishop who has written largely on Ezekiel, the great St. Gregory, has applied it to the examination and correction of our own

[2] Ch. xi. 16.   [3] St. Jer. in Ezek. lib. xii. cap. xl.
[4] Ch. ix. 4.

heart, and building up the soul in righteousness. Thus we know that the temple of God of which so much is said in Ezekiel is in one sense our own soul. Happy he who mourns for all pollutions and abominations that have been there, who puts out from thence all idols, and makes it fit for the indwelling of God. Blessed is he who keeps his heart tender and low to understand His prophets, whether the plaintive voice amidst the ruins of Israel, or the dark harp by the waters of Babylon. Let it not be said of us as it was of the Jews, "We have mourned unto you" with the voice of Jeremiah, but ye lamented not[5]; "we have piped unto you" with the prophecies of Ezekiel, but ye listened as to a lovely song or instrument of music, ye heard and did not.

[5] St. Matt. xi. 17.

DANIEL

And He said unto me, O Daniel, a man greatly beloved.
DANIEL x. 11.

SUCH is the testimony which God Himself bears to the Prophet Daniel, and for this reason we naturally associate him in our minds with the Evangelist St. John; the one as the "man greatly beloved;" the other as "the disciple whom Jesus loved." And what is remarkable, both alike are spoken of in the Church as much for wisdom as for love. Thus it is that to love God is to know Him, and Divine wisdom is ever united with Divine love, as light and heat in the same flame. They that know God must love Him, for He Himself is love, and to them who seek to love Him He imparts this knowledge of Himself. And therefore St. John in his writings speaks of light as much as of love: and it is said to Daniel that, because he is a man of love it is given him to understand.

In both too there was the love of man as conspicuous as the love of God; thus St. John ever dwells on our loving one another; and Daniel seems to have drawn on himself the love of others by his love for them. The first mention of him is that "God had brought him into tender love with the prince of the eunuchs." The heart of the great king Nebuchadnezzar bows before him in worship; and still more knit to him in love is the heart of the king Darius.

He was beloved of them because he loved them. What tender concern does he express for the astrologers: but how much above all for his own people! His exertions with kings are for their sake; his intercessions with God are for their pardon.

And it may be observed that three times as he is designated the "greatly beloved," we find in the margin of our Bibles another reading, "a man of desires;" this may be "a man of love," full of love, all love; love for others, which ever brings love in return, as face answers to face in the clear water: or a man of desires for that which is alone worthy of all desire, all desire towards God, full of earnest, insatiable desire for God; his eyes ever turned to Him, his heart ever pondering, longing, listening for, loving God. On every occasion of need or difficulty did he at once turn to God that he might know what to answer. God was evidently his only rest and confidence; his home, his country, and more than all that he had lost. Three times a day in solemn prayer which nothing could divert did he hold communion with God. Thus also was the beloved disciple afterwards "a man of desires," full of earnest zeal, so that he was called of his Lord "the son of thunder." It was through this love or desire that lying on his Lord's bosom he drank of wisdom.

Oh, what a wonderful expression is this, the man of desires,—this is the highest state of the human soul, to be made up of desire. A soul full of desire is full of prayer. My soul hath a desire, says David, panteth, fainteth, is athirst for God. Of wisdom it is said, "they that drink her shall yet be thirsty[1]." And surely never did a soul of desire so break forth as in those words of the beloved and loving Disciple, "Even so come, Lord Jesus!"

[1] Ecclus. xxiv. 21.

It was these, the desires after God, the love of God, that made Daniel so earnest in seeking Him by humiliation, and fasting, and prayer. It was in thus seeking that he was answered; in this steadfast, unswerving purpose he continued until he was heard[2]. For like reasons in some respects may the character of Daniel be illustrated by a comparison with that of Joseph: in many points they resemble each other: so full was the character of Joseph also of singular love and sweetness; to him God revealed His secrets, as friend does to friend, drew near unto him in visions of the night, and whispered to his secret spirit the interpretations of dreams. He also was brought into love and honour with his successive masters; with the captain of the guard; with the master of the prison; and with the king of Egypt; made by him "the head of the heathen," and "teaching his senators wisdom[3]." But more than all was his love for his own brethren; and he, like Daniel, wept over them in love, and pleaded for them. Again, both were captives and early taught in the school of affliction: the iron was on their limbs and "entered into their soul," both known for purity, both for love, and for wisdom of God; and both were for that reason the best counsellors and best rulers among men, as deriving their wisdom from above. They became wise in human things, by looking away from man unto God. And that which they obtained from above they ever preserved by looking upward: they knew that the pearl of great price was not to be preserved but in a pure heart. If on the walls of the universe they saw and read the fiery Hand which the astrologers and soothsayers could not, it was because in them dwelt the Spirit of Him that wrote.

And this we may see the more strongly, this intimate

---

[2] Dan. ix. 3; x. 2, 3.   [3] Ps. cv. 22. 18.

union of purity of heart with wisdom and Divine love, by the example of Solomon. Of him also it was said while yet young that "the Lord loved him[4]." He also obtained wisdom beyond all men because he sought for it of God. "If any man lack wisdom let him ask of God." But how may "the gold become dim, and the most fine gold changed"!

How was that wisdom clouded, and how did it come to nought! For in him Divine love was lost in earthly, sensual love; whereas Joseph, and Daniel, and St. John were pre-eminently known for purity. In them was fulfilled that the pure in heart shall see God. They were pure in heart; they had visions of God. They saw Him in all His ways, and works, and words; if their knowledge was not like that of Solomon, of the hyssop on the wall and the cedar of Lebanon; yet it was in the spiritual and moral providences, in that which is peculiarly the wisdom of God; so that Pharaoh said of Joseph, "Can we find such a one as this is, a man in whom the Spirit of God is[5]?" And Daniel is ever described by the princes of Babylon as "a man in whom is the spirit of the holy gods," having "understanding and wisdom like the wisdom of the gods."

But in another point likewise did Joseph and Daniel differ from Solomon, that he had not on him as they had that mark of Christ, which is early affliction. By self-chastening thus learned and ingrained deep, their "first love" was preserved fresh and pure to the last. Indeed, even David, the man after God's own heart, and the great Apostle, St. Peter, both fell, though great was their repentance. But of Daniel and St. John it is not recorded that they ever fell away. For in this also is it true that Divine "love never faileth." It is very remarkable that it was while Daniel was yet alive, yea, even while young, for he

[4] 2 Sam. xii. 24. [5] Gen. xli. 38.

had scarcely arrived at middle age, being, as is supposed, but thirty-four years old when, in the prophet Ezekiel, he is united thus with Noah and Job; "Though these three men, Noah, Daniel, and Job were in it, they should deliver but their own souls by their righteousness, saith the Lord God[6]." And not only for his holiness, but for his wisdom also was he so famous, that the same prophet says to the Prince of Tyre, who boasted of his knowledge, "Art thou wiser than Daniel[7]?"

So holy and so wise was he declared to be before death had set the seal on his life. Yet, as St. Augustine observes, though so approved of for holiness and for wisdom, yet he makes the most earnest confession of sin. And indeed very great were his humiliations. He is not a prophet only, but an intercessor with God. It is to be observed that he is not sent to rebuke and reprove his people, as the other prophets had been, but to make himself one with them, to pray for them, and humble himself, as the Priest offered sacrifice for his own sins, and then for those of the people; "confessing my sin," he says, "and the sin of my people[8]." The captivity had done its work; actual idolatry was at end, the voice of reproof was no more raised aloud, but the voice of humiliation and confession was heard as out of the ground; it was Daniel pleading for mercy, fasting and praying, confessing his own sins, and those of his people as if they were his own. And unto this day the Church has no more solemn form of confession than that of the prophet Daniel. Thus Jeremiah and Ezekiel had been sent "to root out, to pull down and destroy," but Daniel to carry out their work, "to build and to plant[9]." For in him repentance had its perfect work, and from the

[6] Ezek. xiv. 14. [7] Ezek. xxviii. 3.
[8] Dan. ix. 20. [9] Jer. i. 10.

desolations of Israel he looked forward and prepared for their restoration.

He was the last of the four great prophets, which four, like the four Evangelists, stand as it were as a whole together, bearing the full witness of God; but Daniel the last, like St. John the last of the Evangelists, stands also like St. John in a different position from the former three. He comes forth the completion and perfection of them in his own person; not as a prophet only, but also as one with those to whom the prophets were sent. Thus we may observe that the part which he bears among the four great prophets is peculiarly his own. For instance, the prophet Isaiah speaks by name long before of Cyrus the restorer and rebuilder of the Temple[1]; Jeremiah foretells the seventy years of the captivity; Ezekiel sees in vision the rebuilding of the Temple: but Daniel carries on all these, and himself takes part in the fulfilment of them. It is he that appeals to Cyrus himself: it is he that numbers the seventy years of Jeremiah, and brings about the accomplishment of them: it is he that gives as it were body and form to the visions of Ezekiel; and stops not at the temporal fulfilment; but goes on to Christ's eternal kingdom, and calculates the years of His coming.

Thus, like St. John among the Evangelists, he may have the eagle for his symbol among the prophets: "They that wait upon the Lord" shall be as the eagle that renews its youth[2], that can rise aloft and gaze upon the sun. The lion, the calf, and the man have their walk on earth; but the eagle "mounts up with wings" towards Heaven, and is there as one of all space. "Her eyes behold afar off," and "her nest is on high;" in the strong place is her abode and her dwelling in the rock[3]. And that Rock is Christ.

[1] Isa. xliv. 28.   [2] Isa. xl. 3. Ps. ciii. 5.   [3] Job xxxix. 28, 29.

And if he is thus as the prophet of God, he then passes, as it were, from the prophet into the saint and martyr; and herein it is given him to resemble, not in character only, but in his history also, the disciple of Divine love; both were martyrs in will, but not in deed; both miraculously delivered from death; both as captives taken into the secret counsels of God, and raised on high to behold His kingdom from afar: both had to wait for it to extreme old age, beholding, like Moses, a further rest for which they longed, but into which they entered not; both were as men not living in one generation only, but belonging to all time; because in visions of God they were present in all succeeding ages to the last. No one, for instance, has so forcibly described these very days in which we live as the prophet Daniel. "Many," he says, "shall run to and fro, and knowledge shall be increased." "But the wicked shall do wickedly[4]." All which is carried out into further description by St. John. Both saw in vision the throne of judgment; the dead, small and great, standing before God; the judgment set, and the books opened[5]; to both it was given to behold "one like the similitude of the sons of men," who was clothed in linen, and girded with fine gold; whose face was as the appearance of lightning, and His eyes as lamps of fire; His feet as brass burning in the furnace; His voice as of many waters, as the voice of a multitude; at whose sight their comeliness was turned into corruption, and they fell with their faces to the ground, till touched and lifted up by Him who is the Resurrection and the Life[6].

Thus was it fulfilled by anticipation, in Daniel, what St. Paul says of the Christian Church: "Ye are come

---

[4] Dan. xii. 4. 10.   [5] Dan. vii. 10. Rev. xx. 12.
[6] Compare Dan. x.; Rev. i.

unto Mount Sion, the heavenly Jerusalem, the company of angels, and to Jesus, the Mediator of the new covenant[7]." Of him more especially might it be said, that he was as a stranger and a pilgrim upon earth, looking for a better country, for a city which hath foundations, whose builder and maker is God. Further, we may observe, that although he did so much for the restoration of Jerusalem and the rebuilding of the temple, yet he himself did not return, but continued an exile and a captive unto the last. And indeed of him and his companions God seems to speak in consolation long before by the Prophet Isaiah, when in describing them he says, "Unto them will I give in Mine house and within My walls a place and a name better than of sons and of daughters, I will give them an everlasting name[8]," which we may well carry on in Daniel's own words, for "they that be wise shall shine as the brightness of the firmament; and they that turn many to righteousness as the stars for ever and ever[9]."

Again, if the sins of forefathers are visited on their children, yet how wonderfully under these visitations do all things work for good for those that love God. Thus we read not long since of the judgment on King Hezekiah, that his treasures should be carried to Babylon and his sons should be captives in the palace of the king of Babylon. And if, as is supposed, Daniel was of the seed Royal, and the descendant of Hezekiah, then was there in this the signal mercy of God, and the remembrance of that good king even in judgment. For Daniel was indeed a captive, but as a captive greater than kings; for Nebuchadnezzar himself fell down and worshipped him[1]; Belshazzar trembled before him; Darius loved, and Cyrus

---

[7] Heb. xii. 22. 24. [8] Isa. lvi. 5.
[9] Dan. xii. 3. [1] Dan. ii. 46.

obeyed and honoured him. The treasures of Jerusalem were there, but he was, as it were, the keeper and defender of them till they should be restored; and when Belshazzar was about to pollute them, Daniel came forth and read the writing, that his kingdom was gone from him, and the restorer of Jerusalem was at the gate.

Indeed where Daniel was, there was the Church of God, the "little sanctuary," He had promised the captives by Ezekiel[2]. As was Melchizedeck among the Canaanites, as Joseph in Egypt, so was Daniel among the Chaldeans: the light of the Heathen, the star appearing in the East, the keeper of Jerusalem in Babylon. If to Joseph was given to interpret dreams, to Daniel far more; to know both the dream untold and the interpretation thereof; if Solomon was given "wisdom exceeding much, and," as it is described, "largeness of heart, even as the sand that is on the sea-shore[3]," in the wisdom given unto Daniel was there largeness of heart, even like as the stars of heaven. For it was a wisdom of things heavenly, kindled by the illumination of Divine love.

Such was the Prophet Daniel, the man greatly beloved, beloved both of God and man; beloved by them because greatly loving both God and man; a man of love, a heart of love, so full of Divine love, that no human things could move him; trained from a child in deep affliction, carried as an exile in the destruction of his home, his country, and his kindred; the family of David laid prostrate in the dust, with his religion a wreck. But wait a little while, and we behold him raised to a wonderful height, beloved of princes, a ruler of kingdoms, the counsellor of counsellors; honoured by the five great emperors of the world in succession, the Babylonian, the Persian,

[2] Ezek. xi. 16.   [3] 1 Kings iv. 29.

the Mede; called by Nebuchadnezzar with the highest appellation he could bestow, even from the name of his own god Belteshazzar, and like that of his own princely son Belshazzar. Yet in all these things was Daniel altogether unmoved, on account of the Divine flame, which outward changes reached not, except to make it burn the more brightly and strongly.

And now what was the one great secret of Daniel? it was desire, a soul full of desire; it was to keep his desire alive, nay, to increase and intensify this desire that his whole life was spent. Other things followed, as his love for man, the love and honour of all; but these were not what he sought, but the love of God. In that he found all. He studied not human things in order to understand them, but he looked to God, the fountain of wisdom. "With Thee is the well of life, and in Thy light shall we see light[4]." As he himself says, "He revealeth the deep and secret things: he knoweth what is in the darkness, and the light dwelleth with Him[5]." The astrologers looked to the stars to know earthly things, but Daniel to the God who made them; the counsellors looked to human laws and customs, but he to God, whose providence ruleth all things, "in the army of Heaven, and among the inhabitants of earth." As it is said of Angels that they learn of earthly things by looking away from earth into the mirror of the Divine mind, thus was it with Daniel. What he wished to understand he set himself, he says, by prayer and fasting to know; when he would come to the knowledge of that which he knew not, he sought it in God by humiliation: "I Daniel," he says, "in those days was mourning; I ate no pleasant bread, neither came flesh nor wine in my mouth, till three

[4] Ps. xxxvi. 9. [5] Dan. ii. 22.

whole weeks were fulfilled; then I lifted up mine eyes and looked⁶."

Hence it was that the more he was exalted, the more did he abase himself; and the higher he was in the favour of God, the more did he lament his unworthiness of that goodness. He knew that Jerusalem should be restored, and understood from the books that the time was come; but on that account he prayed the more earnestly, having faith in God, that it should be. The more confirmed he was in acceptance, the more did he fear God; the more beloved he was of kings, the more fearlessly did he rebuke them: counselling Nebuchadnezzar to "break off his sins by righteousness, and his iniquities by showing mercy to the poor⁷:" and to his successor, Belshazzar, disclosing all the truth. Fearing God, and honouring kings, with fidelity and power, but with love and loyalty unshaken did he reprove them.

It is worthy of consideration, that all the inspired writers, prophets, evangelists, and apostles, indeed all the saints of both the Old and New Testaments, lived under monarchies and kings; none in what is called a free state, or popular government; thus by obedience to man did they learn reverence towards God, and that meekness of spirit which is in His sight of so great price; by looking up to His representatives on earth they were trained to a disposition of loyal love to the King of kings.

All the life and labour of Daniel was to keep alive this heart of desires; for this he fed on pulse, that he might not defile his soul, that his wings might be light to rise heavenward; for this he asked of his three companions, that with him they would "desire mercies of the God of Heaven;" for this "he kneeled on his knees three

⁶ Dan. x. 3. 5.   ⁷ Dan. iv. 27.

times a day, and gave thanks;" for this his sleep was filled with the communings of God as the stars come to view in the night season; for this he "set his face unto the Lord God, to seek by prayer and supplication, with fasting and sackcloth and ashes," in confession of sin; for this he longed for the time as for the morning watch, and calculated the years till Christ's coming, with earnest desire adding to desire, looking and longing for that coming, and hearing in answer these words, "Blessed is he that waiteth [s]."

Such was Daniel, the man of desires; the flame of his soul ever burned upward, and all human events did but stir and fan that flame: he lived among wars and rumours of wars; and not only this, but it was given him to see in visions far more than such in his own times, wars and devastations of armies, aggressions and unjust causes flourishing, and might prevailing; and the time of trouble such as there never was since there was a nation; but none of these things moved him, because he saw them all so fast departing like shadows, and coming to nought, and the Stone cut without hands becoming a great mountain, and breaking to pieces all the kingdoms of the earth; that is, he saw all working together for good, and to the full establishment of the kingdom of Christ, " the Son of Man brought the Ancient of Days," and sitting on His judgment throne. Therefore it was that earthly events, however grievous, troublous, and perplexing, did not shake his confidence in God, because he was a man of desires. These his desires earnestly took hold of God, and of nothing else; these his desires clothed him within and without as it were with a robe of Divine fire; even as the Cherubin, all wisdom; and as the Seraphin, all love.

[s] Dan. xii. 12.

Thus he was not once only saved from death, but all his life was a miracle; to live unharmed with those Heathen kings, was to be all his life in the lion's den; to live amidst those idolatrous nations free from their temptations was to walk in the furnace of fire all his days, and with the smell of fire not passing upon him. And all this because he was a man of desires—of desires that were with God. As such may he be our example in these days of perplexity and war! Our Lord Himself fixes our eyes on Daniel in these the last times. "When ye shall see," He says, "the abomination spoken of by Daniel the prophet;"—"when these things come to pass," He says, speaking of the latter days, "see that ye be not troubled." It is thus in the example of the Prophet Daniel that we may watch the times and the seasons, and in all and through all look to Christ on His throne of judgment, with desire of desires; and seeing Him, may be at peace.

These our passing troubles are but clouds which gather and roll along, and cast their mighty shadows upon the earth before the sun appears.

The very name of Daniel signifies by interpretation the Judgment of God; to that Judgment he ever looked; he had it before his eyes in all things; it was the full manifestation of that Judgment that he saw in vision as the consummation of all: it was ever present with him; and to him alone, of all the sons of men, has it been revealed of that Judgment, that he therein shall be secure, and shall "stand in his lot at the end of the days."

JOEL

The word of the Lord that came to Joel the son of Pethuel.—JOEL i. 1.

GREAT as is the variety in the works of nature, it is no less so in the treasury of God's word. Though by one and the same Spirit, and having mainly one end and object, yet each part differs from every other; and this diversity extends throughout; the prophets, for instance, are quite unlike all the rest; and between the prophets themselves there is a marked distinction of character. We have seen this in the case of the four great prophets; the same richness of variety is even yet more striking in the twelve lesser or minor prophets, as they are called. Not to enter into the case of the others, we may observe this in the three of these minor prophets which are introduced in our Sunday Lessons, Joel, Micah, and Habakkuk. Strongly defined are the individual characters of each, as different members of the same body, while all alike are animated by one life and one Spirit; or as varied instruments of music made use of by one and the same poet or musician, and chosen as best suited for his purpose, according to the character of his message, or the mind he would convey.

Thus the Prophet Habakkuk is remarkable for very striking figurative expressions, which have become familiar in the mouths of all; as e. g. "write the vision and make it plain upon tables, that he may run that readeth;" "they sacrifice unto their net, and burn incense unto their drag;" "the stone shall cry out of the wall, and the beam out of the timber shall answer it;" "He will make my feet like hinds' feet;" "the just shall live by his faith;" "although the fig-tree shall not blossom, neither shall fruit be in the vines," and the like; "yet will I rejoice in the Lord." "The Lord is in His holy Temple; let all the earth keep silence before Him." With these are peculiarly vivid short poetic images, as "God came from Teman;" "He stood and measured the earth;" "the mountains saw Thee;" "the deep uttered his voice, and lifted up his hands on high;" "the sun and moon stood still . . . . at the sight of Thine arrows they went." All this is quite peculiar to Habakkuk; and hence his single sayings are so treasured and remembered.

But Micah is the one of all the prophets chosen to foretell the place of our Lord's birth, Bethlehem Ephrata; being well suited for that purpose, not only as by him our Lord declares the nature of Evangelical righteousness, of mercy being better than sacrifice[1], but because Micah associates the mercies of the Incarnate Son of God with pastoral scenes, well meet for the herald of Bethlehem, with the hills especially of the Sacred Land. As in the Lesson for to-day, "Arise, contend thou before the mountains, and let the hills hear thy voice. Hear ye, O mountains, the Lord's controversy." We are impressed with the majesty of "the everlasting hills," and think as we read of all those Holy mountains which God has made the places of His teaching or His wonders:—the Mount Sinai where the voice of God was heard; the Mountains of Moab with the vision of Balaam; Mount Pisgah with

[1] Micah vi. 6. 8. St. Matt. xii. 7.

that of Moses; Mount Horeb with the still small voice speaking to Elijah; Mount Carmel with Elijah's prayer; Gilead, his birth-place, the mount of healing; Mount Sion, of holiness; the dew of Mount Hermon in the sorrows of David; the Mountain also of the Beatitudes; and Tabor, the Mount of the Transfiguration; and the Mount of Olives with the discourse on the Day of Judgment: and after all these we cannot but add the Mount Calvary. These, "the strong foundations of the earth," stand around, like witnesses of God, as He comes to plead with His people, and appeal to what He has done for them. With Micah the Christian kingdom is "the mountain of the Lord's house, established above the mountains[3]." Such is the proclaimer of Bethlehem, the place of flocks; the prophet of the new law of Christ, the love of mercy, and humble walk with God. His expressions and images are from the field and forest,—of the "mourning owl," and "wailing dragon," and "the bald eagle," and the "noise of the flock;" the Gospel is the rest under the shadow of the fig-tree and the vine; while the remnant of Jacob is "as a dew from the Lord, as showers upon the grass," or as "the flock dwelling solitary in the wood of Carmel." The prophet himself is "as when they have gathered the summer fruits, as the grape gleaners of the vintage, there is no cluster to eat," while his "soul desireth the first-ripe fruit." Thus speaks the Prophet Micah where Jeremiah, in his own characteristic language, says, "where is the love of thine espousals?"

But how different to this is the Prophet Joel; one object fills his mind from first to last, one subject in which he is altogether wrapt; no little sentences of wisdom like Habakkuk, who might be called the prophet of faith; no

[3] Micah vi. 2; iv. 1.

rural images like Micah, who might be termed the prophet of mercy, but one absorbing spirit throughout; and the question is not about expressions, but about the meaning and intent of them. He is beyond all others, and it might be said, solely and entirely the prophet of Judgment. He is full of the trumpet; it is in all he says; the trumpet of Mount Sinai is there, the trumpet of war, the trumpet of calling assemblies, the trumpet to be heard at the last great Day. So that our Church on Ash Wednesday, when she would call on all her people to prepare for judgment, has the Prophet Joel read from the Altar instead of the Epistle; and on the great day of Pentecost itself, the first sermon ever preached in the Christian Church is the declaration of St. Peter in the words of the Prophet Joel[3]. The prophet supplies not only the text, but the sermon. And what is the prevailing tone of this prophet? "The day," "Alas for the day! the day of the Lord," "the day of the Lord great and very terrible;" this is, throughout, his burden. It is one voice, one character, one solemn loud appeal through the whole. No pleasant instrument, as Ezekiel; no pastoral voice, as Micah; no dark sentences upon the harp, as Habakkuk, but the trumpet alone.

But when we come to the detail, and the explanation of particulars, what are we to consider the exact subject of this prophet? it is, but more especially at the beginning, the description of a plague of locusts; such as occurs in eastern countries; the sun is hidden by them, it is "a day of darkness and of gloominess;" "as the morning spread upon the mountains;" "the land is as the garden of Eden before them, and behind them a desolate wilderness;" "Like the noise of chariots on the tops of mountains shall

[3] Acts ii. 16. 21.

they leap, like the noise of a flame of fire that devoureth the stubble." The description is most exact and striking in all its parts. But there is evidently allusion to another subject throughout; another and heavier judgment about to come is associated with the description, and that is the army of the Chaldeans. "A nation is come up upon my land, strong and without number, whose teeth are the teeth of a lion." There was one judgment close at hand, that of the locusts; and there was another yet to come after that, far severer and more enduring, the desolation and captivity of Judah; but yet the prophet speaks as if they were not two distinct things, but one, though in time far apart. The very description itself of the locusts, close and accurate as it is, is at the same time figurative and allegorical of an armed host. In detailing one it foretells the other. Nor is this all; it cannot be so. For we may notice that through the whole there occasionally occur expressions too great for either of these fulfilments, or any thing of a temporal character. It is throughout the great and terrible day of the Lord coming and nigh at hand, "and who can abide it?" In confirmation of which we know that our Blessed Saviour Himself, in His description of the Day of Judgment on the Mount of Olives, takes these expressions of the signs in Heaven from the Prophet Joel, and says they are then to be fulfilled. And St. Peter likewise, on the day of Pentecost, explains these passages in Joel to be the solemn call to repentance before the coming of the Great Day, bringing forward those words to which our Lord had before referred;—"The sun shall be turned into darkness, and the moon into blood, before the great and the terrible Day of the Lord come." And St. John, in the Revelation describing the last days, adduces the like expressions from this prophet: "Put ye in the sickle, for the harvest is ripe : come get you down, for the press is full." These are the words of the Prophet Joel, but in the Revelation St. John mentions this as the saying of the Angel, when "one like unto the Son of Man" descends, sitting upon a cloud, and having "in his hand a sharp sickle." The angel says, "Thrust in thy sickle and reap; for the time is come." And again another angel cries with a loud voice, "Thrust in thy sharp sickle, and gather the clusters of the vine[4]." Then follows in Joel a still more distinct mention of the judgment, "Multitudes, multitudes, in the valley of decision : for the day of the Lord is near."

Now this introducing into the same description many judgments is much to be observed, because it is the case usually in the Bible, with a particular purpose of God, that more than one thing is contained in the same prophecy;— one near and soon to happen, the other more distant; one of things temporal, the other of things eternal. It is the case in our Lord's account of the Day of Judgment; He speaks at the same time of His coming in the fall of Jerusalem, and at the end of the world. Thus the prophecy of Jacob is of some things just about to be, and some after a long time, and some not till the last days. And these descriptions of Joel some explain only of the Babylonian army; others, of the locusts only; others, only of the Last Day; and hence the confusion of interpretation, for it is in fact of all. The vision indeed is but one as present to the prophet's eye; he sees but one scene, though it combines many things—the locusts, the Chaldean army, the array of the last Coming. The events are differing in time, for speaking in the Spirit of God he partakes of the Eternal, and knows not distinction of days; differing in circumstances, but partaking of one character, for they are all of one

[4] Joel iii. 13. Rev. xiv. 14. 18.

judgment of God; many judgments indeed as men behold them, but all leading unto one, and blending into one, and perfected in one, the full and final retribution of God.

Our Blessed Saviour sometimes speaks of things separate in point of time as if they were equally present to Him. For time is short and eternity is long. So is it throughout the Scripture; so will it be with us when released from the body; so even now so far as we partake of the mind of God.

Now the object of thus mixing up things together is partly for the sake of the prophecy itself, that when men see that one sense has been fulfilled, it may be a pledge and earnest to them of the other also. But this is not the only purpose; for it is likewise to teach us that the events of life, even now, to those who will attend to them, do prepare the way and give signals and notes of preparation for the last end of all things; and things are fulfilled in each one of us even now which foretell and foreshadow the great and general consummation. Thus, to take an instance which may come home to us all, some are perplexed in explaining the Scriptural account which speaks of the coming of the Last Day, as speedy and sudden; or of some particular circumstances in that description, as of the failure of the Sun, Moon, and Stars. But each living soul, as he passes through this earthly scene, has a sort of fulfilment of this in himself: for life always seems very short when it is gone, and death always sudden when it has come to each; the sun and the moon being hidden from him, and the stars falling, has in each one of us a fulfilment, when at death this temporal visible scene, this course of night and day, this world in which we behold the sun, moon, and stars, is for ever at an end as far as we are concerned, and our eyes open upon another world which has neither the sun nor moon to lighten it. In the case of each one of us, it is true that "the night is far spent, the day is at hand;" in each it is fulfilled, "Behold I come quickly, and My reward is with Me;" "the sun and moon shall be darkened, and the stars shall not give their light;" "then shall ye see the Son of Man." I do not mean to say that this is the meaning of those sayings, but that thus on a smaller scale we may know that so much is fulfilled among us daily as to keep our faith alive and wakeful respecting the great things foretold of the future.

Another instance of the like kind may be mentioned; when alarmed at any extraordinary visitation men have always been apt to think that the Great Day has come; it is no doubt so intended of God that they should so connect things, and in all His judgments be led to consider the great and the last of all. Now this is what He does here by the Prophet Joel.

I may mention a circumstance which may illustrate herein the mercy and goodness of God. The holy Bishop Ken, whose Morning and Evening Hymns we sing in Church, ever laboured to keep up in his mind a constant and earnest sense of the Last Day; and in a very beautiful Poem[5] of his he represents himself as hearing, in a dream, the sound of the last Trumpet; and that his guardian angel, on his inquiry, told him that this had been his doing; that, grieved at the lukewarmness of mankind, and seeing one of the seven Archangels from God's throne that are to sound the last Trumpet of the Great Day, he had asked him to breathe but one note of that terrible blast in the ear of him of whom he had the charge, in order to awaken him. The holy man goes on to state in his Poem

[5] See "The Trumpet," Bishop Ken's Works, vol. iv. p. 50, edit. MDCCXXI.

that the remembrance of that vision and his thoughts on that occasion made him ever afterwards watchful. To this I may further add the saying of St. Jerome, "Whether I eat or drink, or whatever I do, oh that that Trumpet may ever sound in my ears, Arise, ye dead, and come to judgment!"

We may see then how gracious is this one great lesson which God would impress upon us by His Prophet Joel, of constantly hearing the Trumpet-call and realizing the Great Day. Joel indeed is in this respect the type of the Christian Minister whose office is to "preach" ($\kappa\eta\rho\dot{\nu}\sigma\sigma\epsilon\iota\nu$), that is, to herald or proclaim the kingdom of God, which is as it were to bear the trumpet. They are like the angels whom the Lord sends to gather His elect from the four winds "with a great sound of a trumpet[6]." And of our Lord Himself in the Revelation, when He sent His messages to the Seven Churches, St. John says, "I was in the Spirit on the Lord's Day, and heard behind me a great voice as of a trumpet[7]." Such is His voice in the Prophet Joel. And how trumpet-like, how awakening and alarming throughout is the whole style and strain of this His inspired herald! Some characters are naturally capable of a more sustained and intense contemplation of the great Hereafter than others; and this prophet seems to have been such. Thus when Micah says, "They shall beat their swords into plowshares," Joel on the contrary speaks of their "Beating their plowshares into swords[8]," which is like our Lord's own expression, "I am not come to send peace, but a sword;" "He that hath no sword, let him sell his garment and buy one." As if saying, now is the time for every effort. All is as the season of watching, of earnest

[6] St. Matt. xxiv. 31.   [7] Rev. i. 10; iv. 1.
[8] Micah iv. 3. Joel iii. 10.

preparation, for "the hour is come," "the Day is at hand."

Before concluding, another remarkable point must be mentioned in the Prophet Joel, which is a voice of joy and exultation that is combined throughout with the terrible theme, and pervades each subject of his prophecy. First, when God shall "restore the years which the locusts have eaten;" and, secondly, when on the Day of Pentecost the Spirit shall be poured on all flesh for the restoration of the world; on both of which occasions there occur expressions far beyond any temporal fulfilment; but lastly and more than all, in what is yet to be when the harvest shall have come; when the sun and moon shall fail, but "the Lord shall be the strength of His people," rejoicing over "the remnant which the Lord shall call."

Now in noticing the character of this prophet this circumstance also is full of instruction, as showing that the more we are impressed with a serious expectation of the Great Day, the more shall we be able to look forward to it with joy and comfort. Some have felt this at the near approach of death; so much so that afterwards, on an unexpected recovery, when again taken up by the world, they have complained of losing that peace and joy which they had experienced even at the sight of the King of Terrors, and have missed that light which was around their Lord's presence when He appeared to them in the valley of the shadow of death.

Look always to the Great Day of the Lord, as St. John did, and you will be able to say with him, "Even so come"!

JOB

Ye have heard of the patience of Job, and have seen the end of the Lord.—St. James v. 11.

GOD has been pleased to choose a man in the early ages of the world as an example of patience, and gifted him in a very extraordinary manner, that he might be an inspired teacher unto the very end of time. Patience was the virtue most needful to man in a state of Heathenism and ignorance, yet it is no less so in Christian times; indeed, it may be observed that no grace is spoken of in connexion with the last day more than that of patience. "In your patience," says our Lord, "possess ye your souls." And St. Paul, "The Lord direct your hearts into the patient waiting for Christ[1]." It is set before us as the great perfection of faith. "The trying of your faith," says St. James, "worketh patience: but let patience have her perfect work." And of charity it is said, charity "suffereth long," is long-patient. And above all, in the Apocalypse; the crown of God is in "the patience of the saints." St. John himself is "in the kingdom and patience of Jesus Christ." The praise of Christ is "thou hast borne, and hast patience, and for My name's sake hast not fainted." And "because thou hast kept the word of My patience, I also will keep thee from

[1] 2 Thess. iii. 5.

the hour of temptation which shall come upon all the world[2]." So that the example of Job may be a warm light to cheer and guide in the very night of Antichrist itself; and never more needed than in "the great tribulation." He is for Christians themselves the teacher of patience held out to them by an Apostle; he has been raised as it were into the firmament, there to shine for ever and ever, as a pattern of long-suffering, in the kingdom of God.

And now we cannot but adore the Divine wisdom in choosing this man; and the wonderful manner in which it has been done, when God selected him to put him among the stars to give light unto the world; and why he is so singularly suited for this purpose. For observe how, to clothe his example with attractiveness, and embalm it as a living monument to all ages, God endowed him with a singular power of thought and language; so that for poetic beauty and sublimity there is nothing equal to the Book of Job in the world, from the earliest time to this; there is a greatness of conception in all the words that he utters or details, majesty and simplicity, together with a touching power of reaching the heart; so that it is remarkable how often persons in the deepest affliction are found with the Book of Job in their hands. It is a Divine mirror into which they are given to look, and are comforted: a stream in which we behold ourselves, and at the same time wonders of the deep, jewels of every hue, living things, and reflections of the skies. More than once in our Burial Service the thrilling words of Job fall on our ears; very many of its memorable sentences are in all mouths.

But now Job was a Gentile among Gentiles; and how

[2] Rev. xiii. 10; i. 9; ii. 3; iii. 10.

does this and all other things add a lustre to his example. To teach us patience one is chosen who has no knowledge of the Gospel, nor was Christ revealed to him; he is not even of the sacred nation taught by the Law, by the oracles of God, and the prophets, or the example of the saints, but is one from among the nations, in the earlier and dark times of the world. Nay, he does not appear to have known definitely a future state after death, or that condition of everlasting bliss or grief which makes up for all the evils of this life, and renders its heaviest ills to be but "a light affliction which is but for a moment." For a Christian to be patient who has before him the example of Christ it were not so much; for one to whom the promises of God had been made it were not so much; nor to one who was in covenant with God; but to one instructed only in the wisdom of nature this grace were far more difficult, and therefore by so much the more excellent. And in like manner did all things else respecting him tend to enhance, and perfect, and make bright the example of his patience. For one to suffer poverty, hardship, and sickness, who had always been used to them, the trial of patience had not been so great; but Job was cast down from the very highest state of earthly prosperity. "Thou hast taken me up and cast me down." His former prosperity adds weight to his fall. It were no great trial for one who had always been childless to continue to be so; but for one who had been singularly blessed with children the bereavement was very severe. And again all external hardships are comparatively easy to be borne if health of body remains; but in bodily suffering, as Satan himself said, far more is the temptation to impatience. Yet further, sickness of body itself is far more tolerable if the heart is whole; for "the spirit of a man will sustain his infirmity," says Solomon, "but a wounded spirit who can bear[3]?" whereas anguish and desolation of heart were as the dregs of the cup which Job had to drink. "The arrows of the Almighty," he says, "are within me, the poison whereof drinketh up my spirit; the terrors of God do set themselves in array against me[4]." Yet more—even in desolation of mind it is something to have a comforter in one nearest and dearest, it is a strength of good, and greatly lessens the trial; but to Job all evils were aggravated by the wife of his bosom. And lastly,—the support of martyrs throughout the world has been the countenance of friends who know and value their integrity, and the testimony of their sufferings; but Job's friends laboured to take from him the peace and comfort of a good conscience; he had nothing to support him but the sense of his innocence, and they with much show of wisdom and holiness endeavoured to spoil him of that. Nay, far worse than all, God Himself seemed to have deserted him, and given him up into the hands of Satan.

But now how did every evil in succession add to his crown? In prosperity he greatly feared God amidst blessings so great; but his losses and bereavements drew out his thankfulness; and with unequalled and awful sublimity it is added, "then Job arose, and rent his mantle, and fell down upon the ground, and worshipped." "The Lord gave, and the Lord hath taken away; blessed be the name of the Lord[5]." His wife's evil counsel gave him the opportunity of teaching her wisdom and goodness; his friends' reproaches deepened his humiliation and renunciation of all self-righteousness. It was indeed a contest between God and Satan, and every art of the great enemy was turned to the glory of God, and the perfecting of His

[3] Prov. xviii. 14.   [4] Job vi. 4.   [5] Job i. 20, 21.

saint, whom He foreknew, and chose, and sanctified, and glorified. To the wicked the things that should have been to their wealth are an occasion of falling; but with the good the things that should have been occasion of falling are to them exceeding wealth.

It was not his temptations that caused his patience, but brought it out to view; as the brightness of the firmament comes forth in the darkness. In the time of prosperity he remembered God; he "rose up early in the morning, and offered burnt-offerings" for his sons. And this "continually." Such sacrifices were, though he knew it not, the remembrance of Christ before God, and acceptable to Him. He had the testimony of God beforehand, that there was "none like him in the earth, a perfect and an upright man, fearing God and avoiding evil." And in the course of the book itself, it appears that he had been the very pattern of all goodness; pure in heart, he made a covenant with his eyes; just, hospitable, full of mercy and good fruits, the father of the fatherless, and the friend of the widow, open-hearted, open-handed, open-housed. But one thing he lacked, by tribulation to be brought to the secret knowledge of Christ. To thank God in the midst of blessings, this was much; but from the lowest depth of bereavement to bless God, this was to come near to the hidden mystery of Christ, to the life which is laid up with Christ in God. Fearful indeed and wonderful were his trials, but more fearful and wonderful was his crown. We observed that he was a Gentile, and had not that knowledge which revelation has given us; but by his patience all these wants were supplied. The Gospel had not for him "shed its light on immortality;" but by faith he had what was equivalent to it, he had trust in the Everlasting God; "the eternal God was his refuge," and he felt "beneath him the everlasting arms." He was known of God, and he knew God by faith, and "the knowledge of God is eternal life." He could not speak of eternity because it was not revealed, but beneath his inner soul there was that which leaned on God—the living God—so that his life was with God. And thus "unto the godly there ariseth up light in the darkness;" "He shall never be moved," "for his heart standeth fast, and believeth in the Lord[6]." By patience he put his soul into the hand of God; so that in the destruction of his natural body, by faith he could look forward, and take hold of that great doctrine, the resurrection of the flesh[7]. In the striking expression of St. Augustine, "worms were breeding without, but immortality within[8]."

Again, he knew nothing of Christ as we do; not even it may be as the prophets did, or as Abraham when God's covenant was made with him; but by means of his sore trials in some wonderful and mysterious way he came to the knowledge of Christ Crucified; for in this contest that he underwent by some especial power, or vision of God, that was made known to him, which made all his former knowledge to be as nothing. "I have uttered," he says at last, "that I understood not; things too wonderful for me." "I have heard of Thee by the hearing of the ear, but now mine eye seeth Thee. Wherefore I abhor myself, and repent in dust and ashes[9]." Thus the result of this knowledge was the same as that which appeared in the most signal instances of faith in the Gospels in those who beheld Christ; in St. Peter, in the Centurion, the Canaanitish woman, and others. "Now mine eye seeth Thee, wherefore I abhor myself."

[6] Ps. cxii. 6, 7.
[8] In Ps. xxix. 7. Vol. iv. 196.
[7] See Job xix. 25. 27.
[9] Job xlii. 3. 5, 6.

And now we must consider the trials of Job as leading to this end. When God spake to Elijah, it was not from the whirlwind, nor from the fire and earthquake, but in the still small voice which spake of the meekness and mercies of the Gospel. But to Job, "the Lord answered," it is said, "out of the whirlwind," even as he spoke to Israel out of the fire and earthquake of Mount Sinai. It was out of the whirlwind, the terrible storm of affliction raised by the prince of this world, that God communed with Job; and when He spake it was of His mighty works, of the wonders of His hand in creation; of the gates of death that open at His bidding; of the dwelling-places of the light and the darkness; of the treasures of the snow, of the ordinances of the starry Heavens; of the wild beasts and birds of His hand, the eagle, the unicorn, the Leviathan. For thus God speaks to the natural man of His Almighty power and wisdom, that man may be humbled before Him and learn patience. Thus was Job taught that he might put his hand on his mouth and be humbled before God; and so he was; he rejected not this teaching of God, and thus perfected in the school of patience, he heard at length the "still small voice" which spake of Christ; nay, in his secret spirit, within he beheld Him, and then heard His approving voice.

"Thus," says St. Augustine, "was it given him by inspiration to know beforehand the passion of Christ, and to understand how patiently he himself ought to endure, if Christ in Whom there was no sin yet refused not obedience to His passion, which when Job understood in the pure intention of his heart he added, 'but now mine eye seeth Thee, wherefore I abhor myself, and repent in dust and ashes.' In which great understanding he was displeasing to himself; not as the work of God, but he looked on himself as dust and ashes in beholding the righteousness of Christ in Whom there could be no sin[1]." And in another place the same writer observes of Job, that it was thus Divinely provided that we might see how out of the nations one might belong to the spiritual Jerusalem, which could only be by having revealed to him the only Mediator between God and man, the Man Christ Jesus[2].

All the sufferings of Job were to bring him to this knowledge; before his trials he had the testimony of God that he was beyond all perfect and upright, but this he still needed. Therefore was Satan allowed to try him, and to put forth all his power; and we may be sure from this that the temptations were the most severe that could have occurred to any man; not only in estate, in domestic bereavement, and bodily suffering, but under circumstances which would render these most aggravating. A temper naturally sensitive and quick; his own wife, who should have been his support and helpmate, acting the part of Eve, and becoming herself the tempter; and his friends, that should have comforted him, greatly adding to his sorrows, by attributing them to his own faults. With losses, with wounds, with woes innumerable, with many deaths of those most dear, with reproaches of those that should comfort, he strengthens himself against all with remembrances of a conscience void of offence towards God and man—in hopeless state he maintains still his hope in God, saying, "though He slay me, yet will I trust in Him." After all he had brought upon him the enemy looked in upon him as in mockery, through his wife upbraiding him, and through his friends with much show of wisdom, and

---

[1] De Peccat. Mer. lib. ii. 16, vol. x.
[2] De Civ. Dei, lib. xviii. cap. xlvii. vol. vii.

words smoother than oil, but very swords. In his goods, in his children, in his body had he smitten him, but in all this he magnified God; he had not yet reached his heart; this is what through all he assailed, and all this beautiful and Divine book is of the means he took to insert his poisonous wounds into his soul, but prevailed not. It is not his external calamities, but the wounded spirit that embodies itself in such incomparable eloquence of expression which draws the heart of the afflicted unto Job. Satan had said that a man will give all for his life, but Job shows that his afflictions were worse than death. "Oh that I had given up the ghost," he says, "and that no eye had seen me!" "Why is life given unto the bitter in soul? who long for death, but it cometh not; who rejoice exceedingly, and are glad when they can find the grave." And what was ever so deeply affecting as those his words throughout the seventh chapter and some others? The expressions of his exceeding desolation of heart bring to mind our Lord's own words on the Cross, "My God, my God, why hast Thou forsaken Me?" While under the softness of his friends' words we seem to hear the voice of the great enemy as he spake afterwards through the Jews, "He trusted in God that He would deliver Him; let Him deliver Him now if He will have Him." And then, in his exceeding humiliation, the voice of distressed nature from the lowest depth of affliction in agony of spirit, seems calling out for a Mediator, a Daysman, an Advocate. "If I wash myself with snow water, and make my hands never so clean; yet shalt Thou plunge me in the ditch, and mine own clothes shall abhor me. For He is not a man as I am, that we should come together in judgment. Neither is there any daysman betwixt us[3]."

[3] Job ix. 30—33.

Our Lord Himself in Heaven hears, and seems to take up his words by His prophet: "I looked, and there was none to help; and I wondered that there was none to uphold: therefore Mine own arm brought salvation[4]."

In the first mention of Job it appears that God had set His love upon him. And how was this love shown, but by putting on him this heavy burden of affliction, that thus he might come to know Christ, and to be made like unto Him? He has at the very first the praise of God. "Possessing riches," as says St. Augustine, "he was not possessed by them;" so that when he lost all His gifts he lost not Him that gave. The more poor he was in spirit, the more rich he was in God. He is then cast into the furnace of affliction, and comes out as pure gold, tried in the fire. His friends had said much that was wise and good as became the natural man, according to the wisdom of this world, which is foolishness with God; but they had not come like Job to the knowledge of Christ. This was the great difference. Therefore he whom they had despised had to intercede for them, while they offered sevenfold sacrifices, for they needed expiation for what they had done in ignorance. And he in the likeness of Christ is accepted for them.

To conclude, we see then that great suffering is the reward of great obedience. "My son, if thou come to serve the Lord, prepare thy soul for temptation[5]." None of us knows what may yet await him; if nothing else, yet how the suffering of death, or of sickness which precedes death, may even yet find us out with a deep-searching sorrow such as that of Job.

---

[4] Isa. lxiii. 5.   [5] Ecclus. ii. 1.

And this may be the highest reward of God in this world. "Blessed is the man that endureth temptation; for when he is tried, he shall receive the crown of life, which the Lord hath promised to them that love Him [6]."

[6] St. James i. 12.

ISAIAH

These things said Esaias, when he saw His glory, and spake of Him.—St. John xii. 41.

S T. JOHN here tells us that when the prophet speaks of seeing the Lord sitting on His throne, as described in the sixth chapter of Isaiah, it is of Christ and the glory of His kingdom that he speaks. But the words may be taken as expressing the whole character of the prophecies of Isaiah; "he saw His glory," the glory of Christ, "and spake of Him." Beyond all the prophets he beheld and spake of Christ. And not that only, but the expression *he saw* is peculiarly spoken of Isaiah; his prophecy is called "the vision." "Esay the prophet," says the son of Sirach, "who was great and faithful in his vision[1]." Thus the first words or title of his book is, "The vision of Isaiah, the son of Amoz, which he saw." And again, in the beginning of the second chapter, "The word that Isaiah the son of Amoz saw." A remarkable expression, "the word which he saw," like that of St. John, "That which was from the beginning, which we have seen with our eyes, the Word of Life." But the word "vision" especially belongs to Isaiah, as he seems to behold with the eyes in a vivid and strong manner, and not only to hear of the things which he speaks. As Job says when purified by his trials,

[1] Ecclus. xlviii. 22.

"I have heard of Thee by the hearing of the ear, but now mine eye seeth Thee."

But what is it of which the Evangelist says in the text that Isaiah spoke when he thus beheld Christ? It is of the rejection of the Jews. "He hath blinded their eyes, and hardened their heart: that they should not see with their eyes, nor understand with their heart." This then is the burden of Isaiah. And this vision recorded in the sixth chapter may very well serve to set forth the character, and indeed briefly contains the sum of all his prophecies.

"In the year," he says, "that king Uzziah died, I saw the Lord sitting upon a throne, high and lifted up." As the temporal Israel began to decline and wane away, just before the death of that leprous king who invaded the Priest's office, he beholds the Throne of Christ in the Temple, and the "ministering spirits" giving thanks to the Ever-blessed Trinity, in Whose Name Christians are baptized; and sees the kingdom of Christ filling the world. "Above it stood the seraphims:" . . . "And one cried unto another, and said, Holy, holy, holy, is the Lord of hosts; the whole earth is full of His glory." And then at the sound the door-posts of that visible temple were moved, as ready to depart; and the prophet in humiliation laments his uncleanness, as all the saints do in the manifestation of Christ. "Then said I, Woe is me! for I am undone; because I am a man of unclean lips, and I dwell amidst a people of unclean lips; for mine eyes have seen the King, the Lord of hosts." Here the effect of this spiritual lumination within which God bestows is as it was with Job, who when he says, "but now mine eye seeth Thee," adds "wherefore I abhor myself." So it is with the prophet, "Woe is me! for I am undone."

Such is the spirit which pervades Isaiah's prophecies

throughout. And not less expressive is that which follows. "Then flew one of the seraphims unto me, having a live coal in his hand, from off the altar: and he laid it upon my mouth, and said, Lo, this hath touched thy lips." "And I heard the voice of the Lord, saying, Whom shall I send, and who will go for us? Then said I, Here am I; send me." This alacrity with which he complies, "not disobedient unto the heavenly vision," marks the cheerful love and brave confidence of Isaiah. The very words of his acceptance express the ready obedience of an Apostle, not obedience only, but a willing offer of service. And the Seraphim touching his lips, admitting him as it were into their company about the throne, burning with Seraphic knowledge; and the live coal from the altar; how it all expresses the character of his prophecies; conveying by his words a holy flame into the cold hearts of men, to inspire them with love and Divine knowledge, purifying their hearts as by fire, and this too from the altar; for all is of the sacrifice of Christ, of His atonement and Godhead. Yet wonderful to say, this his Evangelic or Angelic commission is to seal up the eyes and ears of the Jews, for it is added, "And He said, Go, and tell this people, Hear ye indeed, but understand not."

The Spirit of God who marks His manifestations by sensible signs; by the dove at our Lord's Baptism; by the fiery and cloven tongues at Pentecost; He speaks through Isaiah with the altar coal of the Seraphim. And as music partakes of the character of the instrument on which it is played, so the temper of the prophet was no doubt suited to the Heavenly hand and the finger of God. The very mode in which their mission was conveyed characterized the prophets. Ezekiel was given to eat of the roll; the mouth of Jeremiah was touched by the hand of the Lord giving him power of speech; but Isaiah was thus set apart by a yet more solemn and sublime consecration, by the vision of Christ in His Church. Yet further, by Moses in the burning bush was Christ seen as the Everlasting God; by the children of Israel as the Judge in the terrors of Mount Sinai; by St. Stephen standing on the right hand of God to aid; by St. Paul in brightness beyond the sun to convince; by St. John in the Apocalypse as the High Priest that liveth for ever; but by Isaiah as sitting on the throne of His kingdom, and the whole earth full of His glory; and then receiving from the hands of the Seraphim his commission with a loving faith, not as a prophet only, but one might say as an Evangelist and Apostle. It is remarkable, that his very name should signify "the salvation of the Lord!"

And thus we find that when the Gospel was first preached the testimony of Isaiah is referred to as if he had been already the teacher of it all; he bears witness, and witness is borne to him; so that he is more quoted in the New Testament than all the other prophets put together. As soon as John the Baptist begins to preach he refers to the Prophet Isaiah as calling him the "voice crying in the wilderness." When the Bible was given to our Lord Himself to read in His first preaching in the synagogue at Nazareth, it was the Prophet Isaiah from which He read, when He said, "This day is this Scripture fulfilled in your ears[2]." And when He went from thence to Capernaum, it was the prophet Isaiah, says the Evangelist, that described His going as the light springing up in the dark land. When the Baptist sent two of his disciples to inquire if He were the Christ, our Lord called their attention to those particular works which Isaiah had described in

[2] St. Luke iv. 21.

the Messiah. And He Himself when there rejected said, "Well did Esaias prophesy of you[3]." When the Spirit sent Philip to convert the Ethiopian eunuch it was in the Prophet Isaiah that he was reading of Christ. When St. Paul first taught at Rome it was the testimony of Isaiah which he pointed out to his countrymen; it was to the same prophet Isaiah he had so often appealed before in his Epistle to the Romans. And thus it has continued afterwards in the Church. St. Augustine mentions in his Confessions, that when he asked St. Ambrose what book he should read on his conversion, he was told by him the Prophet Isaiah[4]. St. Jerome speaks of wishing to expound him as rather an Apostle and Evangelist than a prophet; as being himself one of those of whom he himself says, "How beautiful on the mountains are the feet of those that preach the Gospel of peace[5]!"

So thoroughly is the Gospel interwoven with Isaiah's prophecies. All the history of our Lord's coming in the flesh is there to be found; the forerunner preparing the way before Him; His birth of a Virgin as our Immanuel; His flight into Egypt; His gentle mode of teaching, with no strife, nor crying, nor voice heard in the streets; His healing miracles, as opening the eyes of the blind, and ears of the deaf; all the particulars of His suffering and passion as by an eye-witness; as the Man of sorrows, set at nought, wounded, smitten with stripes, and stricken, yet silent as a lamb brought to the slaughter; His death and burial; His Resurrection, and His sending of the Comforter; the call of the Gentiles; and His coming again to judgment; and in conclusion of all the final state of the good, and of the wicked, with which his prophecies terminate, of the worm

[3] St. Matt. xv. 7.   [4] Lib. ix. cap. v. vol. i. 276.
[5] Prœm. in Com. Isa.

that dieth not, and the fire that is not quenched. All these he describes expressly; but more than all is his prophecy pervaded and luminated with the Gospel; the vision, the rapt vision into the things of God is so peculiarly his. He is full of warnings and of judgments; and in his near admission unto the throne of God clouds and darkness are round about him; but every cloud is full of light, every judgment is lined or penetrated with the Gospel, its comforts and its glory.

His vision—the range of his spiritual sight—is so extensive, that he mourns not as circumscribed by passing troubles and the rejection of the Jews, but exults and breaks forth into a strain of thankfulness at the call of the Gentiles. "Lift up thine eyes round about and behold; all these gather themselves together and come to thee." "Thou shalt surely clothe thee with them all, as with an ornament, as a bride doeth[6]." Surely if the Seraphims about the throne sing in anticipation of the Gospel it must be in strains such as these of Isaiah. As this prophet says of the Jews, He hath blinded their eyes, that they should not see; so of himself it might be said, He hath opened his eyes and given him to behold His glory. They, when in the midst of it, saw it not: he, though afar off, beheld Him as nigh. They looked upon Him with their bodily eyes, but they beheld Him not: he saw Him in the Spirit so vividly that he spake of His Crucifixion and the scenes of His life as if he had been present. It is as it were vision and not prophecy.

Again; the very words and images with which he describes the Gospel are such that even we, with our knowledge, could find no more glowing or suitable terms with which to speak of it. It is "a tabernacle shadowing from

[6] Isa. xlix. 18.

the heat, a place of refuge, a covert from the storm;" "peace flowing like the river;" "light springing up in the land of the shadow of death;" "sins as scarlet made white as snow;" "salvation appointed for walls and bulwarks;" the wild beasts led by the little child; "the glorious Lord unto us a place of rivers and streams⁷." Nothing could be more descriptive of the prophet himself, in these his Divine gifts, than are his own words, "Thine eyes shall see the King in His beauty; they shall behold the land that is very far off⁸."

Such, then, is the first and greatest of prophets whose writings come down to us; but there is no one whose prophecies are less marked by his own peculiar disposition and character, or which connect themselves so little with the circumstances of his own history. Ezekiel speaks of himself, and Jeremiah much of his own sorrows; but Isaiah does not so. He comes before us indeed in the Book of Kings, but it is only to deliver messages of the same sublime and exalted character as his written prophecies; to Hezekiah on his sickness, and on his recovery, of God's judgments, and the answer of God to the threats of Sennacherib. His miracles, too, are of the same kind, great and wonderful, such as the going back of the sun, and the angel smiting the Assyrian host. "Ask thou a sign," he says in sublimest words to Ahaz, "in the heavens above, or in the depth below." He does not appear mixed up with the events of his time, on which he bore to his people the Divine messages, but seems in spirit apart, as conversing with God. He does not, as David in the Psalms, speak of his own individual trials, in which Christ was the strength of his soul; nor as Jeremiah, suffering with the sins and sufferings of the Jews; but ever sees beyond

⁷ Isa. iv. 6; ix. 2; i. 18; xxvi. 1; xxxiii. 21. ⁸ Isa. xxxiii. 21.

the glories of Christ's kingdom,—and the vast, awful, eternal year. His very first words are, "Hear, O Heavens, and give ear, O Earth," as if about to speak of things which angels as well as men desire to look into.

In like manner of his own history itself nothing is said. It is often spoken of by early writers[9] "as most certain tradition," of which there was no doubt in the Church, that he died a martyr, being "sawn asunder" by Manasses; of whose father, Hezekiah, he had been the friend and counsellor; but these and like trials leading to his martyrdom, are not mentioned in Scripture; it is also supposed that he was, like Daniel, of a princely family, but there is no evidence of this, unless it be in the character of his style of writing. From the throne of kings he is brought near to the throne of God, surpassing in sublimity all the prophets. But in the shadow of that throne he is hidden. Like the Priestly prince Melchizedeck, his earthly belongings are not known, for his life is with Christ in God. In the prophecies which he has to deliver, heavy judgments are conveyed; but they are always the occasion of his looking forward from them to the everlasting mercies which are with God; whatever calamities he had to endure, they are not mentioned by him, for his eyes were looking afar off; and "men have not perceived by the ear," he says, "neither hath the eye seen what God hath prepared for him that waiteth for him[1]." And as the one great subject interwoven with, lying under, in and beyond all his sayings, is the first and the second coming of Christ, so as far as we can learn any thing of his own spirit and temper of mind, it is that especially in which we are to wait for the comings of God. To take and understand his prophecies aright we

[9] St. Aug. Civ. Dei, vol. viii. p. 813. Tertull. De Pat. St. Jerome.
[1] Isa. lxiv. 4.

are to be like him, lifting our hearts above earthly things, heeding them not, seeing them not, on account of the great and glowing flood of light that is poured down afar in the opening of the heavens. "All flesh," he cries, "is grass;" but it is in order to add, "O Zion, that bringest good tidings, get thee up into the high mountain[2]."

To conclude, we observed that ancient writers wished to explain Isaiah rather as an Evangelist than a prophet, now this it is which the Church does for us, and in fact supplies us with the best commentary, by reading this prophet so entirely, both on Sundays and week-days, during this season of Advent. We must all know that passing events, times, and occasions, throw a light upon Scripture, in a marvellous and surprising manner, draw out its meaning, and forcibly apply it, more than any observations of our own could possibly do. And none of us can say how much the reading of Isaiah at this time of Advent has served to furnish us with the fuller understanding of this Evangelical prophet. It thus also serves to carry on and hold up this great light to the last days of Antichrist, as doubtless it has been divinely intended; according to that description given of him in Ecclesiasticus, "He saw by an excellent spirit what should come to pass at the last, and he comforted them that mourned in Sion. He showed what should come to pass for ever, and secret things or ever they came[3]." The time, too, when this great prophet came forward, is to be noticed; it was in the decline of the temporal Israel; all things prepared for their ruin; then it was that the visions of Isaiah were turned to the future; then was faith taught. Something of this kind seems likely to be hereafter.

Again, how was he instated in this his high calling? it

[2] Isa. xl. 6. 9.   [3] Ecclus. xlviii. 24.

was by the coal from the altar on his lips: and what does this signify to us? in an assembly of Christians I need not say; it is the Body of Christ, sacrificed for us, full of His Godhead as with living fire. In approaching we say (*Sursum corda*), "Lift up your hearts," and the answer is, "We lift them up unto the Lord."

The warnings of Isaiah are to us like sounds of the Archangel's trumpet, great, glorious, but very awful. "Hear, O Heavens, and give ear, O Earth," is the sound; for, as the Psalmist says, "He shall call the Heavens from above and the earth, that He may judge His people;" and who are these His chosen? "Gather My saints," He says, "together unto Me; those that have made a covenant with Me with sacrifice."

THE ANTICHRIST

Let no man deceive you by any means: for that day shall not come, except there come a falling away first, and that man of sin be revealed, the son of perdition.—2 THESSALONIANS ii. 3.

ST. PAUL here speaks of the coming of the wicked one before the end of the world, the "man of sin;" and St. John, in his Epistle, speaks of the same under the name of "the Antichrist," or the enemy of Christ, under which name he has ever since been known. St. Paul alludes to it as a subject with which the Thessalonians were well acquainted on account of his instructions; "Remember ye not," he adds, "that, when I was yet with you, I told you these things? And now ye know what withholdeth." And St. John in like manner speaks of it as something which was familiarly known to those early Christians to whom he wrote, "Little children, it is the last time: and as ye have heard that the Antichrist shall come."

Now what I wish to observe is, that these Apostles had evidently made the coming of this wicked man one of the great subjects of their teaching; that when they instructed their disciples on the doctrines of Christ, they gave them warnings about the "man of sin." Because, if it appeared necessary or desirable for the Apostles to do so in those early days, it seems as if it must be the duty of Christian ministers at all times to do the same, to warn their flocks, and instruct them respecting the great enemy of Christ, the wolf that shall lay waste the Christian fold.

But when they search into it, in order that they may teach, they find that they can learn nothing on this awful and important matter, beyond these accidental allusions to it as to a subject once well known. And when we come to inquire of the early writers of the Church in after times, one or two hundred years later, we find that they knew no more than ourselves, having no information beyond what is contained in these passages of St. Paul; and though they were always on the look-out for the coming of this wicked one, and warning others respecting him; yet they say that although it is evident that the first Christians must have known more respecting him, and also of the power that withholdeth, or hinders his coming for a time, yet that knowledge had entirely perished. For St. Paul says to the Thessalonians, " And now ye know what withholdeth ;" but the Church, ever since that time, has not known what it is which keeps down, and prevents the appearance of, that wicked one.

But now we find that there is no important subject revealed in Scripture which stands altogether single and alone, but when we have been informed of it, we then see that there are other places in Scripture where it is more or less alluded to or implied. I will therefore mention some places which have always been supposed by the Church to speak of this wicked man. Our Lord says to the Jews in St. John's Gospel, " I am come in My Father's name, and ye receive Me not; if another shall come in his own name, him ye will receive[1]." And in speaking of the end of the world He says, " When ye therefore shall see the abomination of desolation, spoken of by Daniel the prophet,

[1] St. John v. 43.

stand in the holy place; whoso readeth, let him understand[2]." The word "abomination" in Scripture often means an idol, as we read of the abomination of the Sidonians, and the like; that is, the idol-god which they worshipped. So that our Lord speaks of "the son of perdition" probably under this name. And this is in other words, as St. Paul describes "the man of sin;" "Who opposeth," he says, "and exalteth himself above all that is called God, or that is worshipped, so that he as God sitteth in the temple of God, showing himself that he is God." There are many things on this subject in the Prophet Daniel, and in the Revelation of St. John, but which are difficult to understand or explain. He is spoken of in both of these as the one that "goeth into perdition;" and also, that he shall prevail against, and overcome, the saints; that is, the people of God, or Christians. This overcoming does not necessarily mean that he should conquer them in battle, or any thing of that sort, but that he will deceive them to their ruin. St. Paul says of him, "Whose coming is after the working of Satan, with all power and signs and lying wonders, and with all deceivableness of unrighteousness in them that perish." An expression of St. John in the Revelation is still more strong and fearful than this; in speaking of that time when this wicked man will be revealed, he describes Satan during the whole period of the Christian Church, as being bound or chained by the mighty power of God, but at the end of the world, he says, he "shall be unloosed for a short season." Our Lord in His discourse on the Mount of Olives, says much of this short season so terrible. "For then," He says, "shall be great tribulation, such as was not from the beginning of the creation

[2] St. Matt. xxiv. 15.

which God created unto this time, neither shall be; and except that the Lord had shortened the days, no flesh should be saved; but for the elect's sake, whom He hath chosen, He hath shortened the days." In these places the time is spoken of as being short, and from some expressions in Daniel and St. John's Revelation, it has always been supposed that it will only be for three years and a half.

But now this question will at once occur to us, if it is only to be for three years and a half, how was it of so much concern to the early Christians, that Apostles should warn them so much respecting his coming, and to ourselves now, for we probably may not live to see that time? And again, if this great masterpiece of Satan, which he has been preparing ever since our Lord's Incarnation, this one who is to have the "eyes of man," as Daniel says, although Satan will dwell in him bodily, and give him all power of miracles and lying wonders, so that he will be worshipped as a god; yet still, if it is but one man, and he only continues in full power for so short a time, this can be no great concern to the whole body of Christians of all times. If, for instance, he was to rise at the other end of the world, what concern could he be to the poor of this parish? how could they belong to him, unto their utter condemnation? In short, how could this be a matter of such infinite importance to every Christian of all times, from those Thessalonians whom St. Paul warned even unto the end?

If we look to the passages we have been considering, we shall see the reason of this. Our blessed Lord Himself only went about preaching for three years or three years and a half; He only appeared once in a distant country, for a short time, many hundred years ago; yet we hope that we belong to Him; that we are most intimately united to Him, as much so as those who saw His face in the flesh; that we are made parts of His Body, partake of His Spirit, have our very life hid with Him in God; are knit to Him, are one with Him. In like manner it appears that bad men in all ages of the world may have some connexion with this wicked one; and although they know it not, and think not of it, are all like limbs of one body, of which he is the head; even from Cain, the first murderer, unto the end. It is thus described by good men of old.

Thus St. John in his Epistle says, "this is that spirit of the Antichrist, whereof ye have heard that it should come; and even now already is it in the world." And in another place, "as ye have heard that the Antichrist shall come, even now are there many Antichrists." Even in that early Church, so holy and good, the very pattern to which we look, there were many that belonged to that son of perdition who has not yet appeared. And even then his mark was found. The spirit of the Antichrist was then affecting men's minds so long before he appeared. In like manner St. Paul, when he says that wicked one shall come, adds, and "the mystery of iniquity doth already work." There was some great secret of wickedness which was connected with that wicked one already at work, and no doubt has been at work ever since, but kept under by some constraining power.

The nature also, and the extent of this wickedness, is mentioned. Thus St. John says, "Who is a liar but he that denieth that Jesus is the Christ? He is antichrist that denieth the Father and the Son." And again, "Every spirit that confesseth that Jesus Christ is come in the flesh is of God; and every spirit that confesseth not that Jesus Christ is come in the flesh, is not of God: and this is that spirit" or mark " of Antichrist." Now here every good Christian who will be saved in Christ is described as confessing the Son of God : and it will be seen in these passages that confessing the Son is the same as being guided by His Spirit, and so being found in Christ. And all who are not saved in Christ are said to be those that deny the Son, and they all belong, it is said, to Antichrist. And the same thing is stated in the Revelation, after another manner, where this Antichrist is described. "And all that dwell upon the earth shall worship him whose names are not written in the book of life of the Lamb, slain from the foundation of the world." So that it is clear that whoever does not belong to Christ by living in His Spirit, and being incorporated into His Body, does belong to the great body of Antichrist, that wicked one which is to be revealed. So that we may see it is not a distant matter, nor one that is limited and confined to a short space and a short time; but it is the working of that secret disease within the Church which will at last break out upon the surface, and will then be so intolerable that God will at once put a stop to the world. "For the elect's sake He will shorten the days;" "for a short work will the Lord make upon the earth;" "He will hasten to cut it short in righteousness."

Nothing therefore can be more dangerous and unsuitable in a Christian teacher than to put away from ourselves this name and spirit of Antichrist; as if it were something afar off, belonging to another age or nation; for whatever it may be, it doubtless is at work in our own country, in our own parish, in our own family and household, and, if we do not take great care, in our own heart; for whatever does not bear the mark of Christ Crucified, does bear the mark of His great enemy, who is some day to be manifested upon earth with all the power of Satan, and to be admired and worshipped as God, and to prevail;—until the Lord shall destroy him "by the breath of His mouth," and "the brightness of His coming."

The same will appear in St. Paul's description, as it does in St. John; and here it is more evident in the original Greek than in the English, where it is not "the wicked one," but "the lawless one." St. Paul says, "when that which hindereth is taken out of the way, then shall the lawless one be revealed," for "the mystery of the lawlessness is already at work." What St. John calls the "Antichrist," St. Paul names "the lawless one;" and what St. John mentions as "the spirit of Antichrist already come," St. Paul describes as "the mystery of the lawlessness already working." Even from that time till now corruption has been working against the law and the Spirit of Christ, which will at length give rise to His great enemy in the flesh. And this word "lawlessness" is the same which our Lord Himself uses respecting it, which is translated in our version "iniquity," "because that iniquity shall abound," i. e. that "the lawlessness shall abound" or be multiplied, "love shall wax cold." "The mystery of the lawlessness is working," says St. Paul; and because men received not the love of the truth, God shall send on them a strong delusion, and they shall believe "the lie," or "the false one."

This gathering together through all Christian times of a vast multitude who belong to that wicked one who is to appear at last is set forth in many parts of Scripture; and especially in the Revelation of St. John. It is there represented that Satan has disappeared from sight who used to possess the bodies of men, and to be worshipped in idol temples, and speak through Heathen oracles; he is said to be bound by a chain, but that now he is working secretly in drawing men off from the love and the law of Christ, and when he has sufficiently prevailed he will again be manifest, he will draw all men to him, except a small remnant, by raising up the wicked one, the man of sin, and causing him to be worshipped; and as the Revelation describes it, "Satan will himself be let loose for a short season;" what our Lord calls "the great tribulation." Throughout the Revelation there seems to be a secret gathering as for a great battle at the end; a mustering together throughout the whole period of Christianity which will at last be revealed. "The spirits of devils," it is said, "shall go forth unto the whole world, to gather them to the battle of the great day of God Almighty." "Blessed is he that watcheth." And again it is said, "Satan shall be loosed out of his prison, and shall go out to deceive the nations which are in the four quarters of the earth, Gog and Magog, to gather them together to battle; the number of whom is as the sand of the sea. And they went up on the breadth of the earth, and compassed the camp of the saints about, and the beloved city." The words "Gog and Magog" do not mean any particular place or nation, but are spiritual or mystical expressions, meaning hiding-places; it means the wickedness which is now kept under and hidden will be revealed; and "the camp of the saints" does not mean any particular place, but good people, wherever they are to be found. As our Lord says, of the same, "Then shall many be offended, and shall betray one another, and shall hate one another." "The brother shall betray the brother to death, and the father the son." But by using the words "Gog and Magog," St. John means to say that the account of it all will be found under those names in the Prophet Ezekiel. For

Ezekiel, throughout some long chapters, describes some great and fearful conflict which is to take place, he says, "in the latter days;" and although it is known to be the account of the overflowings of ungodliness, yet it has never been understood.

Now it is not at all known what it is that lets or hinders the manifestation of the wicked one, for though St. Paul says to the Thessalonians, "And now ye know what withholdeth," showing that the Apostles had then explained it, yet it has never been known since. But in the early Church many thought it was the Heathen Roman Empire; and nothing can show more strongly the terrible alarm of the early Christians respecting this "the man of sin," "the son of perdition," than this, that we find it mentioned[3], that they used to pray for the safety of the Roman Empire, and exhorted one another to do so, because it was supposed to be the power that hindereth the coming of the wicked one. They prayed for the continuance even of that Heathen idolatrous empire which at that very time was persecuting them, and putting to cruel deaths those early martyrs, because some supposed that when it was taken away would come the great enemy of Christ. That the Roman empire was the power that hindered was only the opinion of some, who at the same time say that there was also another opinion, that it was the good Spirit of God and His Church that hindered. Now time has shown that it was not the Heathen empire of Rome that hindered, because that has long ago ceased to exist, and the Lawless one is not yet come; and therefore it may be that the Church of God is that power which still keeps under the outbreaking of infidelity. There are many places in Scripture which render this opinion probable with some expla-

[3] As by St. Augustine, Tertullian, Lactantius.

nation. And I think, if we might venture to judge at all for ourselves on such a subject, we should be disposed to think that the Church visible throughout the world, however corrupt it is and unfaithful to her high calling, nay, even as Scripture describes the Holy City of old, "adulterous" in God's sight from its loving the world more than God, yet, I say, that notwithstanding all this, it keeps down the spirit of lawlessness, the great revelation of the man of sin.

However that may be, this is certain, that from the times of St. John and St. Paul there has been going on the secret working of some great wickedness, and that when it is sufficiently strong it will break out in such a manner as to make all the tribulation and all the wickedness that has ever been in the world, and all the horrors of the worst days, to be as nothing in comparison with it. Of what nature it will be is impossible for us to conceive. We might long to know more about this wicked one, and might think ourselves very wise if we could find out. But it is impossible. Nor can any human wit, or learning, or power, afford the slightest protection or escape. "Fear, and the pit, and the snare," says Isaiah, speaking of it, "are upon thee, O inhabitant of the earth. And it shall come to pass, that he who fleeth from the noise of the fear shall fall into the pit; and he that cometh up out of the midst of the pit shall be taken in the snare[4]."

But although it is not given to us to know respecting this wicked one, yet what is of far greater importance, we can avoid having on us his mark, as Holy Scripture calls it; for every one that has on him the mark of this wicked one, the son of perdition, St. John says in the Revelation, will be cast into the lake burning with fire and brimstone[5]. It is impossible, I say, for human ability to escape the

[4] Isa. xxiv. 18.   [5] Rev. xiv. 9, 10.

snare, for it is called the "strong delusion," "all deceivableness of unrighteousness in them that perish." His "coming" is said to be "after the working of Satan with all power," the effect of seducing spirits that will go forth to deceive. But all this we are told will come upon men because they love not the truth. Human wit cannot save us, but the love of God will. It is from the love of God waxing cold that it will take its rise. It will be on account of great corruption and wickedness that God will withdraw His protection; then Satan will have his will and prevail, and will bring forth the man of sin.

We have witnessed many instances of this in what may be called a small and limited scale. A great many countries, once Christian, comprehending many places where the Apostles founded Churches, and which long continued as bright lights of the world; yet now those countries for many hundred years have been followers of the false Prophet Mahomet, a sensual and unprincipled impostor. But what was the reason of their being given over to such a strange delusion as this? It was in this case, because they had become so very corrupt before, idolatrous and sensual. Something of the same kind is now going on in America, in what is called Mormonism; they receive a great impostor, because their minds were before prepared for him. We know to what an extent the god of this world, the spirit of mammon, had eaten out the heart of true Christian faith, before this great manifestation of infidelity went out from among them. For we may be sure that God would never allow such an infatuation as this to prevail, were not men before very far gone from the love of the truth. Many instances of this kind might be mentioned to show that when false prophets arise and deceive many, it is on account of men in those countries provoking God by sins beforehand; and therefore that it is according to the usual mode of God's dealing, that great wickedness will first spread and deepen, before He will give men over to the coming of the wicked one.

But I forbear mentioning these, because it is not desirable to speculate and send our thoughts abroad on this great mystery, but to bring it home to ourselves. There are already, says St. John, many Antichrists, and the spirit of Antichrist is already come. This therefore is what the Revelation calls the mark of belonging to the son of perdition. And what is it? St. John explains, it is he says, "he that confesseth not that Jesus Christ is come in the flesh," for "every spirit that confesseth that Jesus Christ is come in the flesh is of God." And again, "He is Antichrist that denieth the Father and the Son." And we know what our Lord Himself says in the Gospels on denying and confessing Him, that he that denieth Him shall be denied before the angels of God, and he that confesseth Him shall be acknowledged by Him at the last day. And in the same places our Lord explains what it is to deny or to confess Him—that to love father or mother or any thing in the world more than Him is to be not worthy of Him. To confess Christ as our God come in the flesh is to hold to Him in all things in a manner worthy of Him. Wonderful and great is the power of him who in faith abides in Him as God. "The spirit of the Antichrist is in the world," says St. John, "but greater is He that is in you, than he that is in the world." So much greater is the power of Christ than that of the wicked one, that Christ is said to destroy him by "the breath of His mouth." So that very great indeed is our strength if we abide in Him. The power and fearfulness of Antichrist is far beyond any thing we are apt to conceive of him; yet compared with the power of Christ it is absolutely nothing. How then shall we escape, if we neglect so great salvation? Confessing Christ come in the flesh means believing Christ to be God; no belief in Him short of this is what St. John means, or is a saving faith. It is a faith and a confession in which we are to grow more and more, being made by it a part of His living Body, partaking of His life, and as our Lord Himself says, abiding in Him as the branch abides in the vine. This is our safety.

If again we turn to St. Paul's description he says, "The lawless one" cometh, and "the mystery of lawlessness already worketh until that wicked one shall be revealed." The mystery of lawlessness, that must mean some secret working of disobedience. The law of God gives light and converts the soul; the laws of Scripture, the laws of Christ's kingdom on earth, the laws of the Church, and even in some degree the laws of human government, are laws of God, which we are commanded to obey for conscience' sake. But the law of all laws, the highest and best of all laws, is that of the Spirit of God dwelling within us. For even by natural conscience, St. Paul says, that the heathen are a law unto themselves. How much more is the perfect law of God's Spirit within us? Surely it is in obeying this most of all, even in the most trivial matter, that we shall be furthest from the spirit of Antichrist. Obedience to the law of Christ, wheresoever it will carry us, in all matters, bringing every thought into His obedience; this is being armed against the evil day.

A consideration of these times which are to come is calculated to have a very sobering and chastening effect upon our minds: the Jews of old looked forward to a bright earthly future because they expected in the flesh the great Deliverer of mankind, the King of Israel and His kingdom of peace; they had high hopes in looking forward, and therefore they thought much of leaving children behind them and an inheritance in that holy land where the promised Messiah was expected. But the reverse of all this is the case with the Christian; all that he has to look forward to on earth before the coming of the Judge are days of evil such as never before have been, and with them the wicked one being revealed. His earthly hopes are cut off and covered with a black cloud, in order that his treasure may be elsewhere and his heart more turned to Heaven. For this reason it is to be lamented that those which were once Apostolic warnings, sounding throughout the Church, have so much ceased among us. And Christians have been on all sides looking forward to great things upon earth, which has become a great snare to them, leading to impatience and vain, visionary hopes of all kind. Some for earthly liberty, not considering that nothing comes more near to what Scripture calls "lawlessness," which is to prepare the way for the son of perdition. Some think themselves worthy of nothing less than an infallible Church, and sure light, and constant miracles, to prove to them how much God is with them, that seeking for a sign which made our Lord to sigh deeply in spirit, knowing how much it would be so when Antichrist would come in with seducing spirits, and lying wonders, and very high promises. And surely the common evils of life must have lost much of their power to one who considers what is to be on earth before Christ appears; for what are riches and honour in such a world? What is more calculated to teach us in all things moderation of mind? Death is awful, but it loses half its terrors when considered as delivering us from the evil to come upon the earth. This is often alluded to in the Scriptures. It is in speaking of the temptations of Antichrist, and of those that receive his mark being tormented in fire and brimstone for ever and ever, that it is said in the Revelation, "I heard a voice from Heaven, saying, Blessed are the dead that die in the Lord." Blessed indeed will be the dead at that time who have escaped the snare and the sufferings which will be upon the earth. "Wherefore I praised the dead which are already dead more than the living."

Another consideration which this subject will suggest to us is great care for the young, those who are more likely than ourselves to see those days. That they should be baptized and instructed and confirmed. That they should be strengthened in good principles, and for no prospect of worldly advantage exposed to temptation. And that when we can do nothing else we should not cease to pray for them, knowing not what trials they may have to undergo. An early writer[6] speaks of Antichrist as that wicked one who shall put out the sun of this world. This well expresses what Scripture leads us to expect of all spiritual light being in a great manner lost at that time. "His kingdom," says St. John in the Revelation, "was full of darkness." And in allusion to this our Lord Himself seems to say, "Yet a little while is the light with you, walk while ye have the light, lest darkness come upon you." "While ye have the light, believe in the light, and walk as children of the light."

Indeed another great advantage we shall gain by bearing in mind the coming of those evil days is this, that we shall better understand the Holy Scriptures; for they speak very much throughout of those last days. In the

[6] Lactantius.

Prophets there are whole chapters on the subject; but more particularly are there frequent allusions to it even when other lesser matters are spoken of. It has been supposed that the Psalms throughout have an especial reference to the man of sin and his days. An ancient writer in explaining the Book of Job interprets many things of the son of perdition. These passages in the Scriptures need not be mentioned, because if your minds are deeply impressed with this expectation as Christians used to be, you will see it for yourselves, and in the daily reading of the Psalms it will give a force and meaning to many expressions more than you have been used to see in them.

But like a shadow from the heat, a covert from the storm, a resting-place in the water-floods, a light most welcome in the darkness, a delight and counsellor, will be the four Gospels, and what you read therein of Jesus Christ going about and doing good, and healing all that were oppressed of the devil. May we think of these things till we find more and more no consolation on earth equal to that of reading the Holy Scriptures, and communion with God in prayer, and in His blessed Sacraments.

THE END.

April, 1870.

New Works

IN COURSE OF PUBLICATION

BY

Messrs. RIVINGTON,

WATERLOO PLACE, LONDON;

HIGH STREET, OXFORD; TRINITY STREET, CAMBRIDGE.

The Origin and Development of Religious Belief.
By **S. Baring-Gould**, M.A., Author of "Curious Myths of the Middle Ages."
    Part I. Heathenism and Mosaism. 8vo. 15*s*.
    Part II. Christianity. (*In the Press.*)

The Pope and the Council.
By **Janus**. Authorized Translation from the German.
    Third Edition, revised. Crown 8vo. 7*s*. 6*d*.

London, Oxford, and Cambridge

A

Our Lord's Passion;

being the Seventh Volume of a DEVOTIONAL COMMENTARY ON THE GOSPEL NARRATIVE (v. page 28).

By the Rev. **Isaac Williams**, B.D., late Fellow of Trinity College, Oxford.

New Edition. Crown 8vo. 5s.

The First Book of Common Prayer

of Edward VI. and the Ordinal of 1549; together with the Order of the Communion, 1548.

Reprinted entire, and Edited by the Rev. **Henry Baskerville Walton**, M.A., late Fellow and Tutor of Merton College. With Introduction by the Rev. **Peter Goldsmith Medd**, M.A., Senior Fellow and Tutor of University College, Oxford.

Small 8vo. 6s.

A Manual for the Sick; with other

Devotions.

By **Lancelot Andrewes**, D.D., sometime Lord Bishop of Winchester.

Edited with a Preface by **H. P. Liddon**, M.A., Canon of St. Paul's.

Large type. With Portrait. 24mo. 2s. 6d.

The Pursuit of Holiness:

a Sequel to "Thoughts on Personal Religion," intended to carry the Reader somewhat farther onward in the Spiritual Life.

By **Edward Meyrick Goulburn**, D.D., Dean of Norwich.

Second Edition. Small 8vo. 5s.

Apostolical Succession in the Church

of England.

By the Rev. **Arthur W. Haddan**, B.D., Rector of Barton-on-the-Heath, and late Fellow of Trinity College, Oxford.

8vo. 12s.

London, Oxford, and Cambridge

The Priest to the Altar; or, Aids to
the Devout Celebration of Holy Communion; chiefly after the Ancient Use of Sarum.

Second Edition. Enlarged, Revised, and Re-arranged with the Secretæ, Post-Communion, &c., appended to the Collects, Epistles, and Gospels, throughout the Year.
8vo. 7s. 6d.

Walter Kerr Hamilton: Bishop of
Salisbury. A Sketch, Reprinted, with Additions and Corrections, from "The Guardian."
By **H. P. Liddon**, M.A., Canon of St. Paul's.
Second Edition. 8vo, limp cloth, 2s. 6d.
Or, bound with the Sermon "Life in Death," 3s. 6d.

Newman's (J. H.) Parochial and Plain
Sermons.
Edited by the Rev. **W. J. Copeland**, Rector of Farnham, Essex. From the Text of the last Editions published by Messrs. Rivington.
Complete in 8 Vols. Crown 8vo. 5s. each.

Newman's (J. H.) Sermons bearing upon
Subjects of the Day.
Edited by the Rev. **W. J. Copeland**, Rector of Farnham, Essex. From the Text of the last Edition published by Messrs. Rivington. With Index of Dates of all the Sermons.
Printed uniformly with the "Parochial and Plain Sermons."
In One Volume. Crown 8vo. 5s.

Brighstone Sermons.
By **George Moberly**, D.C.L., Bishop of Salisbury.
Crown 8vo. 7s. 6d.

The Characters of the Old Testament.
In a Series of Sermons.
By the Rev. **Isaac Williams**, B.D., late Fellow of Trinity College, Oxford.
New Edition. Crown 8vo. 5s.

Female Characters of Holy Scripture.
In a Series of Sermons.
By the Rev. **Isaac Williams**, B.D., late Fellow of Trinity College, Oxford.
New Edition. Crown 8vo. 5s.

The Divinity of our Lord and Saviour
Jesus Christ; being the Bampton Lectures for 1866.
By **Henry Parry Liddon**, M.A., Canon of St. Paul's.
Fourth Edition. Crown 8vo. 5s.

Sermons preached before the University
of Oxford.
By **Henry Parry Liddon**, M.A., Canon of St. Paul's.
Third Edition, revised. Crown 8vo. 5s.

The Life of Madame Louise de France,
Daughter of Louis XV., also known as the Mother Térèse de S. Augustin. By the Author of "Tales of Kirkbeck."
Crown 8vo. 6s.

John Wesley's Place in Church His-
tory Determined, with the aid of Facts and Documents unknown to, or unnoticed by, his Biographers.

By **R. Denny Urlin**, M.R.I.A., of the Middle Temple, Barrister-at-Law.

With a New and Authentic Portrait. Small 8vo. 5s. 6d.

The Treasury of Devotion: a Manual
of Prayers for general and daily use.

Compiled by a Priest. Edited by the Rev. **T. T. Carter**, M.A., Rector of Clewer, Berks.

16mo, 2s. 6d. ; limp cloth, 2s.

Bound with the Book of Common Prayer. 3s. 6d.

The Guide to Heaven: a Book of
Prayers for every Want. For the Working Classes.

Compiled by a Priest. Edited by the Rev. **T. T. Carter**, M.A., Rector of Clewer, Berks.

Crown 8vo, 1s. 6d.; limp cloth, 1s.

A Dominican Artist: a Sketch of the
Life of the Rev. Père Besson of the Order of St. Dominic.

By the Author of "Tales of Kirkbeck," "The Life of Madame Louise de France," &c.

Crown 8vo. 9s.

The Reformation of the Church of
England; its History, Principles, and Results. A.D. 1514—1547.

By **John Henry Blunt**, M.A., Vicar of Kennington, Oxford, Editor of "The Annotated Book of Common Prayer," Author of "Directorium Pastorale," &c., &c.

Second Edition. 8vo. 16s.

London, Oxford, and Cambridge

Quiet Moments: a Four Weeks' Course
of Thoughts and Meditations, before Evening Prayer and at Sunset.
By Lady Charlotte Maria Pepys.
New Edition. Small 8vo. 2s. 6d.

Morning Notes of Praise:
A Series of Meditations upon the Morning Psalms.
By **Lady Charlotte Maria Pepys.**
New Edition. Small 8vo. 2s. 6d.

Plain Scriptural Thoughts on Holy
Baptism.
By the Rev. **John Wallas**, M.A., Perpetual Curate of Crosscrake, Westmoreland.
Crown 8vo. 6s.

A Manual of Plain Devotions, adapted
for Private and for Family Use.
By the Rev. **John Wallas**, M.A., Perpetual Curate of Crosscrake, Westmoreland.
Second Edition. Small 8vo. 2s.

The History of Tonbridge School, from
its Foundation in 1553 to the present Date.
By **Septimus Rivington**, B.A., Trinity College, Oxford.
With Illustrations. Small 4to. 14s.

The Manor Farm: a Tale.
By **M. C. Phillpotts**, Author of "The Hillford Confirmation."
With Four Illustrations. Small 8vo. 3s. 6d.

London, Oxford, and Cambridge

The Virgin's Lamp:

Prayers and Devout Exercises for English Sisters, chiefly composed and selected by the late Rev. **J. M. Neale**, D.D., Founder of St. Margaret's, East Grinstead.

Small 8vo. 3s. 6d.

Catechetical Notes and Class Questions,

Literal and Mystical; chiefly on the Earlier Books of Holy Scripture.

By the late Rev. **J. M. Neale**, D.D., Warden of Sackville College, East Grinstead.

Crown 8vo. 5s.

Sermons for Children; being Thirty-

three short Readings, addressed to the Children of S. Margaret's Home, East Grinstead.

By the late Rev. **J. M. Neale**, D.D., Warden of Sackville College.

Second Edition. Small 8vo. 3s. 6d.

The Witness of the Old Testament to

Christ. The Boyle Lectures for the Year 1868.

By the Rev. **Stanley Leathes**, M.A., Professor of Hebrew in King's College, London, and Incumbent of St. Philip's, Regent Street.

8vo. 9s.

The Witness of St. Paul to Christ;

being the Boyle Lectures for 1869. With an Appendix, on the Credibility of the Acts, in Reply to the Recent Strictures of Dr. Davidson.

By the Rev. **Stanley Leathes**, M.A., Professor of Hebrew in King's College, London, and Incumbent of St. Philip's, Regent Street.

8vo. 10s. 6d.

Honoré de Balzac.

Edited, with English Notes and Introductory Notice, by **Henri Van Laun**, formerly French Master at Cheltenham College, and now Master of the French Language and Literature at the Edinburgh Academy. Being the first Volume of Selections from Modern French Authors.

Crown 8vo. 3*s.* 6*d.*

H. A. Taine.

Edited, with English Notes and Introductory Notice, by **Henri Van Laun**, formerly French Master at Cheltenham College, and now Master of the French Language and Literature at the Edinburgh Academy. Being the second Volume of Selections from Modern French Authors.

Crown 8vo. 3*s.* 6*d.*

The Greek Testament.

With a Critically revised Text; a Digest of Various Readings; Marginal References to Verbal and Idiomatic Usage; Prolegomena; and a Critical and Exegetical Commentary. For the use of Theological Students and Ministers.

By **Henry Alford**, D.D., Dean of Canterbury.

4 Vols. 8vo. 102*s.*

The Volumes are sold separately as follows:—

Vol. I.—The Four Gospels. *Sixth Edition.* 28*s.*
Vol. II.—Acts to II. Corinthians. *Fifth Edition.* 24*s.*
Vol. III.—Galatians to Philemon. *Fourth Edition.* 18*s.*
Vol. IV.—Hebrews to Revelation. *Third Edition.* 32*s.*

Dean Alford's Greek Testament.

With English Notes, intended for the Upper Forms of Schools, and for Pass-men at the Universities. Abridged by **Bradley H. Alford**, M.A., late Scholar of Trinity College, Cambridge.

Crown 8vo. 10*s.* 6*d.*

London, Oxford, and Cambridge

Elementary Algebra.
By **James Hamblin Smith**, M.A., Gonville and Caius College, and Lecturer at St. Peter's College, Cambridge.

New Edition. Crown 8vo. 6s. 6d.

Elementary Trigonometry.
By **James Hamblin Smith**, M.A., Gonville and Caius College, and Lecturer at St. Peter's College, Cambridge.

Second Edition, Revised and Enlarged. Crown 8vo. 4s. 6d.

Elementary Statics.
By **James Hamblin Smith**, M.A., Gonville and Caius College, and Lecturer at St. Peter's College, Cambridge.

Royal 8vo. 5s.

Elementary Hydrostatics.
By **James Hamblin Smith**, M.A., Gonville and Caius College, and Lecturer at St. Peter's College, Cambridge.

New Edition. Crown 8vo. (*In the Press.*)

Arithmetic, Theoretical and Practical.
By **W. H. Girdlestone**, M.A., of Christ's College, Cambridge, Principal of the Theological College, Gloucester.

New and Revised Edition. Crown 8vo. 6s. 6d.

Also an Edition for Schools. Small 8vo. 3s. 6d.

London, Oxford, and Cambridge

Classical Examination Papers.

Edited, with Notes and References. By **P. J. F. Gantillon**, M.A., sometime Scholar of St. John's College, Cambridge, Classical Master in Cheltenham College.

Crown 8vo. (*In the Press.*)

Materials and Models for Greek and

Latin Prose Composition. Selected and arranged by **J. Y. Sargent**, M.A., Tutor, late Fellow of Magdalen College, Oxford; and **T. F. Dallin**, M.A., Fellow and Tutor of Queen's College, Oxford.

Crown 8vo. (*In the Press.*)

The Story of the Gospels.

In a single Narrative, combined from the Four Evangelists, showing in a new translation their unity. To which is added a like continuous Narrative in the Original Greek.

By the Rev. **William Pound**, M.A., late Fellow of St. John's College, Cambridge, Principal of Appuldurcombe School, Isle of Wight.

In 2 Vols. 8vo. 36s.

The Lyrics of Horace.

Done into English Rhyme. By **Thomas Charles Baring**, M.A., late Fellow of Brasenose College, Oxford.

Small 4to. (*In the Press.*)

A Plain and Short History of England

for Children: in Letters from a Father to his Son. With a Set of Questions at the end of each Letter.

By **George Davys**, D.D., late Bishop of Peterborough.

New Edition, with Twelve coloured Illustrations.

Square Crown 8vo. 3s. 6d.

A cheap Edition for Schools, with portrait of Edward VI.

18mo. 1s. 6d.

Eirenicon, Part III. Is Healthful
Reunion Impossible? A Second Letter to the Very Rev. J. H. Newman, D.D.
By the Rev. **E. B. Pusey**, D.D., Regius Professor of Hebrew, and Canon of Christ Church, Oxford.
8vo. 6s.

A Course of Lectures delivered to Can-
didates for Holy Orders, comprising a Summary of the whole System of Theology. To which is prefixed an Inaugural Address.
By **John Randolph**, D.D. (sometime Bishop of London).
Vol. I. Natural and Revealed.
Vol. II. Historical.
Vol. III. Doctrinal.
3 Vols. 8vo. 7s. 6d. each.

History of the College of St. John the
Evangelist, Cambridge.
By **Thomas Baker**, B.D., Ejected Fellow.
Edited for the Syndics of the University Press, by **John E. B. Mayor**, M.A., Fellow of St. John's College.
2 Vols. 8vo. 24s.

The Annotated Book of Common
Prayer; being an Historical, Ritual, and Theological Commentary on the Devotional System of the Church of England.
Edited by **John Henry Blunt**, M.A.
Fourth Edition. Imperial 8vo. 36s.

London, Oxford, and Cambridge

The Prayer Book Interleaved;

with Historical Illustrations and Explanatory Notes arranged parallel to the Text, by the Rev. **W. M. Campion**, B.D., Fellow and Tutor of Queens' College and Rector of St. Botolph's, and the Rev. **W. J. Beamont**, M.A., late Fellow of Trinity College, Cambridge. With a Preface by the **Lord Bishop of Ely**.

Fifth Edition. Small 8vo. 7s. 6d.

Flowers and Festivals; or, Directions

for the Floral Decorations of Churches. With coloured Illustrations.

By **W. A. Barrett**, of S. Paul's Cathedral, late Clerk of Magdalen College, and Commoner of S. Mary Hall, Oxford.

Square Crown 8vo. 5s.

Light in the Heart; or, Short Meditations

on Subjects which concern the Soul. Translated from the French.

Edited by the Rev. **W. J. Butler**, M.A., Vicar of Wantage.

18mo. 1s. 6d.

Consoling Thoughts in Sickness.

Edited by **Henry Bailey**, B.D., Warden of St. Augustine's College, Canterbury.

Large type. *Fine Edition.* Small 8vo. 2s. 6d.
Also a Cheap Edition, 1s. 6d.; or in Paper Cover, 1s.

Sickness; its Trials and Blessings.

Fine Edition, on toned paper. Small 8vo. 3s. 6d.
Also a cheap Edition, 1s. 6d., or in Paper Cover, 1s.

Help and Comfort for the Sick Poor.

By the Author of "Sickness; its Trials and Blessings."

New Edition. Small 8vo. 1s.

Hymns and Poems for the Sick and

Suffering; in connexion with the Service for the Visitation of the Sick. Selected from various Authors.

Edited by **T. V. Fosbery**, M.A., Vicar of St. Giles's, Reading.

New Edition. Small 8vo. 3s. 6d.

The Dogmatic Faith: an Inquiry

into the Relation subsisting between Revelation and Dogma. Being the Bampton Lectures for 1867.

By **Edward Garbett**, M.A., Incumbent of Christ Church, Surbiton.

Second Edition. Crown 8vo. 5s.

Sketches of the Rites and Customs of

the Greco-Russian Church.

By **H. C. Romanoff**. With an Introductory Notice by the Author of "The Heir of Redclyffe."

Second Edition. Crown 8vo. 7s. 6d.

Household Theology: a Handbook of

Religious Information respecting the Holy Bible, the Prayer Book, the Church, the Ministry, Divine Worship, the Creeds, &c. &c.

By **John Henry Blunt**, M.A.

Third Edition. Small 8vo. 3s. 6d.

London, Oxford, and Cambridge

Curious Myths of the Middle Ages.
By **S. Baring-Gould**, M.A., Author of "Post-Mediæval Preachers," &c. With Illustrations.

New Edition. Complete in one Volume.

Crown 8vo. 6*s.*

Soimême: a Story of a Wilful Life.
Small 8vo. 3*s.* 6*d.*

The Happiness of the Blessed considered as to the Particulars of their State: their Recognition of each other in that State: and its Differences of Degrees. To which are added Musings on the Church and Her Services.

By **Richard Mant**, D.D., sometime Lord Bishop of Down and Connor.

New Edition. Small 8vo. 3*s.* 6*d.*

Anglo-Saxon Witness on Four Alleged Requisites for Holy Communion—Fasting, Water, Altar Lights, and Incense.

By the Rev. **J. Baron**, M.A., Rector of Upton Scudamore, Wilts.

8vo. 5*s.*

Miscellaneous Poems.
By **Henry Francis Lyte**, M.A.

New Edition. Small 8vo. 5*s.*

London, Oxford, and Cambridge

The Holy Bible.
With Notes and Introductions.
By **Chr. Wordsworth**, D.D., Bishop of Lincoln.
Imperial 8vo.

	Part	£	s.	d.
Vol. I. 38s.	I. Genesis and Exodus. *Second Edit.*	1	1	0
	II. Leviticus, Numbers, Deuteronomy. *Second Edition*	0	18	0
Vol. II. 21s.	III. Joshua, Judges, Ruth. *Second Edit.*	0	12	0
	IV. The Books of Samuel. *Second Edit.*	0	10	0
Vol. III. 21s.	V. The Books of Kings, Chronicles, Ezra, Nehemiah, Esther. *Second Edition*	1	1	0
Vol. IV. 34s.	VI. The Book of Job. *Second Edition*	0	9	0
	VII. The Book of Psalms. *Second Edit.*	0	15	0
	VIII. Proverbs, Ecclesiastes, Song of Solomon	0	12	0
Vol. V.	IX. Isaiah	0	12	6
	X. Jeremiah, Lamentations, and Ezekiel	1	1	0
	XI. Daniel. (*In Preparation.*)			
	XII. The Minor Prophets. (*In Preparation.*)			

Manual of Family Devotions, arranged
from the Book of Common Prayer.
By the Hon. **Augustus Duncombe**, D.D., Dean of York.
Printed in red and black.
Small 8vo. 3s. 6d.

Perranzabuloe, the Lost Church Found;

or, The Church of England not a New Church, but Ancient, Apostolical, and Independent, and a Protesting Church Nine Hundred Years before the Reformation.

By the Rev. **C. T. Collins Trelawny**, M.A., formerly Rector of Timsbury, Somerset, and late Fellow of Balliol College, Oxford.

New Edition. Crown 8vo. With Illustrations. 3s. 6d.

Annals of the Bodleian Library, Oxford,

from its Foundation to A.D. 1867; containing an Account of the various collections of printed books and MSS. there preserved; with a brief Preliminary Sketch of the earlier Library of the University.

By **W. D. Macray**, M.A., Assistant in the Library, Chaplain of Magdalen and New Colleges.

8vo. 12s.

Catechesis; or, Christian Instruction

preparatory to Confirmation and First Communion.

By **Charles Wordsworth**, D.C.L., Bishop of St. Andrew's.

New Edition. Small 8vo. 2s.

Warnings of the Holy Week, &c.;

being a Course of Parochial Lectures for the Week before Easter and the Easter Festivals.

By the Rev. **W. Adams**, M.A., late Vicar of St. Peter's-in-the-East, Oxford, and Fellow of Merton College.

Sixth Edition. Small 8vo. 4s. 6d.

Petronilla; and other Poems.

By **Frederick George Lee**, D.C.L.

Second Edition. Small 8vo. 3s. 6d.

London, Oxford, and Cambridge

Consolatio; or, Comfort for the Afflicted.
Edited by the Rev. **C. E. Kennaway**. With a Preface by **Samuel Wilberforce**, D.D., Lord Bishop of Winchester.
New Edition. Small 8vo. 3s. 6d.

The Victory of Divine Goodness;
Including—I. Letters to an Inquirer on Various Doctrines of Scripture; II. Notes on Coleridge's Confessions of an Inquiring Spirit; III. Thoughts on the Nature of the Atonement and of Eternal Judgment.

By **T. R. Birks**, M.A., Incumbent of Holy Trinity, Cambridge; Author of "The Difficulties of Belief," &c.

Second Edition, with Reply to Recent Strictures. Crown 8vo. 5s.

The Doctrine of the Church of England,
as stated in Ecclesiastical Documents set forth by Authority of Church and State, in the Reformation Period between 1536 and 1662. Edited by the Rev. **John Henry Blunt**, M.A. 8vo. 7s. 6d.

The Hillford Confirmation: a Tale.
By **M. C. Phillpotts**.
18mo. 1s.

The Greek Testament.
With Notes and Introductions.
By **Chr. Wordsworth**, D.D., Bishop of Lincoln.
2 Vols. Impl. 8vo. 4l.

The Parts may be had separately, as follows:—
 The Gospels, 6*th Edition*, 21s.
 The Acts, 5*th Edition*, 10s. 6d.
 St. Paul's Epistles, 5*th Edition*, 31s. 6d.
 General Epistles, Revelation, and Indexes, 3*rd Edition*, 21s.

London, Oxford, and Cambridge

Occasional Sermons.

By **Henry Parry Liddon**, M.A., Canon of St. Paul's.
Crown 8vo. (*In Preparation.*)

From Morning to Evening:

a Book for Invalids.

From the French of M. L'Abbé Henri Perreyve. Translated and adapted by an Associate of the Sisterhood of S. John Baptist, Clewer.
Crown 8vo. 5s.

Popular Objections to the Book of

Common Prayer considered, in Four Sermons on the Sunday Lessons in Lent, the Commination Service, and the Athanasian Creed, with a Preface on the existing Lectionary.

By **Edward Meyrick Goulburn**, D.D., Dean of Norwich.
Second Edition. Small 8vo. 2s. 6d.

Family Prayers: compiled from various

sources (chiefly from Bishop Hamilton's Manual), and arranged on the Liturgical Principle.

By **Edward Meyrick Goulburn**, D.D., Dean of Norwich.
New Edition. Crown 8vo, large type, 3s. 6d.
Cheap Edition. 16mo. 1s.

The Annual Register: a Review of

Public Events at Home and Abroad, for the Year 1869; being the Seventh Volume of an improved Series.
8vo. 18s.

** The Volumes for 1863 to 1868 may be had, price 18s. each.

A Prose Translation of Virgil's Ec-

logues and Georgics.
By an Oxford Graduate.
Crown 8vo. 2s. 6d.

Egypt's Record of Time to the Exodus

of Israel, critically investigated: with a comparative Survey of the Patriarchal History and the Chronology of Scripture; resulting in the Reconciliation of the Septuagint and Hebrew Computations, and Manetho with both.

By **W. B. Galloway**, M.A., Vicar of St. Mark's, Regent's Park, and Chaplain to the Right Hon. Lord Viscount Hawarden.

8vo. 15*s.*

A Fourth Series of Parochial Sermons,

preached in a Village Church.

By the Rev. **Charles A. Heurtley**, D.D., Rector of Feuny Compton, Warwickshire, Margaret Professor of Divinity, and Canon of Christ Church, Oxford.

12mo. 5*s.* 6*d.*

Six Short Sermons on Sin. Lent Lectures

at S. Alban the Martyr, Holborn.

By the Rev. **Orby Shipley**, M.A.

Fourth Edition. Small 8vo. 1*s.*

Herbert Tresham: a Tale of the Great

Rebellion.

By the late Rev. **J. M. Neale**, D.D., sometime Scholar of Trinity College, Cambridge, and late Warden of Sackville College, East Grinsted.

New Edition. Small 8vo. 3*s.* 6*d.*

Reflections on the Revolution in France,

and on the Proceedings in certain Societies in London relative to that Event. In a Letter intended to have been sent to a Gentleman in Paris, 1790.

By the Right Hon. **Edmund Burke**, M.P.

New Edition. With a short Biographical Notice.

Crown 8vo. 3*s.* 6*d.*

A Memoir of the late Henry Hoare, Esq., M.A. With a Narrative of the Church Movements with which he was connected from 1848 to 1865, and more particularly of the Revival of Convocation.
  By **James Bradby Sweet**, M.A.
  8vo. 12s.

Yesterday, To-day, and For Ever: a Poem in Twelve Books.
  By **Edward Henry Bickersteth**, M.A., Vicar of Christ Church Hampstead, and Chaplain to the Bishop of Ripon.
  Third Edition. Small 8vo. 6s.

The Perfect Man; or, Jesus an Example of Godly Life.
  By the Rev. **Harry Jones**, M.A., Incumbent of St. Luke's, Berwick Street.
  Crown 8vo. 3s. 6d.

The Sword and the Keys.
  The Civil Power in its Relations to The Church; considered with Special Reference to the Court of Final Ecclesiastical Appeal in England. With Appendix containing all Statutes on which the Jurisdiction of that Tribunal over Spiritual Causes is Founded, and also, all Ecclesiastical Judgments delivered by it since those published by the Lord Bishop of London in 1865.
  By **James Wayland Joyce**, M.A., Rector of Burford, Salop.
  8vo. 10s. 6d.

Sacred Allegories:
  The Shadow of the Cross—The Distant Hills—The Old Man's Home—The King's Messengers.
  By the Rev. **W. Adams**, M.A., late Fellow of Merton College, Oxford.
  New Edition. With Engravings from original designs by Charles W. Cope, R.A., John C. Horsley, A.R.A., Samuel Palmer, Birket Foster, and George E. Hicks.
  Small 4to. 10s. 6d.

London, Oxford, and Cambridge

Liber Precum Publicarum Ecclesiæ

Anglicanæ.
À Gulielmo Bright, A.M., et Petro Goldsmith Medd, A.M., Presbyteris, Collegii Universitatis in Acad. Oxon. Sociis, Latine redditus.

New Edition, with all the Rubrics in red. Small 8vo. 6*s.*

Bible Readings for Family Prayer.

By the Rev. W. H. Ridley, M.A., Rector of Hambleden.
Crown 8vo.

Old Testament—Genesis and Exodus. 2*s.*

New Testament, 3*s.* 6*d.* { St. Matthew and St. Mark. 2*s.*
{ St. Luke and St. John. 2*s.*

Devotional Commentary on the Gospel

according to S. Matthew.
Translated from the French of Pasquier Quesnel.
Crown 8vo. 7*s.* 6*d.*

Sermons on Doctrines. For the Middle

Classes. By the Rev. George Wray, M.A., Prebendary of York, and Rector of Leven, near Beverley.
Small 8vo. 5*s.* 6*d.*

The Religion, Discipline, and Rites of

the Church of England.

By John Cosin, Bishop of Durham. Written at the instance of Edward Hyde, Earl of Clarendon. Now first published in English. By the Rev. Frederick Meyrick, M.A., Rector of Blickling and Erpingham; Prebendary of Lincoln; Examining Chaplain to the Lord Bishop of Lincoln.
Small 8vo. 2*s.*

The New Testament for English

Readers; containing the Authorized Version, with a revised English Text; Marginal References; and a Critical and Explanatory Commentary.

By **Henry Alford**, D.D., Dean of Canterbury.

2 Vols. or 4 Parts, 8vo. 54*s*. 6*d*.

Separately,

Vol. 1, Part I.—The three first Gospels, with a Map. *Second Edition.* 12*s*.

Vol. 1, Part II.—St. John and the Acts. *Second Edition.* 10*s*. 6*d*.

Vol. 2, Part I.—The Epistles of St. Paul, with a Map. *Second Edition.* 16*s*.

Vol. 2, Part II.—Hebrews to Revelation. 8vo. 16*s*.

Thoughts on Personal Religion; being

a Treatise on the Christian Life in its Two Chief Elements, Devotion and Practice.

By **Edward Meyrick Goulburn**, D.D., Dean of Norwich.

New Edition. Small 8vo. 6*s*. 6*d*.

An Edition for Presentation, Two Volumes, small 8vo. 10*s*. 6*d*.

Also a cheap Edition. Small 8vo. 3*s*. 6*d*.

On Miracles; being the Bampton

Lectures for 1865.

By **J. B. Mozley**, B.D., Canon of Worcester, late Fellow of Magdalen College, Oxford.

Second Edition. 8vo. 10*s*. 6*d*.

London, Oxford, and Cambridge

THE "ASCETIC LIBRARY:"

A Series of Translations of Spiritual Works for Devotional Reading from Catholic Sources.

Edited by the Rev. **Orby Shipley**, M.A.
Square Crown 8vo.

The Mysteries of Mount Calvary.
　　Translated from the Latin of **Antonio de Guevara**. 3s. 6d.

Preparation for Death.
　　Translated from the Italian of **Alfonso**, Bishop of S. Agatha. 5s.

Counsels on Holiness of Life.
　　Translated from the Spanish of "The Sinner's Guide" by **Luis de Granada**. 5s.

Examination of Conscience upon Special Subjects.
　　Translated and abridged from the French of **Tronson**. 5s.

KEYS TO CHRISTIAN KNOWLEDGE.

Small 8vo. 2s. 6d. each.

A Key to the Knowledge and Use of the Book of Common Prayer.
　　By **John Henry Blunt**, M.A.

A Key to the Knowledge and Use of the Holy Bible.
　　By **John Henry Blunt**, M.A.

A Key to the Knowledge of Church History.
(Ancient.)
　　Edited by **John Henry Blunt**, M.A.

A Key to the Narrative of the Four Gospels.
　　By **John Pilkington Norris**, M.A., Canon of Bristol, formerly one of Her Majesty's Inspectors of Schools.

RIVINGTON'S DEVOTIONAL SERIES.

Elegantly printed with red borders. 16mo. 2s. 6d. each.

Thomas à Kempis, Of the Imitation of Christ.

Also a cheap Edition, without the red borders, 1s., *or in Cover*, 6d.

The Rule and Exercises of Holy Living.

By **Jeremy Taylor**, D.D., Bishop of Down, and Connor, and Dromore.

Also a cheap Edition, without the red borders, 1s.

The Rule and Exercises of Holy Dying.

By **Jeremy Taylor**, D.D., Bishop of Down, and Connor, and Dromore.

Also a cheap Edition, without the red borders, 1s.

*** The Holy Living and Holy Dying may be had bound together in One Volume. 5s., or without the red borders, 2s. 6d.

A Short and Plain Instruction for the better Understanding of the Lord's Supper; to which is annexed, the Office of the Holy Communion, with proper Helps and Directions.

By **Thomas Wilson**, D.D., late Lord Bishop of Sodor and Man. Complete Edition.

Also a cheap Edition, without the red borders, 1s., *or in Cover*, 6d.

Introduction to the Devout Life.

From the French of Saint Francis of Sales, Bishop and Prince of Geneva. A New Translation.

A Practical Treatise concerning Evil Thoughts: wherein their Nature, Origin, and Effect are distinctly considered and explained, with many Useful Rules for restraining and suppressing such Thoughts: suited to the various conditions of Life, and the several Tempers of Mankind, more especially of melancholy Persons.

By **William Chilcot**, M.A.

With Preface and Notes by **Richard Hooper**, M.A., Vicar of Upton and Aston Upthorpe, Berks.

𝕷𝖔𝖓𝖉𝖔𝖓, 𝕺𝖝𝖋𝖔𝖗𝖉, 𝖆𝖓𝖉 𝕮𝖆𝖒𝖇𝖗𝖎𝖉𝖌𝖊

Imperial 8vo. 21s.

PART I. (CONTAINING A—K).

DICTIONARY OF DOCTRINAL AND HISTORICAL THEOLOGY,

BY VARIOUS WRITERS.

EDITED BY THE

REV. JOHN HENRY BLUNT, M.A., F.S.A.,

EDITOR OF "THE ANNOTATED BOOK OF COMMON PRAYER."

THIS is the first portion of the " *Summary of Theology and Ecclesiastical History," which Messrs. Rivington propose to publish as a* " *Thesaurus Theologicus*" *for the Clergy and Reading Laity of the Church of England.*

It consists of original articles on all the important Doctrines of Theology, and on other questions necessary for their further illustration, the articles being carefully written with a view to modern thought, as well as a respect for ancient authority.

Part II., completing the Dictionary, is in the press.

London, Oxford, and Cambridge

NEW PAMPHLETS

BY THE BISHOP OF ST. DAVID'S.

A Charge delivered to the Clergy of the diocese of St. David's, at his Tenth Visitation, October and November, 1869. With an Appendix, containing an answer to the question, What is Transubstantiation? 8vo. 2s. 6d.

BY THE BISHOP OF LLANDAFF.

A Charge delivered to the Clergy of the diocese of Llandaff, at his Seventh Visitation, August, 1869. With an Appendix, containing Notes on the Doctrine of the Objective Presence. 8vo. 2s.

BY THE BISHOP OF BANGOR.

A Charge delivered to the Clergy of the diocese of Bangor, at his Fourth Visitation, August, 1869. 8vo. 1s.

BY THE BISHOP OF ROCHESTER.

A Charge delivered to the Clergy and Churchwardens of the diocese of Rochester, at his Primary Visitation, in October and November, 1869. 8vo. 6d.

BY THE DEAN OF DURHAM.

The Faith and Work of a Bishop: a Sermon, preached in Westminster Abbey, at the Consecration of the Bishops of Exeter, Bath and Wells, and the Falkland Islands, on St. Thomas's Day, December 21, 1869. 8vo. 1s.

BY CANON SEYMOUR.

Sisterhoods, the Fruits of Christian Love: a Sermon, preached in St. Mark's Church, Gloucester, on the anniversary of St. Lucy's Home and Hospital, December 13, 1869. Published by request. 8vo. 6d.

BY THE REV. F. MEYRICK.

*Denominational Inspection and Religious Examina-*tion in Church of England Schools: a Letter to the Right Hon. W. E. Forster, M.P., on some provisions of the Elementary Education Bill. 8vo. 6d.

NEW PAMPHLETS

Pope Agatho; His Life and Times: a Reprint, intended as a Reply to Archbishop Manning's Pastoral Letter on the Œcumenical Council and the Infallibility of the Roman Pontiff. Edited, with a Preface, by Edmund Tew, M.A., Rector of Patching, in the diocese of Chichester. 8vo. 2*s.* 6*d.*

BY THE REV. HENRY R. BLACKETT.

Education with or without Religion? a Sermon, preached in Christ Church, Woburn Square, Bloomsbury, on Sunday Morning, November 21, 1869, previous to a collection for the Christ Church National, Infant, and Sunday Schools, Little Guilford Street. 8vo. 1*s.*

BY THE REV. W. B. GALLOWAY.

The Unlawfulness of the Marriage of Brother and Sister-in-Law, in the Light of the Word of God; with Ancient Evidence hitherto generally overlooked. 8vo. 1*s.*

BY THE REV. JOHN DAVIES MEREWEATHER.

*On Weekly Communion and Faith in Church Ordi-*nances: a Sermon, preached at Venice, on 24th October, 1869. 8vo. 6*d.*

BY THE REV. W. H. FREMANTLE.

Lay Power in Parishes; the most needed Church Reform. 8vo. 1*s.*

BY THE REV. W. E. SCUDAMORE.

The North Side of the Table; What it was: an Historical Inquiry. 8vo. 1*s.*

The Reformation of the Church of England [A.D. 1514—1547]: a Review, Reprinted by Permission from the "Times," of February 27th and March 1st, 1869. *Second Edition.* 8vo. 6*d.*

Now publishing in Eight Volumes, crown 8vo, 5s. each.

A NEW AND UNIFORM EDITION OF
A DEVOTIONAL COMMENTARY
ON THE
GOSPEL NARRATIVE.

BY THE

REV. ISAAC WILLIAMS, B.D.

FORMERLY FELLOW OF TRINITY COLLEGE, OXFORD.

For Advent and Christmas.

OUR LORD'S NATIVITY.

THE BIRTH AT BETHLEHEM.	THE FIRST PASSOVER.
THE BAPTISM IN JORDAN.	[*Ready.*

OUR LORD'S MINISTRY. SECOND YEAR.

THE SECOND PASSOVER.	THE TWELVE SENT FORTH.
CHRIST WITH THE TWELVE.	[*Ready.*

OUR LORD'S MINISTRY. THIRD YEAR.

TEACHING IN GALILEE.	LAST JOURNEY FROM GALILEE TO
TEACHING AT JERUSALEM.	JERUSALEM.
	[*Ready.*

London, Oxford, and Cambridge

For Lent and Easter.
THE HOLY WEEK.

THE APPROACH TO JERUSALEM.
THE TEACHING IN THE TEMPLE.
THE DISCOURSE ON THE MOUNT OF OLIVES.
THE LAST SUPPER.
INDEX OF TEXTS.

[*Ready.*

For Lent and Easter.
OUR LORD'S PASSION.

THE HOUR OF DARKNESS.
THE AGONY.
THE APPREHENSION.
THE CONDEMNATION.
THE DAY OF SORROWS.
THE HALL OF JUDGMENT.
THE CRUCIFIXION.
THE SEPULTURE.

[*Ready.*

For Ascension-tide.
OUR LORD'S RESURRECTION.

THE DAY OF DAYS.
THE GRAVE VISITED.
CHRIST APPEARING.
THE GOING TO EMMAUS.
THE FORTY DAYS.
THE APOSTLES ASSEMBLED.
THE LAKE IN GALILEE.
THE MOUNTAIN IN GALILEE.
THE RETURN FROM GALILEE

[*Ready.*

Introductory Volume.
THOUGHTS on the STUDY of the HOLY GOSPELS.

CHARACTERISTIC DIFFERENCES IN THE FOUR GOSPELS.
OUR LORD'S MANIFESTATIONS OF HIMSELF.
THE RULE OF SCRIPTURAL INTERPRETATION FURNISHED BY OUR LORD.
ANALOGIES OF THE GOSPEL.
MENTION OF ANGELS IN THE GOSPELS.
PLACES OF OUR LORD'S ABODE AND MINISTRY.
OUR LORD'S MODE OF DEALING WITH HIS APOSTLES.
CONCLUSION.
INDEX OF TEXTS.

[*Ready April 15th.*

A HARMONY of the FOUR EVANGELISTS.

[*Ready May 1st.*

London, Oxford, and Cambridge

CATENA CLASSICORUM,

A SERIES OF CLASSICAL AUTHORS,

EDITED BY MEMBERS OF BOTH UNIVERSITIES UNDER THE DIRECTION OF

THE REV. ARTHUR HOLMES, M.A.

FELLOW AND LECTURER OF CLARE COLLEGE, CAMBRIDGE, LECTURER AND LATE FELLOW OF ST. JOHN'S COLLEGE,

AND

THE REV. CHARLES BIGG, M.A.

LATE SENIOR STUDENT AND TUTOR OF CHRIST CHURCH, OXFORD, SECOND CLASSICAL MASTER OF CHELTENHAM COLLEGE.

Crown 8vo.

The following Parts have been already published:—

SOPHOCLIS TRAGOEDIAE,

Edited by R. C. JEBB, M.A. Fellow and Assistant Tutor of Trinity College, Cambridge.

[Part I. The Electra. 3s. 6d.   Part II. The Ajax. 3s. 6d.

JUVENALIS SATIRAE,

Edited by G. A. SIMCOX, M.A. Fellow and Classical Lecturer of Queen's College, Oxford.   [Thirteen Satires. 3s. 6d.

London, Oxford and Cambridge

CATENA CLASSICORUM—(Continued).

THUCYDIDIS HISTORIA,

Edited by CHARLES BIGG, M.A. late Senior Student and Tutor of Christ Church, Oxford. Second Classical Master of Cheltenham College.
> [Vol. I. Books I. and II. with Introductions. 6s.

DEMOSTHENIS ORATIONES PUBLICAE,

Edited by G. H. HESLOP, M.A. late Fellow and Assistant Tutor of Queen's College, Oxford. Head Master of St. Bees.
> [Parts I. & II. The Olynthiacs and the Philippics. 4s. 6d.

ARISTOPHANIS COMOEDIAE,

Edited by W. C. GREEN, M.A. late Fellow of King's College, Cambridge. Classical Lecturer at Queens' College.
> [Part I. The Acharnians and the Knights. 4s.
> [Part II. The Clouds. 3s. 6d.
> [Part III. The Wasps. 3s. 6d.

ISOCRATIS ORATIONES,

Edited by JOHN EDWIN SANDYS, B.A. Fellow and Lecturer of St. John's College, and Lecturer at Jesus College, Cambridge.
> [Part I. Ad Demonicum et Panegyricus. 4s. 6d.

A PERSII FLACCI SATIRARUM LIBER,

Edited by A. PRETOR, M.A., of Trinity College, Cambridge, Classical Lecturer of Trinity Hall. 3s. 6d.

HOMERI ILIAS,

Edited by S. H. REYNOLDS, M.A. Fellow and Tutor of Brasenose College, Oxford. [Vol. I. Books I. to XII. 6s.

CATENA CLASSICORUM.
The following Parts are in course of preparation:—

PLATONIS PHAEDO,
Edited by ALFRED BARRY, D.D. late Fellow of Trinity College, Cambridge; Principal of King's College, London.

DEMOSTHENIS ORATIONES PUBLICAE,
Edited by G. H. HESLOP, M.A. late Fellow and Assistant Tutor of Queen's College, Oxford; Head Master of St. Bees.
[Part III. De Falsâ Legatione.

MARTIALIS EPIGRAMMATA,
Edited by GEORGE BUTLER, M.A. Principal of Liverpool College; late Fellow of Exeter College, Oxford.

DEMOSTHENIS ORATIONES PRIVATAE,
Edited by ARTHUR HOLMES, M.A. Fellow and Lecturer of Clare College, Cambridge.   [Part I. De Coronâ.

HORATI OPERA,
Edited by J. M. MARSHALL, M.A. Fellow and late Lecturer of Brasenose College, Oxford; one of the Masters in Clifton College.

TERENTI COMOEDIAE,
Edited by T. L. PAPILLON, M.A. Fellow and Classical Lecturer of Merton College, Oxford.   [Part I. Andria et Eunuchus.

HERODOTI HISTORIA,
Edited by H. G. WOODS, M.A. Fellow and Tutor of Trinity College, Oxford.

TACITI HISTORIAE,
Edited by W. H. SIMCOX, M.A. Fellow and Lecturer of Queen's College, Oxford.

OVIDI TRISTIA,
Edited by OSCAR BROWNING, M.A. Fellow of King's College, Cambridge; and Assistant Master at Eton College.

CICERONIS ORATIONES,
Edited by CHARLES EDWARD GRAVES, M.A. Classical Lecturer and late Fellow of St. John's College, Cambridge.
[Part I. Pro P. Sextio.

THEOPHRASTI CHARACTERES,
Edited by A. PRETOR, M.A. of Trinity College, Cambridge; Classical Lecturer of Trinity Hall.

www.ingramcontent.com/pod-product-compliance
Lightning Source LLC
Chambersburg PA
CBHW021337300426
44114CB00012B/982